# JUSTICE AND THE ENEMY

# JUSTICE <small>AND THE</small>
# ENEMY

### NUREMBERG, 9/11, AND THE TRIAL OF KHALID SHEIKH MOHAMMED

# WILLIAM SHAWCROSS

PUBLICAFFAIRS

*New York*

PublicAffairs books are available at special discounts for bulk purchases in the
U.S. by corporations, institutions, and other organizations. For more information, please contact the Special Markets Department at the Perseus Books
Group, 2300 Chestnut Street, Suite 200, Philadelphia, PA 19103, call (800)
810-4145, ext. 5000, or e-mail special.markets@perseusbooks.com.

Library of Congress Control Number: 2011934956
ISBN 978-1-58648-975-5 (HC)
ISBN 978-1-58648-976-2 (EB)

First Edition
10 9 8 7 6 5 4 3 2 1

*For Anthony Smith, constant friend*

*Salus populi suprema lex.*
The safety of the people shall be the highest law.

> — Cicero, *De Legibus,* Book iii, sec. 3,
> derived by tradition from the
> Twelve Tables of Roman law

Laws are formed by the manners and exigencies of particular times, and it is but accidental that they last longer than their causes.

> — Samuel Johnson, "Letter to James
> Boswell," February 3, 1776

# CONTENTS

# INTRODUCTION

THE JUDGMENT OF EVIL IS NEVER SIMPLE. When considering the case of Khalid Sheikh Mohammed, the so-called "mastermind" of the 9/11 attacks on America and of many other murders around the world, I recalled the work of the philosopher George Steiner, who has written at length on the consequences of Nazi crimes. In 1981, Steiner caused a sensation by creating a novella—*The Portage to San Cristobal of AH*—in which a group of Jewish Nazi hunters discover Hitler, deep in the Amazon jungle, three decades after the end of the Second World War. Many prominent Nazis had indeed fled to South America after their defeat in May 1945; the most important to be discovered was Adolf Eichmann, whom the Israelis kidnapped and spirited to Israel in 1960.

In Jerusalem, Eichmann was put on trial, found guilty, and hanged. Hannah Arendt, writing of that trial, famously spoke of "the banality of evil." By this controversial phrase she did not mean that the evil acts of mass murder of Jews for which Eichmann was responsible were commonplace. Rather she felt that it was not the presence of hatred in Eichmann that drove him to send so many people to their deaths, but the absence of imagination. It was the juxtaposition of evil deeds and the failure to make judgments that Arendt called "banal." Eichmann himself maintained after his arrest that he was merely following orders and that he had abdicated his conscience in order to follow the *Fuhrerprinzip*.

But that was not true. In 2011, the German news magazine, *Der Spiegel* published an investigation of Eichmann based on what it said

1

were "formerly confidential, secret and top-secret documents." These included taped conversations Eichmann had with friends in Buenos Aires before the Israelis caught him. On one occasion he boasted of his crimes, "I was no ordinary recipient of orders. If I had been one, I would have been a fool. Instead, I was part of the thought process. I was an idealist." His only regret was in not having murdered all the Jews. "We didn't do our work correctly," he said. "There was more that could have been done." [1]

In the case of the Fuhrer himself, Steiner began to wonder: what if Hitler, as well as Eichmann, had actually escaped his Berlin bunker, had gotten himself to Latin America, and had lived there, hidden, ever since? If, like Eichmann, he was finally discovered, how should he be dealt with—how should he be tried for his crimes?

Steiner, himself a refugee from Nazi Europe, had always been preoccupied by the power of language. He was haunted by an early 1920s photograph of Hitler "standing like a beggar, with a torn raincoat in front of him, and no one is listening to him. But then ten people listened, and then a million. . . . " Hitler's eloquence had been overwhelming and within ten years it had propelled him to be master of Germany and then of Europe "and, had he, for example, decided to woo his Jewish atomic scientists, he might well have been master of everything." [2]

Steiner began to write *The Portage* in 1975, at a time when stories of the horrors perpetrated by the Khmer Rouge were being reported by refugees from Cambodia. He asserted that the book sprang "out of my thinking about the horror and terror of the Holocaust. I insist on this, because this novel is also about Cambodia and Vietnam, El Salvador and Burundi and so on. My feeling is that one has to grapple with the abyss if one can."

In the novella, the Jewish team discovers Hitler and starts to carry him out of the jungle to civilization. But rumors that the Fuhrer has been found flash around the world, as fast as was already possible in those innocent pre-Internet days. The powers who won the war—the United States, the Soviet Union, Britain, and France—all begin to ponder the implications of Hitler's return. Fierce arguments begin over where and how he should be put on trial—and under what jurisdiction. Deep in the jungle, Hitler's Israeli captors have similar debates. What should be done with him? Burn him at the stake? Set him free as a beggar in Israel itself?

In violent rainstorms, the search party's radio breaks down. They have to decide whether to sit out the weather and then deliver Hitler as planned to San Cristobal, or whether the risk of their captive being stolen from them, either by some nation or some media emperor, is too great. They understand that once the world knows that Hitler is being brought out of the jungle, airfields will be dug, roads bulldozed through the trees. "And a million television cameras. And a Hilton. . . . they'd come like locusts. And take him from us. That's the whole point. They'd take him to New York or Moscow or Nuremberg. And we'd be lucky if they allowed us to stand in the anteroom peering over a million heads."

Instead, they decide to conduct their own trial, complete with judge, prosecution, and defense attorneys selected from their own party.

Remarkably, Steiner gives Hitler almost the last word: the climax of the book is Hitler's self-defense. It was from the Jews, he declares, that he learned everything. "To set a race apart. To keep it from defilement. To hold before it a promised land. . . . My racism is a parody of yours, a hungry imitation. What is a thousand-year Reich compared with the eternity of Zion?"

Steiner's Hitler insists that he was not the originator of evil in our time—Stalin, he points out, "had perfected genocide when I was still a nameless scribbler in Munich." Stalin killed thirty million people—far more than he, Hitler. "Our terrors were a village carnival compared with his. Our camps covered absurd acres; he had strung wire and death pits around a continent. . . . How many Jews did Stalin kill, your saviour, your ally Stalin? Answer me that . . . Stalin died in bed and the world stood hushed before the tiger's rest. Whereas you hunt me down like a rabid dog, put me on trial (by what right, by what mandate?)."

Finally, "Hitler" claims that he, the persecutor of the Jews, was also their benefactor; the Holocaust was the principal reason they were able to create Israel. "Perhaps I am the Messiah . . . whose infamous deeds were allowed by God in order to bring His people home."

As his speech ends, Teku, the party's Indian tracker, leaps to his feet and shouts, with startling vagueness, "Proved." As he does so, raucous drumbeats break the air above the clearing where the trial is taking place. The first helicopter from the ravenous world has arrived.

The book caused angry debate when it was published—comments ranged from "masterpiece" to "obscene"—and Steiner was criticized for, inter alia, giving the last word to Hitler. In his own defense, Steiner pointed out that Milton does not provide a real answer to the eloquence of Satan in *Paradise Lost*; nor does Dostoyevsky rebut the overwhelming speech by the Grand Inquisitor in *The Brothers Karamazov*. Steiner also pointed out that he gave the name Teku to the Indian tracker because "it is the Hebrew word used in the Talmud to say that there are issues here beyond our wisdom to answer or decide." [3]

Thirty years later, Steiner's discomfiting meditation on the ambiguity of dispensing justice in an imperfect world seems to have anticipated many of the questions raised in the national and international debates over the best way to bring justice to the leadership of the Al Qaeda terrorist movement.

Brought to trial, Steiner's Hitler was supremely unrepentant. He used the dock as a pulpit from which he not only defended himself but also preached, brilliantly. With his inversion of good and evil, he outwitted his accusers and compounded the victimization of those he had killed. That fictional spectacle anticipated the perversity that many Americans feared would result if, as the Obama administration originally wished, Khalid Sheikh Mohammed went on trial in a civil court in lower Manhattan. The mastermind of the September 11, 2001 attacks on America was also a master demagogue. He would seize the opportunity to inspire his followers around the world to continue Al Qaeda's campaign of mass murder against the American people.

On May 2, 2011, the debate over how to bring America's enemies to account was thrown into even sharper relief when a team of U.S. Navy SEALs carried out a lightning raid in Abbottabad, and killed bin Laden.

"Justice has been done," said President Obama. Not everyone agreed

Since 9/11, America's attempts to balance justice and national security have drawn criticism at home and abroad. Some has been fair but much of it ignores the difficulties and dilemmas that the U.S. government faces in dealing appropriately with twenty-first century terrorists while fulfilling its principal obligation to protect the lives of its own citizens.

This book seeks to examine how to bring justice to an enemy that, unlike at Nuremberg, has not been defeated and that demands nothing less than the destruction of the Western world.

*Chapter 1*

# PRECEDENTS

THE TWENTIETH CENTURY WAS, amongst many other things, the century of mass murder. Totalitarians—Nazis and Communists—killed or caused the deaths of hundreds of millions of people around the world. The grim symbol of the crimes became the mass grave.

In the summer of 1980, I was taken by officials of the Cambodian government to see such graves.* These were a few miles outside the capital, Phnom Penh, and they contained the bodies of thousands of Cambodians who had recently been murdered by their Communist Khmer Rouge rulers.

The Khmer Rouge had been in power between April 1975 and December 1978. They had imposed a form of Maoist autarchy on the country and attempted to return it to what they called Year Zero, an agricultural society supposedly cleansed of all bourgeois and foreign influences. The human costs had been appalling—between one and two million people were thought to have died or been murdered. The Khmer Rouge leadership also made the fatal mistake of attacking their Communist neighbor, Vietnam, and at the end of 1978 the Vietnamese invaded to rid themselves of their troublesome former ally.

Some miles outside of the town, my guide and I were driven to a village where laughing children led us to a shocking exhibition. About six

---

* I described this trip and the memories it aroused in *The Quality of Mercy: Cambodia, Holocaust, and Modern Conscience* (New York: Simon and Schuster, 1984).

pits had been excavated; there were, villagers said, many more. Hundreds of skulls were piled together and limbs were in other piles. Many of the wrists were still tied together with cord or wire—the victims had been forced to kneel on the edge of the pits while Khmer Rouge soldiers clubbed them in the back of the head or shot them. Blindfolds still covered many skulls.

These murders had taken place at the end of 1978 as the Vietnamese armies swept in to overthrow the Khmer Rouge and install another Communist regime more to their liking. Flesh still clung to the hip joints and its terrible sweet rancid smell hung over the fields.

I had been conscious of such horrors since childhood but I had never before seen them with my own eyes. As a child, I listened to fragile 78 rpm records of my father, Hartley Shawcross, the chief British prosecutor at the Nuremberg Tribunal, speaking with gravity and scarcely-controlled emotion to the court.

> On the 5th of October 1943, when I visited the building office at Dubno, my foreman told me that in the vicinity of the site, Jews from Dubno had been shot in three large pits, each about thirty metres long and three metres deep. About fifteen hundred persons had been killed daily. All of the five thousand Jews who had still been living in Dubno before the action were to be liquidated. As the shootings had taken place in his presence, he was still upset.
>
> Thereupon I drove to the site, accompanied by my foreman, and saw near to it great mounds of earth about 30 metres long and 2 metres high. Several trucks stood in front of the mounds. Armed Ukrainian militia drove the people off the trucks under the supervision of an S.S. man. The militia men acted as guards on the trucks and drove them to and from the pit. All these

people had the regulation yellow patches on the front and back of their clothes and thus could be recognized as Jews.

My foreman and I went directly to the pits. Nobody bothered us. Now I heard rifle shots in quick succession from behind one of the earth mounds. The people who had got off the trucks— men, women and children of all ages—had to undress upon the orders of an S.S. man, who carried a riding or a dog whip. They had to put down their clothes in fixed places, sorted according to shoes, top clothing, and underclothing.

I saw a heap of shoes of about eight hundred to one thousand pairs, great piles of underlinen and clothing.

Without screaming or weeping, these people undressed, stood around in family groups, kissed each other, said farewells, and waited for a sign from another S.S. man, who stood near the pit, also with a whip in his hand. During the fifteen minutes that I stood near, I heard no complaint or plea for mercy.

I watched a family of about eight persons, a man and a woman, both about fifty, with their children of about one, eight, and ten, and two grown-up daughters of about twenty to twenty-four. An old woman with snow-white hair was holding the one-year-old child in her arms, and singing to it and tickling it. The child was cooing with delight. The couple were looking on with tears in their eyes.

The father was holding the hand of a boy about ten, speaking to him softly. The boy was fighting his tears. The father pointed to the sky, stroked his head, and seemed to explain something to him.

At that moment, the S.S. man at the pit shouted something to his comrade, who separated off about twenty persons and

ordered them to go behind the mound of earth. Among them
was the family I have mentioned. [1]

These words and images came from the diary of a German engineer,
Herman Graebe, the manager of a German building firm in the Ukraine.
They were part of the evidence produced by the prosecution at Nuremberg.
Eventually I realized that rather than witnessing these terrible mass murders
himself, my father had helped to bring the leaders of Nazi Germany to
justice on behalf of the victims at Dubno and millions of others.

The men in the dock at Nuremberg were architects of a monstrous
regime that almost engulfed the world. However, the evil they embodied
did not die with them, and can be witnessed time and time again through
the horrors of Cambodia and the attacks of September 11, 2001. But the
story of Nuremberg shows how difficult it always is to treat properly
those who commit hideous and unprecedented crimes.

❖ ◎ ❖

The question of how to deal with Nazi war criminals had been discussed
since at least 1942; in August of that year, President Roosevelt had
warned that "the time will come when they shall have to stand in the
Courts of Law in the very countries that they are now oppressing and answer for their acts." [2] In October 1943, at the Moscow Conference of
foreign ministers, the matter came up for discussion amongst the Allies.
U.S. Secretary of State Cordell Hull stated a clear opinion: "If I had my
way," he said, "I would take Hitler and Mussolini and Tojo and their accomplices and bring them before a drumhead court martial, and at sun-
rise the following morning there would be an historic incident." [3]

There was much support for such summary justice at that time. The
Russians, unsurprisingly, were in favor; the British were equivocal. An-

thony Eden, the British foreign secretary, insisted that all legal forms should be observed, though it is not clear quite what he meant.

When Roosevelt, Churchill, and Stalin met for the first time in Tehran in late November 1943, they discussed the fate of the Nazi leaders at the end of a well-lubricated dinner. Stalin proposed a toast "to the justice of the firing squad" for fifty thousand leading German criminals. Churchill demurred and Roosevelt, in an apparent attempt to lighten the conversation, suggested that perhaps forty-nine thousand would be adequate. In his memoirs, Churchill recalled that he had told Stalin that such mass executions were unacceptable. "'I would rather,' I said, 'be taken out into the garden here and now and be shot myself than sully my own and my country's honour by such infamy.'" [4]

However, at the time, Churchill did believe that if the top Nazi leaders were captured by the Allies they should be subjected to summary justice. But he was thinking in terms of a handful, not thousands.

American attitudes in the middle of the war years were mixed. Henry Morgenthau Jr., the U.S. secretary of the treasury, persuaded Roosevelt to accept the quick execution of Nazi leaders. More radically, Morgenthau argued for the "re-pastoralization" of Germany so that it would never again become a powerful industrialized nation capable of creating an aggressive war machine, as it had done so swiftly after its defeat in 1918. He considered it "a question of attacking the German mind." [5]

Morgenthau also proposed deporting millions of Germans: "It seems a terrific task; it seems inhuman; it seems cruel. We didn't ask for this war; we didn't put millions of people through gas chambers. We didn't do any of these things. They have asked for it." [6] When officials in his department questioned the wisdom of dismantling German industry, Morgenthau responded sharply, "Why the hell should I care what happens to their people? . . . For the future of my children and my grandchildren, I don't want these beasts to wage war." When his plan was denounced as immoral, he riposted, "I suppose putting a million or two million people in gas chambers is a godlike action." [7]

There were other American leaders who (at least at times) shared Morgenthau's rage against the Nazis and Germany. In July 1944 (shortly after the D-day landings), Eisenhower expressed a desire to "exterminate all of the General Staff, perhaps some 3,500 people, as well as all of the Gestapo and all Nazi Party members above the rank of Major." He was prepared to allow the Soviets to carry out any such exterminations, except in the case of the Twelfth S.S. Panzer Division, which in June 1944 had killed sixty-four Allied prisoners of war. "I think that the American Army as a unit will handle the Twelfth S.S., every man they can get hold of. They are the men that killed our people in cold blood. . . . We hate everybody that ever wore a Twelfth S.S. uniform." [8]

As the Allies became increasingly confident they would defeat the Nazis, their attitudes changed. When Morgenthau's ruthless if not unrealistic plans were leaked to the press in September 1944, Roosevelt was embarrassed. He sought advice instead from Henry Stimson, the secretary of war, who argued that America's own respect for due process demanded that war criminals be put on trial. So did Judge Samuel Rosenman, Roosevelt's special legal adviser; and so did Justice Felix Frankfurter of the Supreme Court.

Stimson was particularly influential. Mindful of Stalin's Tehran toast to the shooting of fifty thousand Germans, he feared mass revenge killings would tarnish the whole war effort. Concerned by the specter of mass vengeance against the German people, he suggested instead that the entire Gestapo should be interned and then put on trial "as the main instruments of Hitler's system of terrorism in Europe." The men and women running "the Hitler machine" should be punished, rather than the German people at large. [9]

In January 1945, the president received a memorandum from Henry

Stimson, Edward Stettinius, and Attorney General Francis Biddle proposing the creation of an Allied court to try the Nazi leaders for their "atrocious crimes" and for taking part in a "broad criminal enterprise." Significantly, they argued against civil courts and proposed a military tribunal, as this would be "less likely to give undue weight to technical contentions and legalistic arguments." Roosevelt accepted the proposal and took it with him to the meeting with Stalin and Churchill in Yalta in January 1945. There Stalin agreed that "the grand criminals should be tried before being shot." The British were alone in resisting any sort of trial of the Nazi leaders. [10]

When Roosevelt suddenly died in April 1945, just days before victory in Europe, his successor, Harry Truman, enthusiastically endorsed the concept of a trial. Truman was the last U.S. president not to have a university education, but he was well-read in history. He saw that the trial would not only deliver justice to those Nazi leaders who could be seized, but would also establish a documentary record of all that the regime had done and prevent the rise of a new Napoleonic myth. At that time, it was hoped that Hitler, Goebbels, Himmler, Bormann, and Goering would all be captured and tried.

Churchill's preferred plan was to execute the leading Nazis. [11] Just before V.E. Day, the British government submitted an aide mémoire that argued: "HMG assumes that it is beyond question that Hitler and a number of arch-criminals associated with him must, so far as they fall into Allied hands, suffer the penalty of death for their conduct leading up to the war and for the wickedness which they have either themselves perpetrated or have authorized in the conduct of the war." London considered the real charge against Hitler to be "the totality of his offences against the international standard which civilized countries try to observe." Any trial seeking to show the scale of Nazi crimes would be "exceedingly long and elaborate." Moreover, it would be seen by many as a "put up job" designed by the Allies to justify a punishment that had been pre-determined. "Hitler and his advisers—if they decide to take part and to challenge what is alleged—may be expected to be very much alive to any opportunity of turning the tables." [12]

The British were also concerned about Hitler's pre-war aggression being one of the counts of the indictment in any trial. The belief in London was that Germany's unprovoked attacks on other countries "are not war crimes in the ordinary sense, nor is at all clear that they can properly be described as crimes under international law." The British feared that the defense could easily point to many recent precedents in which various countries had declared war and acquired new territory "which certainly were not regarded at the time as crimes against international law." [13]

Such arguments were no longer persuasive in Washington. The War Department now proposed that the German leaders be charged not only with specific atrocities but also for their participation in a broad criminal enterprise.

On May 2, 1945, Truman offered Robert Jackson, a distinguished jurist and an associate justice of the Supreme Court, the position of chief prosecutor at the proposed tribunal and, after short reflection, Jackson accepted. It was an inspired choice, even though there were grumblings amongst the highest American legal circles that a justice should not step down into the arena of a trial—indeed Chief Justice Harlan Fiske Stone disapproved so much that he wrote about "Jackson's lynching party in Nuremberg." Stone's objections were to the use (or misuse) of law. "I don't mind what he does to the Nazis, but I hate to see the pretense that he is running a court and proceeding as to common law. This is a little too sanctimonious a fraud to meet my old-fashioned ideas." [14]

Jackson, on the other hand, had long believed that aggressive war should be declared a crime. He was convinced that the courts had the authority to try those who waged such wars, if only steps were taken to give international law more force. And he also believed that the best should never be the enemy of the good. In 1941 he had argued that "the worst processes of the law" were better than none: "We cannot await a perfect international tribunal or legislature before procribing resort to violence, even in the case of legitimate grievance. We did not await the perfect court before stopping men from settling their differences with brass knuckles." [15]

But Jackson also abhorred the idea of anything that could appear to be a show trial. By coincidence, on the day after Roosevelt died, Jackson made a speech in which he declared that it would be better to shoot the Nazi criminals rather than corrupt the process of law. He made one especially important point that resonates today: "You must put no man on trial under the forms of judicial proceeding, if you are not willing to see him freed if not proven guilty. If you are determined to execute a man in any case, there is no occasion for a trial; the world yields no respect to courts that are merely organized to convict." [16]

Peace in Europe was declared on May 7 (V.E. Day), and only two weeks later Jackson arrived, determined to create the tribunal with all speed. In early July, he made a remarkable journey through the wreckage of the continent—to Germany, Austria, and then to France. He visited Nuremberg, where he was glad to find that the Palace of Justice had survived the Allied bombing. It seemed the ideal place for the trial—except to the Russians, who for some time insisted on Berlin.

In Paris, Jackson was astonished and encouraged to find the vast number of Nazi documents that had already been unearthed. "I did not think men would ever be so foolish as to put in writing some of the things the Germans did put in writing. The stupidity of it and the brutality of it would simply appall you." [17] In short order he persuaded the British to overcome their objections to a military tribunal, set up the machinery required for a trial, and formulate the general principles on which charges against the leading Nazis should be based. It was a superb achievement and an innovative one.

The American case rested on the assumption that the United States had "an inescapable responsibility" to conduct an inquiry and trial of those thought guilty of Nazi atrocities. "To free them without a trial would mock the dead and make cynics of the living." And the alternative of summary executions without definite findings of guilt "would violate pledges repeatedly given and would not set easily on the American conscience or be remembered by our children with pride." [18]

The greatest difference of opinion lay not between Washington and London but between Washington and Moscow. Jackson pointed out that the Russians assumed that wartime declarations by the Allied leaders meant that the accused were already convicted and so no trial before independent judges was needed. In America by contrast these declarations were "an accusation and not a conviction. That requires a judicial finding." [19]

He went on to say, "the reason is the evidence"—not the statements made by heads of state. "The United States feels we could not make political executions. I took that position publicly." [20] He was troubled that other governments did not agree and he wondered whether, if the disagreements were so great, perhaps the only solution would be separate tribunals conducted by each nation according to its own standards.

The British government had by now set up a prosecution team, the British War Crimes Executive. Yet reservations remained. One senior Foreign Office official complained that to allow Russia to be part of any tribunal "will one day be regarded as almost a high point in international hypocrisy." The Russians, just like the Nazis, sought to dominate other nations and they too conducted "atrocities, persecutions and deportations. . . . There have been two criminal enterprises this century—by Germans and Russians. To set up one lot of conspirators as judges of the other . . . robs the whole procedure of the basis of morality." [21] Such arguments had force; they represented a crucial and, at the time, problematic recognition of the moral compromises having to be made by the Allied side.

At the end of June the four powers met at the London Conference to try to reach an agreement. It was not easy and, to Jackson's dismay, the arguments over law and process lasted six long weeks. Jackson insisted, "If we are going to have a trial then it must be an actual trial." The United States would not be party to setting up a judicial body just to ratify a previous political decision to convict. And he was not always diplomatic in attempting to persuade doubters to his point of view, in particular about the nature of aggressive war. Throughout July arguments between the Soviets and their democratic Allies persisted. [22]

Meanwhile Britain had been conducting an immediate postwar general election. The votes of soldiers still serving overseas took time to count and the result was not declared until July 1945. Only a few weeks after victory in Europe, Winston Churchill, the European leader who had done more than any other single man to defeat and destroy the Nazi war machine, lost power to the Labour Party and Clement Attlee became prime minister.

My father, a barrister specializing in criminal law, had served during the war as a regional commissioner organizing civil defense in Britain. Aged forty-three, he became one of the newly elected Labour M.P.s and probably the most senior lawyer on the new government benches. Attlee immediately appointed him attorney general of Great Britain and Northern Ireland. One of his first duties was to take up the position of chief British prosecutor at the planned tribunal.

He became at once aware that the four prosecution teams were still riven with disputes over law, facts, and process. This was hardly surprising—there was absolutely no precedent for such a tribunal. The prosecution would have to be conducted in four languages by lawyers trained in four different legal systems, two of which were in the common law tradition and two in the Roman school of law. Moreover, the Soviet government, unlike the others, was utterly authoritarian and had no understandable framework for due process and the legal protections considered vital to liberal democracies. The Soviets wanted nothing from the trial save propaganda and convictions—public vengeance, and the glorification of the Soviet state. Negotiations between the wartime allies almost collapsed.

Despite these obstacles, in early August 1945 the Allied powers agreed to the framework for the tribunal at Nuremberg. As Francis Biddle wrote, "Robert Jackson's tireless energy and skill had finally brought the four nations together—a really extraordinary feat." [23]

On August 8, the heads of delegation signed the London Charter, which established three main counts against Nazi individuals and organizations. The first was crimes against peace or the waging of aggressive war. The second count dealt with war crimes and held leaders responsible for the misdeeds of the men and women they commanded. The third count—crimes against humanity—was a completely new legal concept and encompassed the persecution of racial and religious groups, as well as the ruthless exploitation of European peoples and resources. Jackson anticipated the complaint that it was merely "victors' justice." But he pointed out that there was no other way "except that the victors judge the vanquished. . . . We must make it clear to the Germans that the wrong for which their fallen leaders are on trial is not that they lost the War, but that they started it." [24]

Problems with the Russians persisted. One of the greatest was over the responsibility for the murder of some twenty thousand Polish officers, found buried with their hands tied behind their backs in the forest at Katyn. The Russians insisted that the indictment must include the charge that the Germans were responsible for this mass murder. The evidence at that time was not conclusive (it later became so) but it strongly suggested that the crime had been committed by the Soviets. Jackson and my father were opposed to this and went together to General Rudenko, the chief Soviet prosecutor, to urge that the charge be dropped from the indictment. He refused and so the democratic Allies felt they were compelled to choose between acquiescence and complete breakdown. They went along with an indictment they knew to be partly a lie; my father wrote later that they informed Rudenko that "the Americans, the British, and the French would not seek to establish this charge nor make any reference to it; the sole responsibility must rest upon the Soviet side of the prosecution." In the end the evidence the Russians produced was (not surprisingly) unpersuasive and the tribunal ignored the charge. No defendant at Nuremberg was punished for Katyn. But the compromise was distasteful.

In Berlin on October 18, 1945, my father lodged the indictment on behalf of the prosecuting powers, rules of procedure were laid down, and the opening of the trial was fixed for thirty days after the indictments were served on the defendants. Everyone then repaired to Nuremberg.

There was much of a domestic nature still to be done. The American army was still reconstructing the court; simultaneous translation and press and telegraph facilities were being installed, accommodation and catering (1,500 lunches a day in the court cafeteria) were still being prepared for all those who were about to descend upon the town to witness this extraordinary spectacle.

All this and much more was completed in time. With speed that seems astonishing in a day when all such processes have become more bureaucratic and laborious, the trial opened on November 20, 1945.

❖ ◉ ❖

There were twenty-two prominent Nazis charged, the most important of whom was Field Marshall Hermann Goering.\* Jackson made a superb opening address, on which he had worked alone and with great care. He pointed out that "less than eight months ago today the courtroom in which you sit was an enemy fortress in the hands of German S.S. troops. Less than eight months ago nearly all our witnesses and documents were in enemy hands. The law had not been codified, no procedures had been established, no tribunal was in existence, no usable courthouse stood here, none of the hundreds of tons of official German documents had been examined, no prosecuting staff had been assembled, nearly all the present defendants were at large and the four prosecuting powers had not yet joined in common cause to try them." [25]

When he came to recount the crimes of which the men in the dock were accused, Jackson's voice sometimes broke. The privilege of opening the first trial in history for crimes against the peace of the world imposed, he said, a grave responsibility. "The wrongs which we seek to condemn and punish have been so calculated, so malignant, and so devastating that civilization cannot tolerate their being ignored, because it cannot survive their being repeated. That four great nations, flushed with victory and stung with injury, stay the hand of vengeance and voluntarily submit their captive enemies to the judgment of the law is one of the most significant tributes that Power has ever paid to Reason." [26]

---

\* Twenty Nazis were in the dock at the start of the tribunal. Martin Bormann was tried in absentia. Kaltenbrunner was ill at the start but later recovered and was brought to court. Ley committed suicide, and Krupp was declared insane.

Jackson was careful to note the propagandistic power of the "broken men" on trial. The prisoners, he said, "represent sinister influences that will lurk in the world long after their bodies have returned to dust. We will show them to be living symbols of racial hatreds, of terrorism and violence, and of the arrogance and cruelty of power. They are symbols of fierce nationalisms and of militarism, of intrigue and war making which have embroiled Europe generation after generation, crushing its manhood, destroying its homes, and impoverishing its life. They have so identified themselves with the philosophies they conceived and with the forces they directed that any tenderness to them is a victory and an encouragement to all the evils which are attached to their names." [27]

Four hours later, after describing in detail the alleged crimes of the Nazis, which he said, "have bathed the world in blood and set civilization back a century," he concluded by saying that that same civilization "does not expect that you can make war impossible. It does expect that your juridical action will put the forces of international Law, its precepts, its prohibitions and, most of all, its sanctions, on the side of peace, so that men and women of good will, in all countries, may have 'leave to live by no man's leave, underneath the law.'" [28]

Over the next 218 days, the evidence against the accused was presented and examined in horrific detail. Thirty-three witnesses were called and examined by the prosecution. Sixty-one witnesses and nineteen defendants testified for the defense. The entire proceedings were conducted, simultaneously translated, and recorded in four languages.

There was one moment of which much has been written—Jackson's cross-examination of Goering. This was not a success. Goering's personality was as large as his frame. He was a wicked man but he was compelling and in some remarkable, sinister way, he came to overshadow the dock if not the larger court. The alternate judge, Norman Birkett, put it like this: "Throughout this trial the dead Hitler has been present at every session. . . . But Goering is the man who has dominated the proceedings and that, remarkably enough, without ever uttering a word." [29]

His ability and his agility became clear as soon as Jackson began his cross-examination. My father later said, in a tribute to Jackson, that Goering should have been cross-examined only by following a basic rule: never ask a question without knowing that there is only one inescapable answer—usually a "yes" or a "no"—"and by that process to lead the witness up to the last fatal but inescapable response." That was how things were done at the criminal bar, where my father had trained. But Jackson had never been a criminal lawyer—his strength was rather advocacy and argument. In this confrontation he saw himself as representing liberal democracy seeking to vanquish the personification of Nazi tyranny. Instead of sticking to specific facts, he delved too deep into history and opinion and gave Goering the chance to digress and discourse at will. Culpably, the trial's four judges did not come to Jackson's aid and stop the defendant's long obfuscations. In the end the British team had to take up the cross-examination and spent that night, in the words of one of its members, "digging up documents signed by Goering personally showing him to be a friend of Himmler, a bandit, and a thug."

My father's view was that Jackson's failure with Goering "was due to his intellectual honesty. His whole case was to expose the evil philosophies with which the Nazis had sought to dominate the world: this inevitably involved him in putting matters of opinion in an argumentative rather than a factual exchange." He faulted the bench for allowing Goering such license. [30]

❖ ◉ ❖

My father made his closing speech to the tribunal on July 26 and 27, 1946. Toward the end, he said that in one way the fate of the men in the dock meant little: their personal power for evil was forever broken. Yet it was crucial that the trial stand as a milestone in the history of civilization, asserting that the rights of the individual transcended the might of the state. "States may be great and powerful. Ultimately the rights of men, made as all men are made in the image of God, are fundamental. . . . And so, after this ordeal to which mankind has been submitted, mankind itself—struggling now to re-establish in all the countries of the world the common simple things—liberty, love, understanding—comes to this Court and cries, 'These are our laws—let them prevail.'"

He ended by asking the court to remember the story of Dubno, which I quoted above: "but not in vengeance—in a determination that these things shall not occur again. 'The father'—do you remember?—'pointed to the sky and seemed to say something to his boy.'"

The verdicts were announced on October 1, 1946. Some mercy was shown, despite the dissent of the Soviet member of the tribunal. Three defendants were acquitted altogether. Seven were sentenced to long terms of imprisonment and twelve were sentenced to death by hanging. The death sentences were carried out on the night of October 16, 1946, on all except Goering who cheated the hangman by crushing a vial of cyanide between his teeth.

Nuremberg was a remarkable achievement. The tribunal was both experimental and contested—as was shown by Churchill's support for summary executions of the Nazi high command, the appetite for vengeance expressed by the American and British publics, and above all the unscrupulous attempts by Stalin to make the trials into a show of propaganda and vengeance.

Justice Jackson believed that the conviction of the Nazi leaders for waging aggressive war would make a crucial contribution to the development of international law. It may have failed in that, but the Trial of the Major War Criminals Before The International Military Tribunal was a vital component in the agonizing process of rehabilitating Germany after World War II. Turning a vicious—albeit defeated—fascist enemy into a responsible democratic ally was an extraordinary accomplishment. Later my father reflected: "Now [that] the principles established by the Nuremberg trial have become an accepted part of international law, the time has come to put all the terrible factual details behind us. In the years since these awful things were done, new generations have grown up in Germany unstained by any guilt borne by some of those that preceded them." [31]

Nuremberg, in the words of Rebecca West, "embodied the rhetoric of progress." [32] It is sometimes presented in too roseate a light, as ushering in a new legal order. It did not do that. However, it was followed by further international actions outlawing crimes against humanity; in December 1946, a general assembly resolution of the newly formed United Nations affirmed Nuremberg's charter and judgment, and then in 1948 the U.N. adopted the Convention on the Prevention and Punishment of the Crime of Genocide. Nuremberg was also instrumental in establishing the protection of civilians as a core component of international law in judging the behavior of state and non-state actors—a key element of the Fourth Geneva Convention of 1949. In 1950 the tribunal also introduced a set of guiding principles for the prosecution and punishment of war criminals and crimes against humanity, today considered to be authoritative law. It created the precedent that is now taken for granted: that the perpetrators of atrocities and war crimes should still, upon the cessation of hostilities, be entitled to a free and fair trial.

And then there was its educational impact. The vast trove of documents amassed for the trial were essential in establishing the awful realities of Nazi rule. After the Eichmann trial in Israel, Hannah Arendt wrote, "Even today, our knowledge of the immense archival material of the Nazi regime rests to a large extent on the selection made for purposes of prosecution." [33] In the end, the historian Gary Bass points out, at Nuremberg, "America and Britain managed to produce something extraordinary. We have created nothing to compare with it since." [34]

At Nuremberg our civilization designed a vehicle to anathemize men imbued with evil. But evil is eternal and re-invents itself in every age. In the 1940s the world confronted and, with immense sacrifice, defeated the horror of fascism. The scale and the nature of the threats are different today but the ideology of Al Qaeda and its Islamist associates shares attributes with Nazism; it, too, is totalitarian, and it, too, has anti-Semitism at its core. In the case of Al Qaeda that intransigent hatred is extended to all "infidels." Just as Hitler planned a "thousand year Reich," so the Islamists call for a global caliphate in which they and their laws prevail absolutely and endlessly.

One can do worse than end this chapter with more words from Justice Jackson on the evils of the regime that the accused at Nuremberg had served. "Civilization can afford no compromise with the social forces which would gain renewed strength if we deal ambiguously or indecisively with the men in whom those forces now precariously survive."

*Chapter 2*

# CRIMES

ON THE AFTERNOON OF SEPTEMBER 11, 2001, Khalid Sheikh Mohammed sat before a screen in Karachi. He was waiting to see the mass homicides he had for years been planning against the United States. On schedule they happened.

Khalid Sheikh Mohammed (or KSM, as he is often, if somewhat too colloquially, called) said later that he was at first disappointed because the towers of the World Trade Center did not instantly collapse when hit by flights American Airlines 11 and United 175, the planes whose hijacking and transformation into missiles filled with men, women, and children he had meticulously organized. Then they did crumble and he rejoiced. A third plane hit the Pentagon as planned. Only the fourth flying bomb, intended for the U.S. Capitol, failed to reach its target and crashed into a field in Shanksville, Pennsylvania.

While Khalid Sheikh Mohammed celebrated in Karachi with his Al Qaeda cohorts, 2,973 people died in these attacks. The scale of the assault was unprecedented on American soil; the scope of Al Qaeda's imagination and ambition was terrifying. America was stunned, grief-stricken, and angry. That evening in Washington, President Bush answered Al Qaeda's act of war with his own vow: "These acts of mass murder were intended to frighten our nation into chaos and retreat. But they have failed. Our nation is strong. A great people has been moved to defend a great nation."

Since that time, the United States and its allies have been engaged in a fierce struggle with Al Qaeda and its affiliates—a worldwide jihadist enemy, with a presence in over sixty countries, that has constantly metamorphosed to meet new attempts by the Western world to defeat it.

As the long search for bin Laden showed, Al Qaeda's leaders have been hard to find, let alone to apprehend and bring to justice. Suffice it to say that they have committed—and have often bragged about—mass murder in many parts of the world, not just the United States.

In his closing address to the jury at the Nuremberg Tribunal, Justice Jackson said that it was his duty "to try and lift this case out of the morass of detail with which the record is full and put before you only the bold outlines of a case that is impressive in its simplicity. . . . I must leave it to experts to comb the evidence and write volumes on their specialties, while I picture in broad strokes the offences whose acceptance as lawful would threaten the continuity of civilization. I must, as Kipling put it, 'splash at a ten-league canvas with brushes of comet's hair.'" [1]

So it is with the crimes of Al Qaeda and its associates.

❖ ◉ ❖

To understand the background of Al Qaeda's attack upon global peace and security in general and the West in particular, it is important to understand the main ideological influences on modern Islamism.

I use the phrase Islamism to connote a collection of ideologies united by the belief that Islam is both a religion and a political system, and that Muslims have a duty to seek unity both religiously and politically. Radical Islamism regards the secular governments in countries with Muslim majorities as creations either of "infidel" colonial powers or of misguided Muslims imitating Western models. To Islamists, any state that is not based exclusively on Islamic law, or sharia, is both "impious" and "illegitimate." Thus it has no claim on the loyalty of Muslims, who have a duty to resist and combat it. Islamism is also characterized by the belief that Muslims have a duty to spread Islam throughout the world. And many, though not all, Islamists espouse such proselytization by force when they consider that necessary. It must be repeatedly stressed that the Radical Islamists are a tiny minority of Muslims. The vast majority of Muslims seek to live honorable, decent lives—and in many parts of the world they have to do so in difficult, sometimes dangerous, circumstances. Indeed, they are often the first to be killed by Radical Islamists.

An important part of the story begins in Egypt, the fulcrum of the Arab world, where, as this book was being completed, history was starting again. In early 2011, a successful rebellion against the autocratic president of Tunisia led to a popular uprising on the streets of Cairo against the thirty-year dictatorship of Hosni Mubarak. Mubarak, a longtime U.S. ally, fell and by March 2011 massive demonstrations had spread fast across borders, threatening many authoritarian regimes throughout North Africa and the Middle East. It was a time of optimism, disappointment, and uncertainty.

Despotism has long been the prevailing characteristic of governance in Arab and indeed other Islamic societies. In response to the mass demonstrations in Cairo, one might recall the great lexicographer Edward William Lane's description of life under Muhammad Ali, the Ottoman pasha of Egypt in the early nineteenth century:

> Most of the governors of provinces and districts carry their oppression far beyond the limits to which they are authorized to proceed by the Basha; and even the sheikh of a village, in executing the commands of his superiors, abuses his lawful power. Bribes and the ties of relationship and marriage influence him and them, and by lessening the oppression of some, who are more able to bear it, greatly increase that of others. But the

office of a sheikh of a village is far from being a sinecure. At the period of when the taxes are demanded of him, he frequently receives a more severe bastinadoing than any of his inferiors; for when the population of a village does not yield the sum required, their sheikh is often beaten for their default. . . . All the fellaheen [peasants] are proud of the stripes they receive for withholding their contributions. . . . Ammianus Marcellinus gives precisely the same character to the Egyptians of his time. [2]

The scholar Reuel Marc Gerecht pointed out that this pattern of authority was hard to shake. Throughout the twentieth century and early into the twenty-first, Egypt remained one of the most effective dictatorships in that part of the world, best known for "Oriental despotism." [3] It is in that context that modern Islamist thought and methods have grown.

Sayyid Qutb is often described as the father of today's Islamist movement, inasmuch as his work was the first to adapt the pre-existing sociopolitical elements of Islam to a modern ideological construct. Qutb came of age in British Egypt in the 1920s, and was profoundly influenced by the growing hostility to Western colonialism and modernity that characterized this period in Egyptian history. He was thus involved early in the work of the Muslim Brotherhood, an extremist network of Muslim charities and organizations formed in 1928 by Hassan al-Banna.

Al-Banna sought to purify Egypt according to Islamic scriptures and to expel the infidel colonial powers, a platform that attracted considerable support. The Brotherhood's radical demands included the destruction of any Western concept of justice, the imposition of sharia law, and the creation of pure Islamic regimes. Sayyid Qutb soon became one of the Brotherhood's most prominent members, and helped to influence its turn towards violent extremism in the years that followed.

Qutb advanced such radical ideas in his own work, writing that Western "civilization that is based on science, industry and material-ism . . . is without heart and conscience. . . . It sets forth to destroy all that humanity has produced in the way of spiritual values, human creeds, and noble traditions." Islamism, by contrast, was both the means and the goal of life on earth. [4]

Although the Nazis were fundamentally irreligious, they and the Brotherhood both rejected bourgeois liberalism and democracy; both were opportunistic, cynical, and totalitarian. During the Second World War, the Brotherhood and other Arab Islamists sought a German vic-tory, hoping that after the British were defeated, the Brotherhood itself could seize power in Egypt. The collaboration between the Third Reich and Muslim extremists was important—the Grand Mufti of Jerusalem, Amin al-Husseini, delivered sermons over Radio Berlin that were broad-cast throughout the Middle East. In one such 1944 oration, the Mufti channeled Hitler by exhorting his audience to "Kill the Jews wherever you find them. This pleases God, history and religion." [5]

Nazi Germany's defeat thwarted the Brotherhood's ambitions and so the group concentrated on terrorism in order to undermine British rule and establish the supremacy of Islam—a modus operandi that spread as political Islam emerged in various parts of the Muslim world. Islamists began to concentrate hatred on the newly-created Jewish state of Israel, which they considered an abomination and an imperialist assault on Islam. Their hatred grew as well for America, Israel's ally and the apogee of Western decadence and sin.

In Egypt, Islamists murdered many senior officials, including two Egyptian prime ministers. In 1949 the government counterattacked and al-Banna was killed. That was the year after Sayyid Qutb was awarded a two-year scholarship to the United States, designed by the Egyptian au-thorities in part to get him out of the country. His personal impressions of the United States during his two-year stay in Colorado are indicative of the distaste for America immanent in much of Islamist thought.

It is hard to imagine many places more demure than Colorado in the late 1940s, but Qutb viewed it as a modern-day Sodom. Haircuts and sports were bad enough but jazz was worse: "music that the Negroes invented to satisfy their primitive inclinations, as well as their desire to be noisy." Worse still was the "animal-like" mixing of the sexes—which encouraged American women's conspicuous sexuality. "The American girl is well acquainted with her body's seductive capacity. She knows it lies in the face, and in expressive eyes, and thirsty lips. She knows seductiveness lies in the round breasts, the full buttocks, and in the shapely thighs, sleek legs— and she shows all this and does not hide it."[6] In other words, the Americans were "shocking," a people who were "numb to faith in religion, faith in art, and faith in spiritual values altogether." The academic Benny Morris later pointed out that there was much in common between the ideologies behind the September 2001 attacks and the words of Qutb: "The white man, whether European or American, is our first enemy. We must .. . make [this] the cornerstone of our foreign policy and national education. We must nourish in our school age children sentiments that open their eyes to the tyranny of the white man, his civilization, and his animal hunger."[7]

In 1948 Qutb published his first major religious work, *Social Justice in Islam*, and insisted that the true Muslim had to cut himself off from the corruption of the world and be totally obedient to Allah. Qutb left the civil service and became a senior member of the Muslim Brotherhood, editing the Brotherhood's principal newspaper and serving on its governing council.

In 1952 the Brotherhood welcomed the overthrow of the pro-British monarchy by nationalist army officers but was outraged when it became clear that their principal ambition was to create a pan-Arab secular movement rather than an Islamist state.

After the Brotherhood tried to assassinate the military's leader, Gamal

Abdel Nasser, in 1954, Qutb and other Brothers were imprisoned or killed. Qutb was tortured and probably avoided death only because he was much of the time confined to the prison infirmary. But he continued to write, and to argue that anything non-Islamic was evil and corrupt. Western society must be destroyed because it contained "nothing that will satisfy its own conscience and justify its existence." He argued that mankind faced only one choice—Islam or *jahiliyya* (the barbaric West), that this was a struggle between God and Satan, and that anyone, Muslim or infidel, who did not accept this Manicheanism must die. [8]

In keeping with Al Qaeda and other modern Islamist movements, Qutb's thinking was infused with anti-Semitism. In the early 1950s, only a few years after the Holocaust, he wrote of "Our Struggle with the Jews," describing Jews as Islam's "worst" enemies, "slayers of the prophets," perfidious and evil. The nature of the Jews, he wrote, "does not allow them to feel the larger human connection which binds humanity together. Thus did the Jews (always) live in isolation." [9] Jews see that rather differently: they see themselves, understandably, facing a never-ending existential threat, one that in the twentieth century morphed through communism and fascism, and at the beginning of the twenty-first century found its most virulent base in Arab anti-Semitism and the dedicated hatred of Islamism.

Qutb was tried for conspiracy and hanged in August 1966, becoming a martyr and a symbol of Islamist resistance. His influence and that of the Brotherhood spread well beyond Egypt, and found particular resonance in the conservative kingdom of Saudi Arabia, where many members of the Brotherhood found refuge and ideological sustenance. This next generation of adherents included Sayyid Qutb's brother, Mohammed, who worked diligently to advance his sibling's work and legend. One of his adherents was Osama bin Laden himself, pampered child of one of the richest families in the Saudi kingdom. Another was Ayman al-Zawahiri, who later became a leading ideologist in Al Qaeda, and after bin Laden's death in 2011, was named his successor.[10] Mohammed Qutb was also a contemporary of the Islamist Abdullah Azzam, who became the ideological godfather of Al Qaeda and Osama bin Laden's own mentor—until bin Laden approved his assassination.

The example of the Muslim Brotherhood looms large for many Islamist movements, particularly in the Arab world, for it was the first to fuse traditional concepts of political Islam with the modern ideological construct and tactical terrorism. Yet Al Qaeda's beliefs and membership derive from an eclectic mixture of Islamist influences—from the more cerebral Islamism of the Brotherhood to the tribalist Wahhabis of Saudi Arabia and the Deobandis of the Indian subcontinent. It is best known as salafism.

❖ ◉ ❖

Just as the influence and violence of the Muslim Brotherhood grew in response to corrupt (and relatively secular) authoritarianism, the most fertile settings for violent Islamism have been states in which the people have, to varying degrees, lacked the freedom to control their own destinies. In many of the countries that have been particularly influential in the development of modern Islamism, religion has been both a vehicle to articulate grievances and a method of state control. Like two threatening weather systems, these instruments of Islam have had a tendency to reinforce one another, often to devastating effect.

The Wahhabi movement, centered in what is now Saudi Arabia, is a two-hundred-year-old reform group originally intended to cleanse Islamic societies. Wahhabis believe in the literal interpretation of the Koran and insist that believers live simple lives; they reject luxury, tolerance of infidels, and every form of "impurity." The school has had a huge impact on modern Islamism and helped form many of Al Qaeda's leaders.

The House of Saud possesses a sword with many sharp edges. The monarchy's control of the spiritual home of Islam has been an enormous source of power; yet that has also left the monarchy vulnerable to the charge of usurping the holy land. And of course, like any monarchical autocracy, the Saudi monarchy suffers the insecurity of the unelected, which, in these times, invites inevitable challenges. In an effort to co-opt those who might aspire to religious revolution, the House of Saud intensified its long-standing commitment to Wahhabism to increase its control of both its own country and the wider Muslim community.

Using its vast income from the export of oil, Saudi Arabia has invested enormously in spreading this doctrine abroad through mosques, madrassas, and broadcast propaganda. Wahhabism has indeed helped to cement the legitimacy and the ideological monopoly of the House of Saud; yet it has also been used as a way of fomenting revolution against all that is considered un-Islamic, and that has sometimes backfired against the Saudi rulers. Bin Laden, for instance, was a product of a Wahhabist background, and took its puritanical lessons to the most radical conclusion: he insisted that the House of Saud was a traitor to Islam because, in order to counter Saddam Hussein, it allowed American military bases in the land of Mecca and Medina.

The history of Islam has given Arab culture a disproportionate influence over the Muslim world, the majority of which is non-Arab. In fact, the demographic strength of the *umma* (community) largely derives from South Asia, which has also exercised an important influence on the global jihadist movement. Arguably, the most significant contribution of this region has been the northern Indian and Pakistani Deobandi school, which holds that Islamic societies have fallen behind the West because they have deviated from the teachings of the Prophet and insists that jihad is the duty of faithful Muslims.

The Deobandi movement originated as a hostile response to both the British Empire and the Hindu majority. After Indian independence,

Deobandi madrassas and clerics were used by the newly-formed Pakistan as a way of binding together the disparate groups of Muslims it now ruled. They became particularly significant following the destabilizing and violent secession of East Pakistan in 1971, and during Zia ul-Haq's military regime, which deliberately fostered Islamist education and law. Since then the parent Indian Deobandi school has distanced itself from political violence; the Pakistani Deobandis, on the other hand, have been closely associated with the Taliban leaders and their brutal methods.

❖ ◎ ❖

Osama bin Laden began his active involvement in the jihadist movement as a financier for the *mujahideen* fighting the Soviet army in Afghanistan in the 1980s. Many jihadis ended up in Peshawar, where virulent interpretations of Wahhabist and Deobandi Islam co-mingled, and Islamist leaders such as Abdullah Azzam propagated the romanticized death-cult of martyrdom that has become a common strain in global jihadism.

In the 1980s, Afghanistan became a holy destination for jihadists—a campaign in which they honed practical experience, forged networks of comradeship and kinship, and achieved their first significant military—and highly symbolic—victory over a world superpower. Moscow's defeat in Afghanistan led perhaps inexorably to the collapse of the Soviet Union for it showed to the Russian and many other peoples that the Marxist promise of history's unilinear march toward a glorious communist future was a lie. And it was this victory that emboldened jihadists, and Al Qaeda in particular, to wage war on the other hated superpower—the United States.

Al Qaeda is thought to have come into being in 1988, towards the end of the Afghan-Soviet War. As Michael Burleigh has pointed out, Al Qaeda was unique in that it drew its recruits from a variety of social, religious, and nationalist backgrounds, which he observes "gradually dissolved into a new global jihadi salafist identity that picked and mixed from secular geopolitics and several extreme Islamic traditions in a thoroughly eclectic, post-modern fashion." [11]

Throughout the 1990s bin Laden inspired, planned, directed, and celebrated attacks against the Saudi regime and its American allies. He declared war on the United States first in 1996 and then again in 1998, claiming that America was waging war against Muslims, God, and his messenger, Muhammad. He called for the murder of any American, anywhere on earth, as "the individual duty of every Muslim who can do it in any country in which it is possible to do it." [12] In an American television interview, he asserted that in this war, American deaths were more valuable than any other and that he would make no distinction between American soldiers and civilians. "We believe that the worst thieves in the world today and the worst terrorists are the Americans. . . . We do not have to differentiate between military or civilian. As far as we are concerned they are all targets." [13]

Bin Laden and Al Qaeda offered disaffected Sunni Muslims a way of life that might be more properly called a way of death. It has proved tragically attractive to a small, but nonetheless worrying, minority of young men in the Muslim lands of North Africa and the Middle East and, increasingly, beyond. It has become a powerful barrier to the march of change, a march which, one must acknowledge, is often unsettling if not deeply disruptive of traditions around the world.

Although Al Qaeda is a resolutely Sunni organization, the Shiite Islamic Revolution in Iran had an enormous effect on the jihadist imagination. Ayatollah Khomeini's surge to power in 1979 was an astonishing victory for all proponents of political Islam, and was a powerful rebuke and humiliation for the West. There is much in common between bin Laden's vision of hatred and of death and the views put forward by Khomeini, who warned in a speech in December 1984:

> If one allows the infidels to continue playing their role of cor-rupters on Earth, their eventual moral punishment will be all the stronger. Thus, if we kill the infidels in order to put a stop to their [corrupting] activities, we have indeed done them a service. For their eventual punishment will be less. To allow the infidels to stay alive means to let them do more corrupting. [To kill them] is a surgical operation commanded by Allah the Creator. . . . Those who follow the rules of the Koran are aware that we have to apply the laws of qissas (retribution) and that we have to kill. . . . War is a blessing for the world and for every nation. It is Allah himself who commands men to wage war and to kill. [14]

In considering the pronouncements of both Khomeini and bin Laden, one is drawn back to the description of Hitler by Justice Jackson at Nuremberg. Hitler, he said, "was a mad 'Messiah' who started the war without cause and prolonged it without reason. If he could not rule, he cared not what happened to Germany." So it is with Khomeini, bin Laden, and other leaders of the Islamist revival. They may not be, by their own standards, mad—but nor was Hitler. Their madness resides in the fact that for them dogmas, not consequences, matter.

Thus, despite the rhetoric of Islamists who routinely accuse the Western powers of responsibility for all the ills of the Muslim world, the truth is that over the last half century, by far the greatest numbers of Muslims killed around the world have been murdered by other Muslims. In East Pakistan (now Bangladesh), between a half million and one million people were slaughtered in 1971 by the Pakistani army in an attempt to prevent secession. In the devastating war between Iran and Iraq in the 1980s, there were an estimated 1.5 million military casualties, and thousands of civilians were also killed. The Algerian civil war that began in 1992 claimed over 150,000 lives. In Darfur, between 200,000 and 500,000 civilians (mostly non-Muslims) are estimated to have been killed by the Islamist government in Khartoum. In Iraq, the vast majority of the estimated 106,000 civilians who lost their lives after the United States overthrew Saddam Hussein in March 2003, were killed by other Muslims.*

Almost every day of every year brings more accounts—not news any more—of Muslim men, women, and children being murdered in the latest suicide bombing by followers of Al Qaeda and other such groups. The Radical Islamist reach for power is almost always bloody; and where Radical Islamists achieve power—as in Afghanistan, Sudan, and Iran—they practice mass murder on a scale not equaled in the world except by Nazi and Communist rulers.

This cult of death, embraced by both Sunni and Shia extremists, has been described by the philosopher Roger Scruton as "both a protest against modern nihilism and a form of it—a last-ditch attempt to rescue Islam from the abyss of nothingness by showing that it can still demand the ultimate proof of devotion." [15] But Scruton also points to the responsibility of globalization in the rise of international Islamism. Western money, Western banking, Western communications, Western concepts of the individual, even Western architecture, since the 1960s have reached ever further and deeper across the globe. Globalization has changed the world forever. For good, in the eyes of its advocates, who point to the rising prosperity that follows free trade and the greater intermingling of peoples. But to its critics, "it means the loss of sovereignty, together with large scale social, economic, and aesthetic disruption." Worse still, Western habits, Western morals (particularly

---

* The most reliable source for casualties in Iraq has been www.iraqbodycount.org.

sexual), and Western television are seen as temptations, not freedoms, "and the normal response to temptation is either to give in to it or to punish those who offer it." Globalization thus "offers militant Islam the opportunity that it has lacked since the Ottoman retreat from central Europe." It has created "a true Islamic *umma*, which identifies itself across borders in terms of a global form of legitimacy. . . . This new form of globalized Islam is undeniably threatening, since it satisfies a hunger for membership that globalization itself has created." And it has created an international army ready to do battle with the enemies of God, wherever they are. [16]

❖ ◉ ❖

Khalid Sheikh Mohammed's own background and influences mirror the diverse nature of Al Qaeda. He is both a product of the various strands of violent Islamism that have permeated the Muslim world, and a natural-born killer who has devoted most of his adult life to a path of jihadist mass murder. His defining characteristic is said to be his egoism.

He was born in Kuwait in 1965 to Baluchi parents, who had escaped the poverty of Baluchistan (in western Pakistan) by emigrating to the increasingly wealthy Gulf state. He spent a comfortable childhood in Kuwait with eight siblings and his nephew Ramzi Yousef, three years his junior. When his father died before he began school, his elder brothers took over his religious and academic education. He was radicalized during the course of several summers at desert camps where, according to *The 9/11 Commission Report*, he became "enamored of violent jihad." In 1980, he joined the Muslim Brotherhood at the age of sixteen. [17]

In 1984, he went to study in the United States and was enrolled in Chowan, a small Baptist college in North Carolina, and subsequently attended the North Carolina Agricultural and Technical State University, where he obtained a degree in mechanical engineering. His distaste for America grew while he was there, rather like Sayyid Qutb almost forty years before.

The Arab students at these schools tended to divide almost viscerally. Some happily enjoyed what they saw as the opportunities of American life—the alcohol, the women, the cars—while others, including Khalid Sheikh Mohammed, rejected these pleasures as decadent and became increasingly religious. The devout segregated themselves from their peers; they lived together, ate together, and prayed together. Khalid Sheikh Mohammed's high school teacher later claimed that he had decided that most Americans did not like Arabs and Islam because of Israel.

According to one U.S. intelligence summary, "KSM's limited and negative experience in the United States"—which included a brief jail stay because of unpaid bills—almost certainly propelled him on his path to becoming a terrorist. He stated that his contact with Americans, while minimal, confirmed his view that the United States was "a debauched and racist country."

While KSM was completing his studies in the United States, his three elder brothers moved to Pakistan to support the jihad against the Soviets in Afghanistan. KSM joined them in the late 1980s and spent much of his time in Peshawar, where the Deobandis had, and continue to have, considerable influence. According to *The 9/11 Commission Report*, he later joined the jihadist forces fighting in the Bosnian war between the Bosnian Muslims and the Serbian nationalists. Then, apparently seamlessly, he moved to work as a government engineer in Qatar before committing himself more permanently to the path of jihadist murder.

Khalid Sheikh Mohammed's first major terrorist success came in 1993 when he helped finance the first bombing of the World Trade Center. Indeed, this was a family plot—it had been devised by Ramzi Yousef, his nephew. Yousef, aka Abdul Basit Mahmud Abdul Karim, was under thirty years old when he arrived in New York, claiming to be an Iraqi dissident and requesting asylum. He was welcomed into the country he planned to attack. Basing himself among the Arab community in Brooklyn, he assembled a gang of petty criminals committed to radical Islam.

Yousef worshipped at mosques in New Jersey where the preacher was often the extremist Sheikh Omar Abdel Rahman who, for inexplicable reasons, had been given an entry visa from Sudan. The Egyptian government considered the blind Sheikh Rahman dangerous and sought his extradition but, in the name of free speech, the U.S. government tolerated the Sheikh's rabble-rousing diatribes against America and Israel.

To attack the World Trade Center, Yousef and his crew, using funds KSM had raised for the purpose, bought and assembled 1,500 pounds of explosives, a huge bomb. On February 26, 1993, they loaded their homemade weapon aboard a rented van and drove it into the garage of the Center. The bomb detonated at midday, killing six people and injuring thousands. The blast tunneled through seven floors and caused massive damage: the repairs cost some half a billion dollars.[18]

Yousef managed to flee the country that night, while others of their group, including the blind Sheikh, were arrested. They were indicted and tried for complicity in a wide-ranging series of terrorist plots, including the murder of Meir Kahane, a fanatical Israeli rabbi shot dead in New York in 1990; the Trade Center bombing; and plans to blow up several other vital sites in Manhattan, including the Lincoln and Holland Tunnels, F.B.I. headquarters, and the United Nations. After a protracted trial in federal court in the Southern District of New York, they were sentenced to life imprisonment. During the proceedings, the prosecution was required by the standard practice of conspiracy cases to reveal the names of unindicted co-conspirators. The list included Osama bin Laden—it was the first time that his name had surfaced in such a context. Then resident in Sudan, he was thus put on notice that the U.S. authorities were aware of his activities. The presiding judge in the trial, Michael B. Mukasey, who became attorney general during the second administration of George W. Bush, said later that that case made clear to him that the United States was facing a military, not a criminal, problem in Islamist terrorism, and captured terrorists should be dealt with in military not civilian court.[19]

Ramzi Yousef joined Khalid Sheikh Mohammed in Karachi, and they both traveled to Manila, where KSM posed as a Qatari businessman in the timber business, one of many identities, and acquired a young Filipina dentist as a girlfriend. He hired a helicopter to show off to his girlfriend and to survey the city while he and Yousef made new plans to cause terror and to kill.

An early ambition was to assassinate Pope John Paul II during his pilgrimage to the Philippines. They thought he would be easier to murder than their principal target, President Bill Clinton. Yousef refined and extended his expertise as a bomb maker; he developed a tiny new bomb that could be easily smuggled onto a plane in parts, the batteries hidden in the heels of shoes. Studying airline timetables, they worked out how five men could in a single day board twelve flights and hide under seats bombs primed and timed to explode on later flights. KSM called this Operation *Bojinka*. According to Terry McDermott, "The math was simple: 12 flights with at least 400 people per flight. Somewhere in the neighborhood of 5,000 deaths. It would be a day of glory for them, calamity for the Americans they supposed would fill the aircraft." [20]

In December 1994 Yousef made a test run of *Bojinka* on a Philippine Airlines plane. In the lavatory he concocted a bomb from parts he had smuggled on board and then strapped it under his seat. It exploded on a later flight, tearing to pieces a young Japanese engineer, Haruki Ikegami, and almost bringing down the plane.

At the beginning of 1995, they fixed on January 14 for their mass airline bomb plot and started brewing the explosive nitroglycerine in their Manila apartment. The infernal swill of chemicals took on its own life and smoke filled the apartment building. The police arrived. Yousef and

KSM succeeded in fleeing and made it back to Pakistan. The Pope was spared attack and so were the passengers of many airliners.

Betrayed by an informer in Pakistan, Ramzi Yousef was arrested at a guesthouse by Pakistani and U.S. security and flown to New York. His guilt was never in doubt and, in the U.S. District Court for the Southern District of New York, he was convicted, along with two others, of planning the *Bojinka* plot. In a statement to the Court, Yousef boasted, "Yes, I am a terrorist, and proud of it as long as it is against the U.S. government and against Israel, because you are more than terrorists; you are the one who invented terrorism and are using it every day. You are butchers, liars, and hypocrites."[21] He was sentenced to life imprisonment, with no chance of parole, and was incarcerated in the Supermax federal prison at Florence, Colorado.

Khalid Sheikh Mohammed was staying in the same guesthouse as Yousef, but he escaped detection by Pakistani or U.S. officials. Using one of his many passports, he returned to Qatar, where he was protected by sympathizers. But as a result of U.S. pressure on the government of Qatar to arrest him, he was forced to flee to Afghanistan, where he met Osama bin Laden.

Bin Laden had been living in Afghanistan since 1996, when, under U.S. and Saudi Arabian pressure, the government of Sudan decided that hosting him was no longer in its interest. He had flown east and became the honored guest of Afghanistan's Taliban, the recently-founded ultra-Islamist regime notable for its fundamentalism and its brutality. Outside Kandahar, the Taliban allowed bin Laden to set up training camps for terrorists who, armed with the necessary Islamist zeal and knowledge of modern tradecraft, could be dispatched all over the world to commit mass murder.

Khalid Sheikh Mohammed began to plot with bin Laden in Afghanistan in 1998. He was aware that bin Laden was keen to embark on major operations against the United States and its interests. He gave bin Laden details of the first World Trade Center bombing in 1993 and other terrorist plots in which he had been involved. He also outlined for the first time his vision of training Al Qaeda gangs to hijack numbers of planes and, turning them into massive missiles crammed with people, crash them into buildings in the United States. [22] His original proposal envisaged planes flown at ten targets, including the C.I.A. and F.B.I. headquarters, nuclear power plants, and skyscrapers on the East and West coasts.

In a revealing detail, KSM later said that he was determined that he himself should be in charge of the tenth hijacked plane. He intended to land the plane at a U.S. airport, slaughter all the male passengers on board and then, before the massed media, deliver a speech attacking the United States for its support of Israel, the Philippines, and repressive Arab governments. As the U.S. government's 9/11 Commission later reported, "this vision" showed KSM's true ambitions: "This is theater, a spectacle of destruction with KSM as the self-cast star—the super terrorist." [23] And that is an important part of what he has always sought. His passion for grandstanding and jihadist propaganda would, one must imagine, be on display in any court where he is arraigned. His record suggests that he would try to dominate the proceedings as Goering dominated Nuremberg. *

---

\* In his eloquent closing speech for the prosecution at Nuremberg, Justice Jackson said that "Goering stuck a pudgy finger in every pie." It was an odd phrase for such a serious speech but it was understood by everyone in the courtroom who had watched Goering dominate the proceedings. Rebecca West agreed with Jackson: "The courtroom was not small, but it was full of Goering's fingers. His soft and white and spongy hands were forever smoothing his curiously abundant brown hair, or covering his wide mouth while his plotting eyes looked facetiously around, or weaving impudent gestures of innocence in the air." And "he was the only one of these defendants who, if he had the chance, would have walked out of the Palace of Justice and taken over Germany again, and turned it into the stage for the enactment of the private fantasy which had brought him to the dock." [Rebecca West, *A Train of Powder* (New York: Macmillan, 1955), 21, 7.]

Nineteen ninety-eight was a crucial year for Al Qaeda, one in which it achieved its greatest successes to date and learned that it could continue to operate relatively undisturbed. Osama bin Laden repeated his declaration that Al Qaeda was at war with the United States. He asserted that America's presence in Saudi Arabia, its alliances with other Arab states, and its hostility toward Saddam Hussein gave Muslims no alternative. He claimed that all Muslims must kill Americans and their allies "until the Aqsa Mosque [in Jerusalem] and the Haram Mosque [in Mecca] are freed from their grip and until their armies, shattered and broken-winged, depart from all the lands of Islam, incapable of threatening any Muslim."[24]

He went on to say: "By God's leave, we call on every Muslim who believes in God and hopes for reward to obey God's command to kill the Americans and plunder their possessions wherever he finds them and whenever he can. Likewise we call on the Muslim *ulema* and leaders and youth and soldiers to launch attacks against the armies of the American devils and against those who are allied with them from among the helpers of Satan."[25]

In his most serious and enduring threat, bin Laden also declared that it was his duty as a jihadist to acquire and use weapons of mass destruction (WMD) against the enemies of God. This was an ambition that he often repeated in both private and public communications. The threat grew after the Egyptian Islamist group, Islamic Jihad, controlled by Ayman al-Zawahiri, merged with Al Qaeda. Zawahiri and his colleagues brought valuable technological expertise in WMD matters to the more ideological Al Qaeda. Bin Laden told *Time* magazine that "Acquiring [WMD] for the defense of Muslims is a religious duty." From that point on, Al Qaeda camps in Afghanistan trained hundreds of Islamist extremists in the production and use of chemical, biological, and radiological weapons.[26] The possession of weapons of mass destruction by

Islamists was far more terrifying than their possession by the Soviet Union; the specter has lurked in the minds of American policy makers ever since, and after 9/11 came to dominate them.

Al Qaeda's threat had been growing for several years. On June 25, 1996, Islamist terrorists, almost certainly controlled by Iran, had a bloody success in Saudi Arabia. They detonated a sewage truck filled with explosives close to the Khobar Towers, a building in the town of Khobar that housed U.S. Air Force personnel. Nineteen Americans and one Saudi were killed; 372 people of many nationalities were wounded, some of them seriously.

In August 1998, bin Laden activated a longstanding Al Qaeda plot to destroy the American embassies in Nairobi and Dar es Salaam. Neither was adequately protected and two truck bombers were able to blow up their lethal loads on August 7, 1998, exactly eight years after U.S. forces first arrived in Saudi Arabia. In Dar es Salaam, much of the blast was absorbed by a water tanker but it still killed eleven Tanzanians and wounded another eighty people. In Nairobi the carnage was far worse: twelve Americans and 201 Kenyans were killed. Another 4,500 people were injured, many of them terribly. Kenya's medical services were quite unable to cope with carnage on this scale. The U.S. flew many of the worst injured to hospitals in Europe. Israel sent teams of sniffer dogs that were able to find scores of victims buried under the rubble.

In both attacks, most of those innocent Africans who died were Muslims. After the embassy bombings, bin Laden issued a statement justifying the murder of his co-religionists: "When it becomes apparent that it would be impossible to repel these Americans without assaulting them, even if this involved the killing of Muslims, this is permissible under Islam." [27]

The American response was not a success. President Clinton ordered Tomahawk Cruise missiles to be launched against several of bin Laden's training camps in Afghanistan. These killed six people. U.S. officials said they would have hit bin Laden himself had he not left one target an hour before it was struck. A chemical factory in Khartoum that had been mistakenly linked to Al Qaeda was also destroyed by Tomahawks. (U.S. officials believed that the factory had been producing VX nerve gas for the Iraqi regime of Saddam Hussein, another sworn enemy of the United States.)

Altogether, the Clinton administration's reaction to the embassy bombings seemed to demonstrate weakness rather than resolve and was thus another boost to the Islamist cause. Bin Laden was able to announce, "By the grace of God, I am alive." His myth in the Islamic world was promoted and the group began to boast of its vast ambitions.

The millennium celebration of the birth of Christ was an obvious moment for Al Qaeda extravaganzas—Jordanian police discovered a plot to blow up the Radisson Hotel in Amman at a time when it would be filled with American Christians. On the U.S.-Canadian border, a vigilant customs officer stopped a clearly nervous Algerian, Ahmed Ressam, who was trying to enter the U.S. in a car containing bomb-making materials and plans to target the Los Angeles International Airport. Plots were discovered throughout Europe, where inadequate asylum laws had allowed Islamist groups to multiply. One gang of would-be bombers, organized from London, had made themselves a film that contained scenes of Strasbourg's Christmas market; over the images of the shoppers, the soundtrack, in Arabic, announced, "These are the enemies of God as they stroll about. You will all go to hell. God Willing." [28]

Mercifully, vigilant police work thwarted this plot to attack Strasbourg. At their trial, the defendants refused to speak except to scream such slogans as "You are all Jews. I don't need the court. Allah is my defender. Our only judge is Allah." [29]

One millennium attack that succeeded was a suicide bombing assault on the United States Navy destroyer U.S.S. *Cole* when it was refueling in Aden Harbor on October 12, 2000. A small boat came up alongside the ship and its Al Qaeda crew exploded a massive bomb that killed seventeen American sailors and injured over forty more. Neither President Clinton, in the last months of his presidency, nor his successor, President Bush, undertook any direct military response to this brutal attack upon the U.S. navy.

By this time, Osama bin Laden had approved Khalid Sheikh Mohammed's plan for an aerial assault on prominent targets in the United States. (Interestingly, KSM did not swear *bay'ah* (a pledge of loyalty) to bin Laden at this stage because he wished to be able to ignore any later decision by the Al Qaeda leadership to cancel his plan of attack.[30]) Bin Laden pledged to finance these attacks and to provide manpower from Al Qaeda's Afghan training camps. KSM oversaw the planning and execution, helping the hijackers travel and selecting the targets—these were narrowed down to the World Trade Center, to symbolize American capitalism; the Pentagon; and the Capitol, which was considered to be the source of U.S. support for Israel. Bin Laden also wanted to target the White House, but this idea was dropped for fear that, if the president was not in residence, the attack would be seen as a failure.

Khalid Sheikh Mohammed recruited potential pilots who were sent to the U.S. to enroll in flying schools, and thugs whose job was to overpower crew and passengers during the attacks. His eventual indictment alleged in plain but chilling words, "In or about 1999 and 2000, in Afghanistan and Pakistan, Khalid Sheikh Mohammed trained the hijackers to use short bladed knives by killing sheep or camels."[31]

In the course of 2000 and early 2001 more and more of these gangs made their way to the United States. All of the logistics—relatively simple—were commanded and controlled by Khalid Sheikh Mohammed, and the men's expenses, remarkably modest for such an ambitiously destructive operation, were transferred from the United Arab Emirates by another of his nephews.

Cunning and limited use of the Internet and cell phones allowed the plotters to communicate relatively freely and undetected. There were, during the long conspiracy, various moments at which the U.S. authorities came close to uncovering the plot. In August 2001, just weeks before 9/11, one recruit, Zacarias Moussaoui, was arrested at his flight school in Minnesota after his erratic behavior aroused suspicion. He was held on immigration-violation charges and concerns that he might be a suicide hijacker actually reached the highest levels of the C.I.A. But the F.B.I. failed to obtain a warrant to search his laptop, which might well have revealed the wider plot. There were other intelligence hints of an impending attack that intelligence officials in the Bush administration should have pursued more diligently.

On the morning of September 11, 2001, the long-planned mass murder took place. Four planes were hijacked by Khalid Sheikh Mohammed's men and three successfully bombed their targets: the twin towers of the World Trade Center in New York and the Pentagon. Only the fourth plane failed to reach its target, the U.S. Capitol; the passengers, having learned that they were now part of a massive flying bomb, rebelled against the hijackers who, about to be overpowered, plunged the plane into a field in Pennsylvania. In addition to the 2,973 people who were murdered that day, some 3,000 children lost a parent and a new age of anxiety began.

That evening, President Bush told the shocked American people that "Our way of life, our very freedom came under attack in a series of deliberate and deadly terrorist acts." He did not at this stage blame radical Islamists for the attacks, but he promised that America would fight back and would make no distinction between the terrorists themselves and anyone who harbored them.

There was a very real fear at the time that the attacks of 9/11 were but the first in a series and that the next assault might well involve weapons of mass destruction. The Bush administration decided at once that the law enforcement response to terrorism was now inadequate; it would need to go beyond law enforcement to include military, financial, and diplomatic weapons in the defense of U.S. national security.

On September 18, the U.S. Congress authorized President Bush "to use all necessary and appropriate force against those nations, organizations, or persons he determines planned, authorized, committed, or aided the terrorist attacks that occurred on September 11, 2001, or harbored such organizations or persons, in order to prevent any future acts of international terrorism against the United States by such nations, organizations or persons."

This monumental mandate was unlimited in terms of time and geography. It was passed 98–0 in the Senate and 420–1 in the House of Representatives. From then all the force and power of the United States would be brought to bear to defeat America's terrorist enemies on and off the battlefield, all over the world. There was almost no dissent, at home or abroad. America's allies rallied to its defense. For the first time in history, NATO invoked Article 5, which pledges members to defend each other and declared its support for a fellow member under attack. The British Prime Minister, Tony Blair, was particularly robust in his response, immediately expressing full support for the United States in what he, too, called this new war. Later he recalled, "The most common words that day were 'war,' 'evil,' 'sympathy,' 'solidarity,' 'determination,' and, of course, 'change.' Above all, it was accepted that the world had changed. How could it be otherwise?" [32]

As America grieved and girded, Khalid Sheikh Mohammed celebrated in Karachi—the most cosmopolitan city of America's Muslim ally Pakistan— and bin Laden rejoiced in his Afghan hideout. In a conversation recorded with his deputy, Ayman al-Zawahiri, and a visiting Saudi militant, Khaled al-Harbi, whose mother had reported that she had received many, many calls of congratulation, bin Laden waxed lyrical about the effects of the crimes he had authorized Khalid Sheikh Mohammed to commit:

> The sermons they [the hijackers] gave in New York and Washington, made the whole world hear—the Arabs, the non-Arabs, the Indians, the Chinese—and are worth much more than millions of books and cassettes and pamphlets [promoting Islam]. Maybe you have heard, but I heard it myself on the radio, that at one of the Islamic centers in Holland, the number of those who have converted to Islam after the strikes, is greater than all those who converted in the last eleven years.

*Chapter 3*

# CONVENTIONS

"THE MOST SERIOUS CHALLENGE that faces modern civilization [is] war and international lawlessness." [1]

So spoke Justice Jackson in 1949, just three years after judgment was reached against the major Nazi war criminals. Nineteen forty-nine was also the year in which the international community (a nebulous concept at the best of times), appalled by the horrors of the Second World War, renegotiated and redefined the Geneva Conventions, the rules by which wars between states are always now supposed to be fought.

Jackson believed that Nuremberg had tackled the nineteenth-century concept that state sovereignty permitted any nation to declare war at any time, for any purpose and finally laid to rest "the vicious assumptions that all war must be regarded as legal and just, and that while the law imposes personal responsibility for starting a street riot, it imposes none for inciting and launching a world war." [2]

Nuremberg's value to the world lay less in how faithfully it interpreted the past than in how accurately it forecast the future. "It is possible that that strife and suspicion will lead to new aggressions and that the nations are not yet ready to receive and abide by the Nuremberg law." But he was confident at least that at Nuremberg, "in place of what might have been mere acts of vengeance we wrote a civilized legal precedent and one that will lie close to the foundations of that body of international law that will prevail when the world becomes sufficiently civilized."

An important part of the attempt to make the postwar world less savage was the rewriting of the Geneva Conventions that same year. The inspiring history of the Geneva Conventions is well known. They took form after the publication in 1862 by Henri Dunant of *A Memory of Solferino*, in which he wrote of the horrors he had witnessed at that battle. To alleviate them, he proposed the creation of neutral relief groups to provide humanitarian aid in time of war. So the Red Cross was born and the first Geneva Convention on protecting wounded and sick soldiers on land in time of war was passed in 1864. The second Convention, enacted in 1907, extended those protections to those who needed it on the sea. The third Convention, guaranteeing decent treatment for prisoners of war, was concluded in 1929.

In 1949, all three Conventions were updated and a fourth Convention was created. The basic intention was to protect innocent civilians by deterring violations of the laws of war. To that end, the Convention also offered protection to combatants who followed the laws of war.

The fourth Convention imposed obligations on occupying powers vis-à-vis civilian populations; it outlawed torture, collective punishment, and the resettlement by an occupying power of its own civilians on territory under its military control. Common Article 3, common to all four Conventions, was especially important because it covered, for the first time, non-international armed conflicts, including civil wars, internal armed conflicts that spill into other states, or internal conflicts in which third states or a multinational force intervenes. It established fundamental rules from which no derogation was to be permitted and has been described as, in effect, a mini-Convention within the Conventions.

Among its requirements was humane treatment for all persons in enemy hands, specifically prohibiting murder, mutilation, torture, cruel, humiliating and degrading treatment, the taking of hostages, and unfair trial. It required that the wounded, sick, and shipwrecked be cared for. It granted the International Committee of the Red Cross the right to offer its services to the parties of the conflict. It called on all parties to the conflict to bring the Conventions into force through special agreements. And it recognized that the application of these rules did not affect the legal status of the parties to the conflict.

The updated Geneva Conventions came into force in October 1950. One hundred ninety-four states have since ratified them and they claim universal application. But many states throughout the world pay little regard to them. Indeed it is doubtful whether a single captured American soldier has ever been treated according to the Conventions since 1950.

❖ ◎ ❖

Once it became clear that Osama bin Laden, resident of Afghanistan and leader of Al Qaeda, was the evil leader and financier behind the attacks on September 11, 2001, the U.S. government immediately demanded that the Taliban rulers of Afghanistan hand him and his colleagues over. When that request was refused, the U.S. launched Operation Enduring Freedom, a swift and successful light footprint assault on the Taliban government and an unsuccessful attempt to capture or kill bin Laden himself. None of this was controversial at the time.

America's prompt response to 9/11, including the immediate use of military force against the terrorists and their sponsors, was appropriate. If, as its critics later proposed, the U.S. government had treated the attacks as a criminal offense rather than an act of war, there could never have been such a quick reaction. But it was also evident that existing domestic and international laws were not designed to cope with what was being called a "new kind of war," involving primarily stateless actors who cared nothing for any rules of war. The 1949 Conventions were part of the international legal system designed after the most destructive war in history; the new United Nations was intended to prevent traditional armed conflicts between states and their uniformed armed forces or civil wars. The postwar structures have helped avoid such total war as developed after 1939. But today the threats to peace are rarely such as Hitler posed—an aggressive nation-state greedy for conquest. The threats today are more often from failed states (Afghanistan, Somalia), rogue nations (Iran, North Korea), global terrorism (Al Qaeda and its associates in the Arabian Peninsula and in the Mahgreb), and the proliferation of weapons of mass destruction. Postwar rules do not always match the realities of present-day conflicts.

Until 9/11 the United States had reacted relatively cautiously and sporadically to terrorist attacks abroad; it had taken a primarily law-enforcement approach, however shocking these assaults had been. Such attacks had become an increasing threat through the 1970s and 1980s and they showed the limits of America's effective jurisdiction. For example, on March 1, 1973, a reception at the Saudi embassy in Khartoum was stormed by eight Black September terrorists who took hostage Ambassador Cleo A. Noel Jr.; his deputy, George Curtis Moore; a Belgian diplomat, Guy Eid; and two others. The U.S. government refused to negotiate and the terrorists killed Noel, Moore, and Eid. Their demands for an escape plane were rejected and they eventually released the remaining hostages and surrendered to the Sudanese authorities.

A court of inquiry sentenced the terrorists to life imprisonment, but these sentences were reduced to seven years and they were handed over to the custody of the Palestine Liberation Organization—which sent them to Egypt. Three of them disappeared from Egyptian custody and were never recaptured. The remaining men served out their sentences. The United States also tried to prosecute Yasser Arafat, the P.L.O. leader, in the United States for his role in the murders, but concluded that it lacked the legal jurisdiction to do so.

President Reagan was determined to extend America's reach and enable it to pursue terrorists more effectively by judicial means. In October 1984 Congress passed legislation that gave U.S. courts jurisdiction over certain terrorist acts committed outside the United States. This had an important effect: from now on the administration was able to demand, often forcefully, that governments either prosecute or turn over to the U.S. any person suspected of carrying out attacks on Americans within their jurisdiction.

The first terrorist incident involving the new policy occurred in June 1985 when TWA Flight 847 was hijacked and flown to Lebanon by Hezbollah terrorists; they brutally beat and murdered one young man, Robert Stethem, because he was a U.S. Navy diver. The hijackers got away from the scene of the crime but the U.S. charged all four of them. One was called Mohammed Ali Hamadi and in January 1987 he was arrested for another offense at Frankfurt airport. According to Victoria Toensing, then a U.S. Justice Department lawyer in the Terrorism Unit, the German authorities had an "Oh damn" moment when they realized they had detained one of Stethem's murderers. [3] Fearing Islamist reprisals, they were not eager to accede to U.S. demands for his extradition. The first excuse was Germany's policy not to extradite suspects whose crime might carry a death penalty sentence, common in the U.S. but increasingly eschewed in Europe. Even when the U.S. agreed not to call for the ultimate sentence for Hamadi, Germany refused his extradition. Instead, under fierce U.S. pressure, he was eventually tried in Germany. He was convicted and sentenced to life—but the German government released him in 2005 and allowed him to disappear back into the Middle East. [4]

As a result of the Reagan–era legislation, the United States was able to pressure other countries—Pakistan, for example—either to prosecute terrorists on their soil or to hand them over to the U.S. for trial. And so, because the U.S. could and would now demand extradition or prosecution, terrorists knew that many countries would hold them accountable even for crimes committed outside their jurisdictions.

The law enforcement paradigm was never absolute before 9/11; for example, in 1986, President Reagan used warplanes to bomb Colonel Gaddafi in revenge for the Libyan attack on a Berlin nightclub frequented by U.S. soldiers. Unfortunately for his thousands of future victims at home and abroad, the Colonel survived the raid. He was able to continue promoting murderous civil wars in Africa as well as terrorism elsewhere for years to come.

The continuing difficulties of bringing terrorists to justice were highlighted by the Lockerbie murders. In December 1988 Pan Am Flight 103 exploded as it flew over Lockerbie, Scotland, en route from London to New York. One hundred eighty-nine of the two hundred fifty-nine victims on the plane were Americans. The Reagan administration was only weeks from leaving office and feared that bringing those responsible to justice would be a protracted, perhaps even futile process. It was far worse than anyone expected.

After long investigations, Libya was identified as the culprit and finally, following complex diplomatic and judicial negotiations, two Libyan men were accused and were detained in Libya in 1991. Although the aim of the attack had been to kill as many Americans as possible, the Libyan government was able to insist that their trial take place in the Netherlands, a country that was unconnected to the offense. The court heard the case under Scottish law, for it was in Scottish skies that the plane exploded; eleven Scots on the ground were also killed. The trial did not end until early 2001, when one of the defendants was found not guilty and released; the other, Abdul Basset Ali al-Megrahi, was convicted and given a life sentence, which required him to serve at least twenty-seven years in Scotland. However, al-Megrahi developed prostate cancer, and in 2009, under immense pressure from Libya, the Scottish government announced that because he had only three months to live, he would be released on compassionate grounds. One of Colonel Gaddafi's sons, Seif al-Islam al-Gaddafi (who had recently been courted by some of Europe's leading bankers and had filed his dissertation at the London School of Economics in 2007) came on a presidential plane to fly him home to Libya, where he was welcomed as a triumphant hero. Almost two years later, in early 2011, when a popular revolt began against the Gaddafi regime, al-Megrahi was still alive. This shocking penultimate act in the drama caused outrage. Despite financial compensation paid by the Libyan government, justice was not done to the victims of Lockerbie.

❖ ◎ ❖

After 9/11, law enforcement was still used against terrorists in the United States, but the emphasis shifted to military responses in the war which Al Qaeda had declared on the U.S. A legal framework for this change was provided by John Yoo, the deputy assistant attorney general in the Justice Department's Office of Legal Counsel. He argued that "the scope and the intensity of the destruction is one that in the past had only rested within the power of a nation-state, and should qualify the attacks as an act of war." [5] The war paradigm certainly suited both the national and international shock over the attacks on September 11.

Perhaps as important was the public definition of this new war. What could one call it? Not wishing to use the word Islam in its identification of the enemy, the White House created a new concept and declared a "War on Terror," an imperfect description that would lead to both confusion and derision even among allies of the United States. As Benjamin Wittes observes in his closely argued book, *The Law and the Long War*, "Just as the word 'war' doesn't quite describe the War on Terror intellectually or in practical terms, it doesn't quite work legally either—at least not if the goal is a legal architecture that grants the president the powers he needs yet also generates the sort of accountability for the use of those powers that might sustain them with long-term public confidence."

Even more complicated than naming the type of war was defining the legal status of the enemy. At one level, they were no more than a motley gang of murderers—their ideological motive was irrelevant in terms of law. Yet Al Qaeda was also an international organization that had, long before 9/11, carried out a sustained, worldwide campaign against the United States. The fact that it was a non-state actor did not make it any less belligerent than a sovereign state. And the fact that its members refused to heed the laws of war made them, in one sense, more dangerous than a conventional state enemy, by virtue of their unpredictability. As a result, the Bush administration concluded that members of Al Qaeda and its affiliates should be treated as "unlawful combatants."

This is a long-accepted term under the laws of war but unfortunately its meaning is now contested, particularly between the U.S. and Europe. The United States considers that an unlawful combatant can be targeted and detained but is not entitled to the privileges of a prisoner of war under the Third Geneva Convention—neither the benefits in captivity nor the combat immunity that prohibits prosecution for anything other than war crimes. By contrast European states consider that the capturing power must bring any person to trial if it denies them P.O.W. treatment.

Critics of the Bush White House argued that its rationale was untenable and that the administration's analysis of Al Qaeda could make the entire world a battlefield. But universal conflict was indeed Al Qaeda's stated ambition and it would seem strange to argue that the very fact that made the organization Al Qaeda so dangerous—namely its multinational presence and its refusal to follow the laws of war—should constrain the ability of the U.S. to deploy all possible force to defeat it. As far as President Bush—and most Americans—were concerned, the U.S. was now compelled to fight an essential, legitimate, and defensive war against the unprovoked aggression of Al Qaeda and its associates.

Al Qaeda deployed "unlawful combatants," but what was the status of Afghanistan's Taliban? President Bush determined that Geneva did apply to the U.S. conflict with the Taliban; but he decided that Taliban fighters did not follow the rules of war, so they too were unlawful combatants who did not merit P.O.W status. Furthermore, the president declared that Common Article 3 of the Geneva Convention did not apply to either the Taliban or Al Qaeda because it applied only to "armed conflicts not of an international character occurring in the territory of one of the High Contracting Parties," a definition that encompassed civil wars or internal conflicts that spill into other states. This was clearly not that.

Under the 1949 rules, only legal combatants could be legal prisoners of war. To qualify as such a combatant must be (1) commanded by a person responsible for his subordinates, (2) wear a uniform or some other fixed emblem that is recognizable at a distance, (3) carry arms openly, and (4) observe the rules of war.

A vital legal and moral point that is often ignored by America's critics is that these protections were put in place to protect not only soldiers, but also civilians. The Conventions offer rights to combatants who follow the rules of war—but not to those who defy them. As Jack Goldsmith, a former senior lawyer in the Bush administration, wrote in his book *The Terror Presidency*, Geneva means that "if a soldier wears a uniform and complies with the basic laws of war, he would be treated well if caught. But if (as terrorists do) he wears ordinary clothes and hides among civilians, he endangers the innocent and acts treacherously toward rival soldiers, and thus receives no rights under Geneva."[6] Al Qaeda fighters have never attempted to observe the Geneva Conventions. President Bush later said that they "represent no nation, they defend no territory, and they wear no uniform. They do not mass armies on borders, or flotillas of warships on the high seas. They operate in the shadows of society; they send small teams of operatives to infiltrate free nations; they live quietly among their victims; they conspire in secret; and then they strike without warning." [7]

And so the White House argued that to offer P.O.W. protections to Al Qaeda and associated belligerents would be not only legally unsound but also morally dangerous. Stephen Hadley, the former national security adviser, later pointed out, "We defended the Geneva Conventions, and Al Qaeda violated them in every respect. They would hide among civilians to protect themselves and they would kill innocent civilians to achieve their objectives. There could not be anything more inconsistent with international standards for how you conduct a conflict. And, in light of that, we were supposed to treat them like normal P.O.W.s? Why is that a humane, forward-thinking policy?" [8] The U.S. position was clear—to give captured terrorists the same rights as prisoners of war would be to demean and devalue all that had been achieved on behalf of P.O.W.s during the twentieth century.

That seemed sensible. But there was a problem: it was called Protocol I and it made this interpretation far more controversial than it appeared in the immediate aftermath of 9/11.

In 1977, acceding to pressure from the Soviet bloc and such organizations as the Palestine Liberation Organization (P.L.O.), the United Nations added two new Protocols to the Geneva Conventions. These were supposed to take account of the increase in non-international armed conflicts and wars of national liberation. Protocol I extended the rights of prisoners of war to fighters of many kinds including those, like the P.L.O., who wantonly concealed themselves among civilians. As Jack Goldsmith later pointed out, this effort "dovetailed with the agenda of the nascent human rights movement and the traditional protector of the laws of war, the International Committee of the Red Cross." [9] They both saw Protocol I as a chance to import more demanding human rights standards into the laws of war. But there was a price for this—it meant a rejection of Geneva's reciprocity requirements: Protocol I would give basic protections "to even the most vicious and law-defying combatants." This provided a significant incentive for terrorist groups to ignore the rules of law, as they would "gain strategic and tactical advantages through their own noncompliance of the law and their adversaries observance of it." [10]

The Carter administration signed the Protocol I treaty, but held off on ratification and so it did not became part of U.S. law. Ten years later President Reagan announced that the United States would not ratify the Protocol; he declared that to give terrorists Geneva Convention protections would aid "the intense efforts of terrorist organizations and their supporters to promote the legitimacy of their aims and practices." [11]

At the time, President Reagan's decision was greeted with widespread approval, including from newspapers that were not his natural supporters, such as the *New York Times* and the *Washington Post*. Given its consistent and strongly expressed opposition to President Bush's actions some fifteen years later, the *New York Times'* view is particularly relevant. In 1987 it carried an editorial headlined "Denied: A Shield for Terrorists," which agreed with President Reagan that giving terrorists the legal status of P.O.W.s was "fundamentally and irreconcilably flawed."

Despite the U.S. government's rejection, the Protocol was ratified by the great majority of the United Nations' members, including all of America's European allies. Since then many of them have tended to view America's refusal to ratify as reactionary and contrary to the spirit of international law. They also consider that even without U.S. ratification, Protocol I is binding on the United States. This argument accounts for much of the transatlantic divide over detention issues. European states seem to have difficulty accepting that America's refusal to ratify has serious moral grounds—including the protection of civilians against brutal and illegal terrorist combatants.

In the United States after 9/11, when further attacks were thought to be imminent, and when intelligence from captured terrorists was deemed to be essential, the attitude that the Bush administration had inherited from President Reagan seemed correct. Indeed, at the time even Eric Holder, a Democratic lawyer and President Obama's future attorney general, approved the Bush administration policy and said on CNN, "One of the things we clearly want to do with these prisoners is to have an ability to interrogate them and find out what their future plans might be, where other cells are located. . . . Under the Geneva Convention . . . you are really limited in the amount of information you can elicit from people. It seems to me that given the way in which they have conducted themselves, however, that they are not, in fact, people entitled to the protection of the Geneva Convention."[12]

On November 13, 2001, President Bush took a further important step away from the use of the criminal law enforcement paradigm and towards the application of military justice for captured terrorists. He issued a military order on the "Detention, Treatment, and Trial of Certain Non-Citizens in the War Against Terrorism." Its intent was *"to protect the United States and its citizens, and for the effective conduct of military operations and prevention of terrorist attacks, it is necessary for individuals subject to this order . . . to be tried for violations of the laws of war and other applicable laws by military tribunals."*

The new military courts were to be based closely on a military tribunal created by Franklin Roosevelt in 1942, which the Supreme Court had unanimously upheld.

❖ ◉ ❖

Military commissions have long been a recognized part of American and international legal practice. U.S. presidents have claimed the authority to conduct them under Articles I and II of the U.S. Constitution. Article I, Section 8, clause 10 provides authority for national trials for those who commit criminal offenses against "the Law of Nations." Article II gives the president the title "commander-in-chief," which authorizes him to establish military commissions. George Washington used a military tribunal to try Major John Andre, a British spy and confederate of Benedict Arnold. They were used extensively in the U.S.–Mexico war of 1846–1848, and eight conspirators involved in President Lincoln's 1865 assassination were tried before a commission.

The role of military commissions has been examined on many occasions by the Supreme Court. Among the most important of these judgments is the American Civil War case of *Ex Parte Milligan* (1866). In this case Lambdin Milligan, a civilian and a member of the "Sons of Liberty," was sentenced to death by a military court in Indiana, along with four others, for plotting to steal Union weapons, liberate prisoners of war, and overthrow the government and other duly constituted authorities. Milligan appealed to the circuit court for release under the 1863 Habeas Corpus Act, but the court split on whether or not civilian courts had jurisdiction over appeals from military tribunals. The Supreme Court made the significant ruling that military rule could not supersede the civil courts where they were operating properly—as they were in Indiana. The Court ordered Milligan's release.

The most significant case, which is often discussed in the context of the case of Khalid Sheikh Mohammed, is *Ex Parte Quirin* (1942). Richard Quirin was one of eight Nazi saboteurs arrested in the United States in June 1942. All were Germans who had lived in America in the 1930s and two were American citizens. They returned to Germany before the war began and the Nazis trained them to infiltrate the U.S. to conduct sabotage and espionage. Hitler wanted to cripple U.S. factories and demoralize the population. In June 1942 they were landed by U-boat on the coasts of Long Island and Florida.

They were barely competent. Two gave themselves up quickly and informed on the other six, who were quickly rounded up by the F.B.I. They were interrogated on the assumption that they would receive a civilian trial. But President Roosevelt intervened—he wanted a military trial, and he wanted executions. On June 30 he wrote to Attorney General Francis Biddle, saying that the death penalty was "called for by usage and by the extreme gravity of the war aim and the very existence of our American government." He had no doubts about the men's guilt and said, "it seems to me that the death penalty is almost obligatory." The president's intention was to demonstrate to Germany and his own public that the United States would not tolerate either espionage or sabotage. He told Biddle, "I want one thing clearly understood, Francis. I won't give them up. . . . I won't hand them over to any U.S. marshal armed with a writ of habeas corpus. Understand?" [13]

The difficulty was that there could be argument over what capital crime the men had committed. Biddle decided that a special military commission would be the best way of dealing with this difficult case. It would be swifter, it should be able to prove violations of the laws of war, and it would be able to administer the death penalty. It would also prevent the defendants from seeking a writ of habeas corpus and any matters of national security could be kept secret.

The president agreed [14] and on July 2, 1942, less than three weeks after the Germans had landed, he issued Proclamation 2561, "Denying Certain Enemies Access to the Courts of the United States," which created a military tribunal. The Proclamation stated: "The safety of the United States demands that all enemies who have entered upon the territory of the United States as part of an invasion or predatory incursion, or who have entered in order to commit sabotage, espionage, or other hostile or warlike acts, should be promptly tried in accordance with the law of war." It explicitly denied the eight men access to civilian court.

In a second executive order, Roosevelt constituted the commission, appointing Major General Frank McCoy as president with three major generals and three brigadier generals under him. The attorney general led the prosecution; defense counsel were assigned. The commission was allowed to admit any evidence that would "have probative value to a reasonable man."

The eight Germans were charged, inter alia, with having "secretly and covertly passed, in civilian dress, contrary to the law of war," through U.S. military and naval lines and defenses for the purpose of committing acts of sabotage, espionage, "and other hostile acts" to destroy certain war industries, war utilities, and war materials within the United States.

The trial was held in complete secrecy, so that no information should be made available to the enemy; papers as different as *The Nation* and the *New York Times* approved this wholeheartedly. The defendants all testified that they had no plans to conduct sabotage in the United States. Some conceded they had originally intended to do so, but claimed that they had changed their minds on the long voyage over the Atlantic.

Defense counsel argued that the commission had no jurisdiction in this matter, that the defendants were not in a war zone and thus the charges of violations of the law of war could not apply. Counsel further argued that the men should be prosecuted in federal court, not under a military commission.

Biddle was robust in his prosecution, and insisted that the case was "not a trial of offenses of law of the civil courts but . . . a trial of the offenses of the law of war, which is not cognizable to the civil courts." The prosecution emphasized the deterrent value of punishment, and insisted that the commander-in-chief had authority to act thus in a time of war.

The defense application for a writ of habeas corpus was denied but its request that the Supreme Court convene a special session to consider the validity of the jurisdiction of the military commission was granted. Therefore, three weeks into the military trial, the proceedings had to be put on hold. In arguments that would have resonance sixty years later after 9/11, the defense maintained that nothing in the charges justified the appointment of a military commission by the president and that, moreover, only Congress had the constitutional authority to declare martial law, which was necessary for the creation of military tribunals. The defense also argued that the Milligan precedent, that enemies could not be tried in a military commission when civilian courts were open, suggested that the military commission was unconstitutional.

But Biddle insisted that the defendants had "no capacity to sue in . . . any court" because they were enemies of the U.S. Habeas corpus was intended to protect American citizens, not subjects of a country "with which we are at war, or who are subject to its orders."

Ultimately, the government's case relied upon an expansive theory of presidential power in times of war: "The President's power over enemies who enter this country in time of war, as armed invaders intending to commit hostile acts, must be absolute." [15]

Members of the Supreme Court were concerned lest Roosevelt might order that the Germans be executed even before they had issued a ruling and so they made haste. On July 31, 1942, the Court released a brief opinion, limited to the issue of the jurisdiction of the military commission, which the Court decided did have the authority to try the saboteurs. It offered no explanation at the time, but promised one in the future.

Four days later, on August 3, 1942, the commission found all eight men guilty and sentenced them to death. President Roosevelt commuted the sentences of the two men who had surrendered and informed on their comrades. The remaining six men were electrocuted on August 8, 1942.

Subsequently the Supreme Court did issue its longer opinion giving a more detailed account of its reasoning. In a crucial consideration, the opinion distinguished between lawful combatants (uniformed soldiers) and unlawful combatants (enemies who enter the country in civilian dress). The justices affirmed that the latter were subject to trial and punishment by military tribunals—an important precedent for the Bush administration after 9/11.

Given his subsequent role at Nuremberg, the draft opinion of Justice Robert Jackson—which was not released as part of the Court's opinion—is of particular interest.* In this, Jackson would have granted sweeping powers to the president. He concluded that (1) the president has the inherent authority to create military tribunals, (2) this authority could not be regulated by Congress, and (3) this power was by virtue of his position as commander-in-chief.

Jackson stated, "[I]t is abundantly clear to me that it is well within the war powers of the President, as commander-in-chief, to create a non-statutory Presidential military tribunal of the sort here in question." Nonetheless, Jackson maintained that the president's power should be "discharged, of course, in the light of any obligation undertaken by our country under treaties or conventions or under customs and usages so generally accepted as to constitute the laws of warfare." [16]

Jackson also questioned the Court's ability to review the president's actions. He concluded that dealing with enemy prisoners of war was a foreign policy and military issue that touched upon issues of national security and political questions that were wholly out of the province of the judiciary. Jackson also decided that legislation, such as the Articles of War, was not applicable to enemy combatants; rather it was meant to protect U.S. civilians in times of martial law.

---

* Jackson withdrew this opinion because the men had already been executed and he judged it therefore no longer relevant.

Jackson's view was very similar to that of President Bush when he set up military courts after 9/11, almost sixty years later. "I was confident the military tribunals would provide a fair trial," Bush wrote in his memoirs. He argued the new system struck the right balance between protecting the American people and upholding civil liberties.

It was not so easy for President Bush as it was for President Roosevelt. In 1942, there was widespread support for the president's decisive, even abrupt method of dealing with the German saboteurs. People accepted that America was at war and that the president had the right and the duty to lead. Indeed, the American Constitution specifically gave power in wartime to the commander-in-chief, limited to some extent by Congress but scarcely touched by the Supreme Court. Alexander Hamilton wrote in Federalist No. 78 that the executive "holds the sword of the community," the legislature "commands the purse," while the judiciary "has no influence over either the sword or the purse." Until the end of the twentieth century, lawyers remained largely aside from the conduct of war and the Supreme Court deferred to the presidency.* But by the time of Al Qaeda's attack on 9/11, the power of the judicial branch in matters of national security had grown apace, and attitudes, at home and abroad, were very different.

---

* In his 1951 study "The Supreme Court and the Commander in Chief," the scholar Clinton Rossiter noted that the Court "has refused to speak about the powers of the President as commander in chief in any but the most guarded terms. It has been respectful, complimentary, on occasion properly awed, but it has never embarked on one of those expansive flights of dicta into which it has been so often tempted by other great constitutional questions." [Gabriel Schoenfeld, *National Affairs* 7, (2011).]

*Chapter 4*

# RESPONSES

ON NOVEMBER 25, 2001, the first American was killed in the war in Afghanistan. He was Johnny "Mike" Spann, a C.I.A. officer operating in the north of the country.

In the early weeks of the U.S. campaign to overthrow the Taliban and oust Al Qaeda, thousands of their fighters were rounded up and detained in various makeshift camps around Afghanistan. There was almost nowhere to put them and some prisoners were even flown to American ships in the Arabian Sea. Several hundred others were taken to a mud-walled nineteenth century fort, Qala Jangi, near Masar-i-Sharif.

It was immediately clear that captured enemies in this war were not like conscript prisoners of previous wars who were often relieved to be safe in P.O.W. camps. "The Islamist fighters would not stop fighting once captured," wrote Jack Goldsmith, "but would instead use any means at their disposal to kill their enemies." Ferocious fights against the Americans were frequent and at the end of November 2001, a group of captured Arabs who had been fighting with the Taliban used hidden weapons to take over the fort, killing Johnny Spann and others. It took U.S. forces and their Afghan allies a week of brutal combat to subdue the revolt.

U.S. commanders knew that it would take time to build appropriate detention facilities in Afghanistan and urged the Bush administration to find another prison quickly. "Get those guys out of here," General Tommy Franks told the Pentagon. [1]

Detention of captured enemy combatants is completely legal under the rules of war. After considering various sites, including the maximum security Disciplinary Barracks at Fort Leavenworth, Guam, and a prison ship in the Arabian Sea, the U.S. government settled on the U.S. naval base at Guantanamo in Cuba. It was isolated, well defended, and technically not part of the United States, which it was thought might lessen judicial intervention on behalf of the detainees. "The least worst place," Secretary of Defense Donald Rumsfeld called it.

For similar legal reasons the Clinton administration had temporarily confined thousands of Cuban and Haitian boat people in Guantanamo; Clinton did not wish to give the refugees the same legal rights as Americans. The Bush administration could thus claim that Guantanamo had precedent on its side. But it had not reckoned on international perceptions and the power of the civil liberties and human rights movement. During the Second World War, the United States and the British detained hundreds of thousands of German and Italian prisoners of war, who were treated decently without there having to be any debate about their rights. A tiny number of those detained in the United States instigated habeas corpus petitions but not a single one of these was granted by a U.S. court.

At the end of the war in 1945 there were no international lawyers clamoring to represent the Nazi defendants. Perceptions were dominated by anger at the way in which Hitler had provoked the war, by the graves filled during his fascist rule, and by the consequences for all those millions of people who now tried to pick their lives out of the rubble. And yet justice stayed the hand of vengeance.

The first Al Qaeda and Taliban detainees arrived in Guantanamo on January 11, 2002. They were temporarily housed in Camp X Ray, which the Clinton administration had built for refugees.

The U.S. then suffered a serious setback: the Pentagon's Public Affairs office released photographs of some of the first detainees. They were wearing orange jumpsuits and blacked-out goggles, and many of them had their hands tied. They were confined in what seemed to be wire cages. These images were instantly beamed around the world and created an uproar that never ended.

American and international human rights groups began to agitate on their behalf. The Bush administration made a significant mistake in not consulting adequately either Congress or its allies. Its refusal to apply the Geneva Conventions and some provisions of human rights treaties to the "unlawful combatants" it captured, though legally and historically defensible, was widely condemned.

The abuses that occurred in the early days of Guantanamo have been well and frequently documented. It became clear that in the haste to make sense out of the battlefields in Afghanistan, a significant proportion of the men captured and brought to Guantanamo were innocent. They were not all "the worst of the worst," as Donald Rumsfeld had declared. On the other hand, many of them were indeed dangerous men bent on inflicting great harm on America and the West.

Geneva required that "a competent tribunal" assess whether individual combatants should receive P.O.W. status, but this was denied on the grounds that the president had made a "group status determination" that the detainees were all enemy fighters. As Jack Goldsmith wrote later, "Whatever its legal merits, this was an inadequate response to concerns that particular *individuals* were not enemy fighters but instead were innocent farmers scooped up in Afghanistan." [2] It was not easy to sort the farmers from the fighters. It is to be condemned that some were interrogated harshly. Some blameless men were detained too long. But genuine terrorists were also released and many of them went on to do further harm.

The detainees were from forty different countries and some of them turned out to be Muslim citizens of America's European allies, amongst whom the view developed that the U.S. was overreacting to 9/11, that the War on Terror was an exaggerated exercise, and that many laws were being broken in its name. There was immediate pressure from many countries for the return home of their nationals.

Jack Goldsmith pointed out that the administration had legal basis for all that it did but it also chose "to push its legal discretion to its limit, and rejected any binding legal constraints on detainee treatment under the laws of war. President Bush settled instead on treating the detainees 'humanely and, to the extent appropriate and consistent with military necessity, in a manner consistent with the principles of Geneva.'" This formulation sounded good. But it was very vague.[3]

It was certainly not good enough for the administration's critics. Amnesty International called Gitmo "the gulag of our times." The senior Democratic senator, Dick Durbin, compared U.S. behavior there to that of "Nazis, Soviets in their gulags, or some mad regime—Pol Pot or others—that had no concern for human beings." Tom Bingham, one of the greatest legal minds in Britain, a law lord and former chief justice, wrote a well-regarded book, *The Rule of Law*, which included stinging indictments of U.S. policies in the War on Terror. Of Guantanamo, he wrote, "the Pentagon is said to have conceded that the United States has detained more than 80,000 people, of whom nearly 800 were held for a time at Guantanamo Bay. Some of these were as young as thirteen, and there were very few terrorists among them."[4]

The views of a legal scholar such as the late Lord Bingham should not be taken lightly. On the other hand, the United States was having to grapple with an area of law in which new kinds of warfare were not adequately addressed. As the House of Commons Foreign Affairs Committee in London concluded after its visit to Guantanamo in 2006, "the Geneva Conventions are failing to provide necessary protection because they lack clarity and are out of date."

In an effort to counteract the vociferous complaints, and to be seen to abide by its own values, the United States invested millions of dollars in Guantanamo's facilities and over time transformed it into one of the best equipped and managed detention centers in the world. Food was prepared according to halal dietary requirements. All detainees were given Korans; the Muslim call to prayer sounded five times each day and arrows across the camp pointed the way to Mecca. The detainees could play games, learn languages, and take books (in at least sixteen languages) from the library. According to the Guantanamo librarian, Harry Potter books were said to be especially popular. The detainees had health care equal to that given to the U.S. troops. [5]

But whatever the U.S. did to ameliorate the camp, the early perceptions of Guantanamo as a cruel and illegal hellhole proved indelible. *Newsweek* magazine ran a story in May 2005 alleging that U.S. interrogators at Gitmo had flushed a Koran down a lavatory in order to upset prisoners. This was untrue, but it sounded like a reprise of the horrors of ill-disciplined abuse at Abu Ghraib prison in Baghdad. The article provoked riots across Muslim countries; in Afghanistan seventeen people died in the violence.

Predictably, *Newsweek*'s and similar horror stories garnered far more attention than the testimony of an expert for the Organization for Security and Cooperation in Europe, who stated, after a visit, that Guantanamo inmates were treated much better than any in Belgium's jails. Alain Grignard, the deputy head of Brussels' federal police anti-terrorism unit, said, "it is a model prison. . . . I know of no Belgian prison where each inmate receives its Muslim kit." He thought that the inmates' ability to practice their religion, their food, clothes, and medical care were all better than in Belgium. He agreed that detention without the expectation of release was "mental torture" but Guantanamo itself improved every time he visited. [6]

The Bush administration made serious efforts to send home all the detainees who were deemed safe (and who had safe homes to go to), to clarify the legal rules applicable to detention and to hold substantive discussions with its allies on the complicated legal issues involved. The Pentagon tried to make the prison transparent, organizing visits by over a thousand journalists and scores of members of Congress, as well as by European parliamentary groups, human rights organizations, and lawyers visiting their detainee clients.

Some detainees remained obdurate. Michael Mukasey wrote that on a visit there in 2008, when he was U.S. attorney general, "I saw the plastic face shields that guards must wear when they approach or enter cells to protect them from the cocktails of urine, feces, and semen that are regularly hurled at them along with verbal and physical abuse. I saw the collection of weapons fashioned by detainees to attack guards, as well as the rigorous standards imposed on the guards in responding to these provocations. Any lapse of behavior or demeanor by a military guard results in swift discipline or transfer." [7]

From 2002 to the present day, Guantanamo remained a symbol to America's enemies and to many of its friends, as well as to human rights groups in the United States and around the world, of America's disregard for the rule of law. [8] The much bigger and more poorly appointed U.S. detention center at Bagram in Afghanistan never excited equal interest, though conditions for detainees there were worse and it offered less access to legal representation than the base on Cuba.

❖ ◎ ❖

Guantanamo was not the only problem that the Bush administration's policies created. Similar, near-universal opprobrium was heaped upon the administration when the president acknowledged in 2006 that, after 9/11, the

C.I.A. had set up secret prisons in allied countries around the world for the detention and interrogation of Al Qaeda suspects. Prisoners were also covertly flown or, in the sinister jargon, "rendered" to other countries where their humane treatment could not be guaranteed. Worse still, the U.S. employed what were called, in an awful euphemism, "enhanced interrogation techniques," on selected Al Qaeda prisoners. When revealed, many lawyers and commentators immediately denounced these techniques as torture, a description vigorously resisted by the administration.

It is outside the scope of this book to map in detail the difficult frontier between illegal torture and legitimate interrogation. Michael Ignatieff, Canadian academic and liberal politician, has pointed out, "Torture is probably the hardest case in the ethics of the lesser evil. A clear prohibition (against torture) erected in the name of human dignity comes up against a utilitarian case also grounded in a dignity claim, namely, the protection of human lives."[9]

The U.S. is a signatory to the U.N. Convention Against Torture, which bans not only torture but also "other acts of cruel, inhuman, or degrading treatment or punishment which do not amount to torture." And the 1996 War Crimes Act made a crime of any grave breach of the Geneva Conventions, including Common Article 3, which prohibits outrages upon personal dignity, including humiliating and degrading treatment.

I have already stressed the U.S. government's desperate search for intelligence on Al Qaeda's structures and plans after 9/11. The White House believed that the threat of another, far more serious attack, was so great and the United States' knowledge of Al Qaeda's operations was so slight, that the rapid and effective interrogation of captured enemies was crucial. Thus it was that the Bush administration decided that if significant captured combatants, who were thought to have vital information, refused to cooperate with their interrogators, they could be subjected to the so-called "enhanced interrogation techniques."

One advocate of this form of interrogation was Douglas Feith, an undersecretary of defense for policy in George W. Bush's first administration. He argued that in this age, human beings themselves are potentially devastating weapons—as were the hijackers on 9/11. "The new situation means that weapons are now in people's heads—so getting it out is crucial." [10] Failing to make terror suspects talk could fatally compromise national security. John Lloyd of the *Financial Times* pointed out that although torture is hideous, it can work and is widely practiced. "Torture—ironically, at a time when human rights, democracy, the rule of law and the protection of women's rights are being globalized—now suggests itself as a response to the most urgent problems of security." [11]

The "enhanced interrogation techniques" approved by President Bush were carried out by C.I.A. officers; they required numerous levels of authorization prior to use and were put into effect under carefully controlled circumstances including medical supervision. Some of them were undoubtedly painful, but none of them was intended to inflict intense pain—like, say, the pulling out of fingernails—or to cause lasting physical damage. They included sleep deprivation, walling (in which the prisoner is slammed against a false wall that is flexible so as not to cause physical harm), slapping, forced nudity, and prolonged wall standing.

Most contentious of all was waterboarding, which has been variously described as a grotesque relic of the Spanish Inquisition and a safe, effective, though very unpleasant method of interrogation. In the method employed by the C.I.A., the prisoner is strapped with his head down on a tilted board; his face is wrapped in damp cloths onto which water is poured for twenty to forty seconds. This gives the sensation of drowning, causing a reflexive feeling of suffocation and panic. The rules stated that waterboarding could take place only with a physician present to monitor the prisoner's reaction.

Members of the U.S. Special Forces and other elite troops have long had to experience a form of waterboarding as part of their SERE (Survival, Evasion, Resistance, and Escape) training program. Some officials and commentators argued that if waterboarding was part of U.S. troops' training, it could not really be torture. However, when the writer Christopher Hitchens, with characteristic élan, voluntarily subjected himself to waterboarding at the SERE training center in North Carolina, he was required to sign a waiver that stated "waterboarding . . . participant can receive serious and permanent (physical, emotional, and psychological) injuries and even death." Hitchens underwent the procedure and decided that as far as he was concerned it was indeed torture. [12]

According to U.S. government records, out of the thousands of terrorist suspects captured after 9/11 about a hundred were put into the C.I.A. program and about a third of these were questioned using the "enhanced" techniques. Despite the attention given to it by the world's press and human rights organizations, it is important to stress that waterboarding was not widely used—altogether only three suspected terrorists were ever subjected to the treatment. [13]

President Bush later insisted that all these interrogation methods were "designed to be safe, to comply with our laws, our Constitution, and our treaty obligations. The Department of Justice reviewed the authorized methods extensively and determined them to be lawful." [14] Some senior members of the armed forces disagreed and wished to maintain what was sometimes called a "tradition of restraint" on interrogation and detainee treatment. Donald Rumsfeld accepted some of the enhanced techniques being used by members of the armed forces but never allowed any waterboarding at Guantanamo. The techniques remained contentious amongst those few administration officials who knew of them. Nonetheless, Rumsfeld later insisted that as a result of the C.I.A. interrogation program, "a major fraction of Al Qaeda's senior leadership has been captured or killed since 2001." [15]

Given the abuse that was heaped upon the Bush administration for its interrogation methods, one should note that it kept leading Democrats informed of the methods of interrogation being used and that at the time they made no objections. Bush wrote later, "At the time, some were concerned we weren't pushing hard enough. But years later, once the threat seemed less urgent and the political winds had shifted, many lawmakers became fierce critics." Some of them then alleged that they had been kept in the dark and that Bush had ordered torture in secret. One of those who complained thus was Nancy Pelosi, Democrat from San Francisco, who became Speaker of the House. However, administration records indicate that she, and many other members of Congress, had been fully briefed about the use of "enhanced interrogation techniques" and that they had raised no concerns or questions at the time. Subsequently Pelosi acknowledged this and claimed that she had not complained because she did not know that waterboarding was actually employed. [16]

Nor was the program, which was certainly a departure from past policy, quite as revolutionary as its critics believed. Benjamin Wittes, author and senior fellow of the Brookings Institution, wrote later, "High minded prohibitions of all coercive tactics have [long] coexisted with policies that, in the granular terms of actual implementation, have allowed a great deal more flexibility than the top-line rhetoric would suggest." And he quoted William Levi's study of declassified C.I.A. and Pentagon interrogation manuals, which authorized techniques just short of torture: "Almost without exception, the techniques approved at any one time post–9/11 for military interrogations of unlawful combatants . . . would have been understood to fall within the constraints of the Geneva Conventions for protected Prisoners of War." [17]

After 9/11, the Harvard law professor and lawyer Alan Dershowitz considered the famous dilemma of the "ticking time bomb scenario" in an article entitled "Want to Torture? Get a Warrant." He proposed the issuance of warrants permitting the torture of terrorism suspects, if there were an "absolute need to obtain immediate information in order to save lives coupled with probable cause that the suspect had such information and is unwilling to reveal it." He argued that it would be less destructive to the rule of law to regulate the process than to leave it to the discretion of individual law enforcement agents. [18]

The British and Northern Irish governments had used similar techniques (except waterboarding) against Irish Republican Army (I.R.A.) suspects in Northern Ireland in the early 1970s. In 1978 the European Court of Human Rights (ECHR) had determined that the five techniques used (wall standing, hooding, subjection to noise, deprivation of sleep, and deprivation of food and drink) "as applied in combination undoubtedly amounted to inhuman and degrading treatment" but "did not occasion suffering the particular intensity and cruelty implied by the word torture." [19]

Another insight on torture is provided by Nigel Biggar, Regius Professor of Moral Theology at Oxford University. He has argued that if the use of violent force in war is justified in the pursuit of peace—if a man can legitimately shoot at another—"then what's so wrong with verbal threats, sleep deprivation, or even waterboarding? Can't these, too, be administered without sadistic pleasure or malice and in proportion to what's necessary to extract life-saving information? I imagine that they can. In which case, their proper name is 'aggressive interrogation' rather than 'torture.'" [20]

Such careful, nuanced observations suggest that the whole debate on what constitutes torture is more complex than the angry critics of the U.S. government from both home and abroad would acknowledge.

In the specific cases of the three Al Qaeda prisoners waterboarded by the C.I.A., it seems very likely, as George W. Bush and other U.S. officials have insisted, that the process yielded important intelligence. However, against this must be set both moral concerns and the political harm done to the United States throughout the world by such "techniques." Whether they were effective or not (and no form of interrogation is always effective), there is no question that their use does severe damage to the reputation of the government applying them.[21] And, as the political scientist Michael Walzer wrote in a famous 1973 essay, "The Problem of Dirty Hands," about the politician who feels he has to make the decision to use torture to save lives. "His choices are hard and painful and he pays the price not only while making them but forever after."[22]

The whole argument came to the fore once again after Osama bin Laden was found and executed by U.S. Navy SEALs in May 2011. Former officials of both the Bush administration and some serving members of the current Obama administration suggested that important parts of the intelligence that eventually led to his hiding place in Abbottabad, Pakistan, had originally derived from enhanced interrogation of detainees including Khalid Sheikh Mohammed. Others denied this. As we shall see, the fierce debate began again.

The dilemma of the lesser evil endures.

After his triumph on 9/11, Khalid Sheikh Mohammed was a hero among those few people in Al Qaeda who knew of his role in masterminding the attacks. He was promoted within the organization, becoming in effect the operations chief for Al Qaeda's next international attacks.[23] As first C.I.A. officers and special forces soldiers, and then U.S. combat forces, entered Afghanistan in pursuit of Al Qaeda, Khalid Sheikh Mohammed helped many of its operatives flee into Pakistan and on towards the Middle East. He later claimed that he had planned a second wave of hijacking attacks on the United States to follow 9/11, but shifted his attention to Britain, partly because of the increased security measures in the U.S. and partly because of the British government's strong alliance with Washington. He also claimed to be involved in dispatching the failed "shoe-bomber" Richard Reid, a hulking British misfit and convert to Islam, to blow up a transatlantic flight at the end of 2001. Reid had explosives in his shoes and his attempt at mass murder was thwarted only because alert passengers overpowered him before he could ignite this bomb. As a result of his failed attack airline passengers have been compelled since then to remove their shoes at airport security—another indignity imposed upon the world's patient public by Islamist terror.

Khalid Sheikh Mohammed later claimed credit for other plots both planned and realized. One of the most nauseating was the 2002 murder of Daniel Pearl, a reporter for the *Wall Street Journal* who was beheaded by an Al Qaeda gang when he was following up post-9/11 leads in Pakistan. Pearl was killed at least in part because he was Jewish and Khalid Sheikh Mohammed took evident pleasure in it, boasting that he had committed the crime himself "with my blessed right hand."

That was not all; according to Indonesian security and to the arrested Indonesian terrorist known by his *nom de guerre* Hambali, after 9/11 Khalid Sheikh Mohammed also provided funding for attacks throughout Southeast Asia. The most destructive of these was the bombing of Bali nightclubs by Islamic extremists in October 2002 that killed 202 people and wounded another 240.

By no stretch of imagination or law could such vicious attacks fall under the accepted definitions of legal warfare between high contracting parties to the Geneva Conventions. Under none of the laws of war could Khalid Sheikh Mohammed qualify for P.O.W. status when captured.

An important step in that direction was made in March 2002 when Abu Zubaydah, Al Qaeda's logistics specialist, was seized in Pakistan after a gunfight in which he was badly wounded. The C.I.A., anxious not to lose a valuable source of intelligence, had him nursed back to health. The F.B.I. subsequently interrogated him; he gave some important information and then is reported to have "clammed up." [24] Given his high value as a source of information, the decision was made to subject him to several of the "enhanced interrogation techniques," including waterboarding. [25] George W. Bush later said that "Zubaydah revealed large amounts of information on Al Qaeda's structure and operations. He also provided leads that helped reveal the location of Ramzi bin al-Shibh, the logistical planner of the 9/11 attacks." [26]

After Ramzi bin al-Shibh was captured, he did not need to be waterboarded. He quickly cooperated with his questioners and apparently confirmed that he had been plotting a British version of 9/11—flying planes into Heathrow Airport and central London. In November of that year, Abd al-Rahin al-Nashiri, the Saudi accused of planning the bombing of the U.S.S. *Cole* in Aden Harbor in 2000, was also arrested. Unlike Ramzi bin al-Shibh, al-Nashiri resisted interrogation and was the second Al Qaeda detainee to be waterboarded.

On March 1, 2003, Khalid Sheikh Mohammed himself was seized in Rawalpindi after an informer had gone to the bathroom and managed to text, "I am with KSM." That brought the C.I.A. and Pakistani security to the hiding place. When they stormed the house, Mohammed shot a Pakistani soldier in the foot before he was overpowered. Captured with him was another Al Qaeda official, Mustafa al-Hawsawi, who was described as the paymaster of 9/11. The Pakistanis also found that they had stumbled into an Aladdin's Cave of computers, cell phones, documents, and other "pocket litter" providing invaluable intelligence. [27] (The informer not only survived but was also given by the U.S. government a $25 million reward and a new identity in the States. According to President Bush he explained his actions thus: "I want my children free of these madmen who distort our religion and kill innocent people." [28])

A photograph of Khalid Sheikh Mohammed, looking fat and unkempt, was published around the world after his arrest. (Ever the egotist, he was later said to be infuriated by it.) He was at first boastfully defiant. He asserted that he would talk only when he was in New York and could see his lawyer—which was what had happened to his nephew Ramzi Yousef after his arrest. But times had changed since 9/11 and the U.S. had no intention of affording him such privileges. Instead, he was bundled off into a succession of the secret "black site" prisons created and maintained by the C.I.A., the most important of which was in Poland. [29]

According to President Bush and other members of the administration, Khalid Sheikh Mohammed at first refused to talk and spewed contempt for his interrogators, telling them that Americans were weak and without resilience; they would never be able to stop Al Qaeda. His C.I.A. jailers understood that he had been trained to resist interrogation. Asked about future attacks, he taunted them: "Soon you will know." According to classified documents later leaked, he threatened a "nuclear hellstorm" if Osama bin Laden were captured or killed. He claimed that Al Qaeda had hidden a nuclear bomb in Europe for detonation if any harm came to Al Qaeda's leader. This frightening assertion was unprovable but it added to the Bush administration's real fear of Al Qaeda's well stated ambitions to use weapons of mass destruction against the West. [30]

In his memoirs George W. Bush records that George Tenet, director of the C.I.A., asked permission to use the "enhanced interrogation techniques" including waterboarding on their prisoner. Bush writes that he thought about Daniel Pearl's widow, about all those who had died on 9/11, and about his duty to protect the United States from another act of terror. "'Damn right,' I said." [31] In 2010, Bush was still unrepentant: "Yeah, we waterboarded Khalid Sheikh Mohammed. I'd do it again to save lives." [32]

Khalid Sheikh Mohammed's resistance was described by one American official as "superhuman." Altogether he is reported to have been waterboarded 183 times—but there is a dispute over what exactly that meant. According to former administration officials, 183 refers to the number of times water was poured onto him rather than the number of separate waterboarding sessions. This may sound like hairsplitting, but in a discussion about such a complex, contentious issue, precision is desirable.* According to U.S. officials, when he finally broke, he was not grudging to his interrogators. Instead he began to give seminars on Al Qaeda's structures, personnel, logistics, communications, plans, and ambitions. In 2004 and 2005 the C.I.A. compiled two classified documents on the cornucopia of information he provided: "Khalid Shaykh Muhammad: Preeminent source on Al-Qa'ida" and "Detainee Reporting Pivotal for the War Against Al-Qa'ida."

---

* The International Committee of the Red Cross (ICRC), which first visited Guantanamo in 2002, was able to speak to Khalid Sheikh Mohammed after he and the other detainees held in secret sites were moved there in 2007; the ICRC report was subsequently leaked and published in the *New York Review of Books*. The ICRC complained strongly about the slowness of the Bush administration to respond to its concerns about the men's treatment; it also asserted that C.I.A. medical staff committed a "gross breach of medical ethics" by agreeing to oversee the abusive interrogations. Marc Thiessen, former speechwriter to President Bush and author of *Courting Disaster*, used the same ICRC report to dismiss the notion that KSM was waterboarded 183 separate times. He pointed out that the report, based on information from KSM himself, stated that the number 183 referred not to the number of waterboarding sessions but to the number of splashes of water on the face in each session. There were five waterboarding sessions. "During each application, which could last no more than 40 seconds and usually lasted much less, there could be several dozen splashes. To say KSM was waterboarded 183 times is the equivalent of walking out into a rainstorm and getting hit by 10,000 rain drops and saying that you were in 10,000 rainstorms." [Marc Thiessen, "McCain Is Wrong: KSM Was Not Waterboarded 183 Times," *Enterprise Blog*, American Enterprise Institute, May 16, 2011.]

Although heavily censored before declassification in 2009, these papers make for extraordinary reading. The first stated that since his capture, Khalid Sheikh Mohammed "has become one of the U.S. government's key sources on Al Qaeda." He had provided numerous reports "that have shed light on Al Qaeda's strategic doctrine, plots and probable targets, key operatives, and the likely methods for attacks in the U.S. homeland, leading to the disruption of several plots against the United States. Information from KSM has not only dramatically expanded our universe of knowledge on Al Qaeda's plots but has provided leads that assisted directly in the capture of other terrorists."[33]

❖ ◎ ❖

Before the fifth anniversary of 9/11 in September 2006, President Bush made an important, contentious speech at the White House to families of some of the 9/11 victims. He said that after 9/11 the U.S. and its allies had launched operations around the world to capture or kill terrorists plotting against the United States. "These are enemy combatants who are waging war on our nation. We have a right under the laws of war and we have an obligation to the American people, to detain these enemies and stop them from rejoining the battle."[34]

It was then Bush revealed both the hitherto secret C.I.A. "black sites" for "high-value" significant captured terrorists and the enhanced interrogation techniques first used on Abu Zubaydah, after he stopped talking. "And so, the C.I.A. used an alternative set of procedures. These procedures were designed to be safe, to comply with our laws, our Constitution, and our treaty obligations. . . . The procedures were tough, and they were safe, and lawful, and necessary." Some three weeks later, the president told the Reserve Officers Association, "The questioning of these and other suspected terrorists provided information that helped us protect the American people. They helped us break up a cell of Southeast Asian terrorist operatives that had been groomed for attacks inside the United States. They helped us disrupt an Al

Qaeda operation to develop anthrax for terrorist attacks. They helped us stop a planned strike on a U.S. marine camp in Djibouti, and to prevent a planned attack on the U.S. consulate in Karachi, and to foil a plot to hijack passenger planes and to fly them into Heathrow Airport and London's Canary Wharf."

Bush also argued that the victims' families had a right to see justice delivered to those suspected of being the killers and announced that he was transferring the remaining fourteen denizens of the secret C.I.A. program to Guantanamo for trial before the military commissions that he had authorized after 9/11. However, the commissions remained problematic. The Pentagon had taken thirty months to work out the procedures and to prepare for the first trial. Bush was frustrated by the deliberate approach, as he later revealed in his memoirs. "No doubt it was a complex legal and logistical undertaking. But I detected a certain lack of enthusiasm for the project." He was correct—the military hierarchy was not keen to undertake a large caseload of military trials. Much more important, the commissions themselves had been struck down by the Supreme Court only a few weeks before Bush made his speech.

The crucial case that the Court had been considering involved Salim Hamdan, who was believed by some intelligence officers to be a more significant Al Qaeda operative than his frequent description as Osama bin Laden's driver suggested. He was captured in Afghanistan in a car carrying a surface-to-air missile. After he was charged in 2004, his lawyers demonstrated that military commissions would not necessarily ease the path of the government. Diligent on behalf of Hamdan, they filed a lawsuit challenging the legality of the commissions.

The Appeals Court upheld their validity. But *Hamdan v. Rumsfeld* then went to the Supreme Court and in June 2006, that court decided by a 5–3 majority that the commissions violated Common Article 3 of the Geneva Conventions because they had been established without explicit authorization of Congress. In other words, unlike Franklin Roosevelt in the case of *Ex Parte Quirin*, Bush needed specific Congressional approval. Without that, the majority of the Supreme Court decided, the commissions were not a "regularly constituted court. "

The Supreme Court's majority opinion in *Hamdan v. Rumsfeld* was both contentious and hugely important. Donald Rumsfeld later called it "a staggering blow"[35] to both the military commission system and the administration's position on wartime detentions.

Jack Goldsmith thought the majority opinion was "informed more by the atmospherics of executive extravagance and a seemingly waning terrorist threat than by strict analysis of legal materials." He, and other lawyers, disagreed with the Court's interpretation of Common Article 3 in this case. But that is the nature of law—perpetual argument. The decision meant that at least a part of the Geneva Conventions did after all apply in the War on Terror and it gave detainees far more rights than the administration had ever considered legally necessary. Altogether it was a devastating defeat for the Bush administration.

In his speech, Bush made provocative remarks about the Geneva Conventions. He claimed that the provisions of Common Article 3* referred to in *Hamdan v. Rumsfeld* were "vague and undefined" and argued that the

---

\* In his memoir Donald Rumsfeld wrote that U.S. lawyers had advised the Bush administration in early 2002 that Common Article 3 did not apply to the conflict with Al Qaeda because it referred to detainees in conflicts "not of an international character"—in other words, civil wars. "Now, Common Article 3 was deemed by the Supreme Court to apply to that conflict, even though Al Qaeda is an organization, not a state, and was not a party to the Geneva Conventions, and even though the conflict is of an international character." Rumsfeld said that although he disagreed with the Supreme Court, he did agree "that there should be a proper standard of care for all detained enemy combatants, even those technically not entitled to P.O.W. privileges." [Rumsfeld, *Known and Unknown* (New York: Penguin Group USA, 2011), 593.]

Court's interpretation could put at risk military and intelligence personnel involved in the capture and questioning of terrorists.

As a consequence, Bush announced he was immediately asking Congress to pass clarifying legislation that would determine what was specifically forbidden in the handling of enemies under the War Crimes Act, and to make explicit that America was meeting its obligations under Common Article 3 of the Conventions. Finally he wanted Congress to make it clear that captured terrorists could not use the Conventions as a basis to sue American officials in American courts. "We're engaged in a global struggle—and the entire civilized world has a stake in its outcome. . . . We're fighting for the cause of humanity against those who seek to impose the darkness of tyranny and terror upon the entire world." [36]

Bush aroused much anger for his observations about the Geneva Conventions.* But he was not alone; concern was growing that the Conventions needed revision. I have already quoted the British Parliament's Foreign Relations Committee's criticisms; the British Minister of Defense, John Reid, also called for them to be re-examined in face of the realities of asymmetric war at the start of the twenty-first century. Reid said that the Conventions had been written fifty years before, and "We risk trying to avoid twenty-

---

* Alberto Gonzalez, a legal aide to President Bush and subsequently attorney general, caused a furor when it was revealed that, in a memo to the president, he had called some of the provisions of Geneva "quaint." He was referring to requirements that captured fighters be given "commissary privileges, scrip, athletic uniforms, and scientific instruments." He later explained, "The old ways may not work here ... I never meant to convey to the president that the basic values in the Geneva Convention were outdated." The memorandum was at once rebutted by Secretary of State Colin Powell. But the British Parliament and government subsequently came to similar conclusions. [Robert Boorstin, Memorandum on the Geneva Conventions, *American Progress,* May 18, 2004, www.americanprogress.org/issues/kfiles/b79532.html.]

first-century conflict with twentieth-century rules, which when they were de-vised did not contemplate the type of enemy which is now extant." Now, with Al Qaeda and other Islamists, said Reid, the West was fighting an enemy "which obeys no rules whatsoever" and "We now have to cope with a delib-erate regression towards barbaric terrorism by our opponents."[37]

Tiring of the conventional pieties of America's critics, Reid said that it was not "sufficient just to say [Guantanamo] is wrong" and the world had to protect itself against the declared ambition of terrorists to ac-quire weapons of mass destruction.[38] It was worth noting that John Reid came from the opposite end of the political spectrum from George W. Bush—he was a senior Cabinet minister in Britain's left-of-center Labour government. Yet his analysis of the inabilities of the Geneva Conventions to meet the challenges of warfare in the twenty-first century was very similar.

On September 28, 2006 Congress passed the Bush administration's newly-crafted Military Commissions Act, the most far-reaching con-gressional action in the War on Terror. The Act authorized military commissions and defined the crimes they could try; it defined breaches of the Geneva Conventions' Common Article 3 narrowly; it immunized C.I.A. personnel who had inadvertently violated the Con-vention; and it sought to remove habeas jurisdiction from military courts.

On October 17, 2006 President Bush signed the new Act into law. He wrote later that he believed that "the American people understood the need for intelligence professionals to have the tools to get infor-mation from terrorists planning attacks on our country. And they did not want Guantanamo detainees brought to the United States and tried in civilian courts with the same constitutional rights as common criminals."[39]

In a newly constructed courtroom in Guantanamo Bay, Salim Hamdan was once again put on trial. He was charged under the new law with material support for terrorism and convicted. His sentence gave him credit for time already served and he was released to Yemen after another five months in Guantanamo. This mild sentence did not suggest that the new military commissions would be the ruthless instrument of the government's will that their critics claimed.

❖ ◎ ❖

On February 11, 2008 the U.S. employed the new military commission system to charge Khalid Sheikh Mohammed together with Ramzi Binalshibh, Mustafa Ahmad al-Hawsawi, Ali Abd al-Aziz Ali, and Walid Bin Attash for the attacks on 9/11. They were charged with terrorism, mass murder, providing material support for terrorism, conspiracy, the hijacking of planes, attacking civilian objects, causing serious bodily injury, and destroying property in violation of the laws of war. The charges included almost 3,000 individual counts of murder—one for each of the people killed in the 9/11 attacks—and listed 167 overt acts allegedly committed by the defendants in that assault.

In the charge sheet, Khalid Sheikh Mohammed was alleged to be "the mastermind of the 9/11 attacks by proposing the operational concept to Osama bin Laden as early as 1996, obtaining the funding from bin Laden and overseeing the entire operation." [40]

Bin Attash was charged, inter alia, with administering an Al Qaeda training camp in Afghanistan where two of the hijackers were trained. Binalshibh was accused of having helped to find flight schools for the hijackers and having provided funds for the conspiracy. Ali was accused of sending some $120,000 to the hijackers for their expenses and flight training and facilitating their travel to the United States. Hawsawi was charged with providing the hijackers with money, food, clothing, travellers' checks, rental cars, and credit cards.

Khalid Sheikh Mohammed called the military tribunal before which he was arraigned "an inquisition," but he made the most of it. He behaved as a showman, "tossing self-aggrandizing broadsides from his perch at the front of a courtroom and then retreating into self-satisfied smiles."[41]

He seemed determined to seize responsibility for almost every well-known terrorist outrage that had occurred around the world in recent years. He appeared to be trying to show that he was far more important than bin Laden himself. Among his boasts were these:

1. I hereby admit and affirm without duress that I was a re-sponsible participant, principal planner, trainer, financier (via the Military Council Treasury), executor, and/or a personal participant in the following:

2. I was responsible for the 1993 World Trade Center Operation.

3. I was responsible for the 9/11 Operation, from A to Z.

4. I decapitated with my blessed right hand the head of the American Jew, Daniel Pearl in the city of Karachi, Pak-istan. For those who would like to confirm, there are pic-tures of me on the Internet holding his head.

5. I was responsible for the Shoe Bomber Operation to down two American airplanes.

6. I was responsible for the Filka Island Operation in Kuwait that killed two American soldiers.

7. I was responsible for the bombing of a nightclub in Bali, Indonesia which was frequented by British and Australian nationals.

In December 2008, Khalid Sheikh Mohammed and his four co-defen-dants sent a note to the military judge of their tribunal saying that they wished to confess and plead guilty. The sooner they could be executed and become martyrs, the better—that was their message. "KSM had expressed this sentiment earlier that year, telling his military judge, 'This is what I wish: to be a martyr for a long time,' Mohammed said. 'I will, God willing, have this.'" [42]

But the force of his personality was such that the human rights lawyers and military lawyers representing his co-defendants feared that Mohammed had intimidated the others into pleading guilty, so that they could contribute to the greater glory of his own martyrdom.

At the same time, Anthony Romero, executive director of the American Civil Liberties Union (ACLU), which arranged for the defendants' civilian defense attorneys, declared, "It is absurd to accept a guilty plea from people who were tortured and waterboarded." In his view, "the question for us is whether we want to lend a patina of legitimacy to this legal farce." [43]

The military commissions were not a farce. They were certainly far too slow—this was in part because of bureaucratic nervousness in the Pentagon but in greater part because the ACLU and other such organizations used every legal device to undermine them and delay them.

During the 2008 election, much of the criticism of President Bush was shrill. British tabloid newspapers liked to portray him as an idiotic gun-slinging monkey in cowboy gear. At home and abroad he and the hated "neo-cons" were attacked with a lack of restraint, bordering on hysteria, for launching the war in Iraq.

Iraq is not the subject of this book but it is appropriate to note two things. There is no question that the U.S. mismanaged the early stages of the occupation of Iraq after the overthrow of Saddam Hussein in 2003. But the vast majority of civilian deaths were caused by Sunni and Shia terrorists, not by U.S. troops. Indeed it is important to stress that from the moment that the United States invaded to overthrow Saddam, the worst abuser of human rights in the region, Al Qaeda determined to murder as many innocent Muslims as possible in the hope of creating bloody chaos in which the U.S. mission to create a reasonable government would fail. This grotesque campaign of mass murder was only brought under control at the end of 2007 after President Bush defied all conventional wisdom in Washington and authorized a surge of U.S. troops under General David Petraeus to crush the sectarian murderers. This was a courageous decision and the correct one. (When, in early 2011, mass demonstrations demanding democracy broke out across the Arab world, Iraq was the only nation already to have a directly elected government. It was a corrupt and disappointing government but it was not a tyranny.)

The complexities of reality were at all times hard for those who loathed President Bush to acknowledge. Some Democrats accused him of using methods reminiscent of the Taliban and Saddam Hussein. "Bushitler" became a term used by his enemies on the left. One Congressman complained that he was asking for legislation to make him a dictator. [44]

Throughout 2008, Senator Barack Obama campaigned for the presidency on similar positions, using fierce rhetoric against many of President Bush's policies in the War on Terror—and indeed against that very concept. He claimed that Bush ran prisons "which lock people up without ever telling them why they're there or what they're charged with." He maintained that Bush's military commissions undermined "our Constitution and our freedom" and that they were an affront to American values.

With President Obama's inauguration in January 2009, the public priorities of the United States changed dramatically. But one problem remained constant and acute: how best to deal with the evil that Al

Qaeda and other Islamist groups had unleashed upon the world. It is one of the defining issues of our time and one that Obama, like Bush, would find difficult to confront.

As Tony Blair put it, the struggle is not against a small group of fanatics who can and should be crushed, "Or at least, it is not only that. It is also a fundamental struggle for the mind, heart, and soul of Islam."

The West is a participant in this struggle but it has to be won within Islam. "Such struggles don't last an electoral cycle; they last a generation."[45]

*Chapter 5*

# COURTS

BARACK OBAMA STUDIED NUREMBERG in law school. Campaigning for the presidency in summer 2008, he referred to the trial when speaking about a recent 5–4 Supreme Court decision, *Boumediene v. Bush*, which gave Guantanamo detainees the right to challenge their detention in federal court.* He praised the opinion as a triumph for American democracy, linking the ruling to the respect for due process that, he said, Nuremberg exemplified. "During the Nuremberg Trials," he asserted,

---

\* Lakhdar Boumediene was a naturalized Bosnian who was captured in Bosnia in 2002 and taken to Guantanamo. *Boumediene v. Bush* was a writ of habeas corpus submission made in federal court on his behalf. The 5–4 split decision of the Supreme Court demonstrated the huge differences of opinion within the country over the detention and trial of prisoners in Guantanamo. The majority opinion, written by Justice Kennedy, reviewed the history of habeas corpus since the Magna Carta in 1215 and found that the U.S. did have de facto sovereignty over Guantanamo, and that prisoners there did have habeas corpus rights. The decision struck down one section of the 2006 Military Commissions Act as unconstitutional, but left the rest of it intact. Justice Scalia led the four dissenters, Chief Justice Roberts, Justice Alito, and Justice Thomas.

The majority opinion was a great victory for Boumediene, who was released in 2009, and for the human rights groups that had defended him and so many other Guantanamo cases. The decision guaranteed independent review of the executive's hitherto unchecked power to hold suspects indefinitely. But the divided justices offered no guidelines on how the lower courts should handle such    *(continues)* "part of what made us different was even after these Nazis had performed atrocities that no one had ever seen before, we still gave them a day in court and that taught the entire world about who we are but also the basic principles of rule of law. Now the Supreme Court upheld that principle yesterday." [1]

To all of which perhaps the most appropriate answer is: up to a point. By arguing in the *Boumediene* decision that the 2006 Military Commissions Act still failed to protect the rights of detainees adequately, the Court in effect placed itself above both the executive and the legislature in a sensitive area of counterterrorism. This was controversial enough. At the same time the judgment itself represented an unprecedented extension of constitutional rights to foreign-born enemy combatants, which four of the nine justices thought wrong.

The dissenters, led by Justice Scalia, found no breach of the Constitution in the Military Commissions Act, and they argued that the high number of new terrorist acts committed by those already released from Guantanamo "illustrates the incredible difficulty of assessing who is and

---

cases and it took some time for consistency to develop amongst different judges of the U.S. District Court for the District of Columbia, which heard the cases. The national security analyst Thomas Joscelyn commented, "This two-fold dynamic (no guidelines plus judicial inexperience) was bound to be problematic, as even the district judges (who asked Congress to intervene) have recognized. And history has proven Scalia right. The first batch of habeas rulings was, by and large, inconsistent with America's national security concerns. Over time, the habeas rulings have improved, but only because the D.C. Circuit Court has repeatedly issued much-needed clarifications." [ Scott Johnson, "The Holder Hangover (And Whence it Comes)," Powerline Blog, January 31, 2010.]

who is not an enemy combatant in a foreign theater of operations where the environment does not lend itself to rigorous evidence collection."

In a demurral that was nicely modest about his profession, Justice Scalia pointed out, "Henceforth, as today's opinion makes unnervingly clear, how to handle prisoners in this war will ultimately lie with the branch [the judiciary] that knows least about the national security concerns that the subject entails." [2]

Nuremberg was rather different.

The top Nazis captured at the end of the war in 1945 were indeed given their "day in court." But that court was a military tribunal, with unique procedures very different from those applied in any domestic criminal court. I believe it was a necessary and successful exercise, but aspects of it remain controversial. To some it will always remain "victors' justice."

Nuremberg was created specifically for the circumstances the world faced after V.E. Day in May 1945. Its rules were tailored to the needs of that moment. In one sense it was very much like the military commissions created by the U.S. government after 9/11—not because it was a military tribunal but because it was a special court designed for a particular moment in history.

Senator Obama was correct to suggest that the rights of the Nazi defendants were far better protected than they would have been in any Nazi court (or Soviet court, for that matter)—but they certainly did not enjoy the rights of defendants in U.S. federal courts. The idea that the Nazis should have had the protections afforded to Americans by the United States Constitution never occurred to Justice Jackson or any of the other jurists involved in the tribunal.

But this issue did arise in 1950 in the case of *Johnson v. Eisentrager*. German soldiers, who were fighting alongside the Japanese in China after Germany surrendered, claimed that their trial and imprisonment after they were captured by the U.S. Army violated their rights under Articles I and III of the Constitution, their Fifth Amendment rights, and others besides.

The government, in the name of Secretary of Defense Louis A. Johnson, argued that non-resident aliens had no access to U.S. courts in wartime and no habeas corpus rights either. The government recognized that prisoners had rights under the Geneva Conventions but the Constitution gave them no right to immunity from trial or punishment.

In his majority opinion for the Court, Justice Jackson agreed with much of the government's position. He poured scorn on the idea that such prisoners should be entitled to habeas corpus rights. He wrote that there were "inherent distinctions" justifying different treatment of enemies and non-enemies, aliens and residents. The Court found that the Germans had lost their habeas rights not just because they were enemy aliens, but because as such they lacked "comparable claims upon our institutions" and because, as enemies, their access to the courts could have been "helpful to the enemy." Moreover, if the Fifth Amendment invests "enemy aliens in unlawful hostile action against us with immunity from military trial, it puts them in a more protected position than our own soldiers." Most crucially of all, Jackson argued, "We hold that the Constitution does not confer a right of personal security or an immunity from military trial and punishment upon an alien enemy engaged in the hostile service of a government at war with the United States." [3]

It would be hard for a Supreme Court opinion to be stronger in its rejection of the idea that illegal enemy combatants should have the same rights as American citizens.

Justice Jackson knew whereof he wrote.

At Nuremberg, the defendants' rights were governed by the charter annexed to the London Agreement of August 1945, crafted by Jackson and his colleagues from the other Allied powers, that created the Tribunal. [4] The charter's provision for "fair trial" was brief. It insisted only that the indictment be prepared, translated into German, and explained to the defendants, and that the proceedings be simultaneously translated so that the defendants could follow the course of their trial—and the German population could be enlightened as to the crimes that had been committed in its name. The accused were granted the right to conduct their own defense or to have the assistance of counsel, as well as the right to present evidence and to cross-examine any witnesses testifying against them.

On the question of rights of appeal, the charter was succinct. Nothing of the sort was allowed. The charter stated "The judgment of the Tribunal as to the guilt or the innocence of any Defendant shall give the reasons on which it is based, and shall be final and not subject to review."

In other words, the law enforced by the victorious Allies at Nuremberg was, in many ways, rather less generous to the Nazi defendants than Barack Obama recalled. It gave fewer rights to the accused than did the military commissions created in the United States during the Bush administration. Any German in the dock at Nuremberg would be astonished to learn of his rights, privileges, and entitlements, if he were suddenly transferred by time machine to the court in Guantanamo.

In Bush's 2002 Military Commissions Order (which critics described as setting up "kangaroo courts"), there was a presumption of innocence, and the standard of proof had to "have probative value to a reasonable person," which was similar to the Rules of Procedure for the Nuremberg Tribunal. However, at Nuremberg, the rules were less lenient towards the accused: they could be tried in absentia, had no right against self incrimination, and had no right to challenge the judges—all of which were the opposite at Guantanamo. The differences grew further in 2009, when many restrictions were imposed on the admissibility of unlawfully obtained evidence.

The Germans would also have been surprised if there had been a throng of highly qualified, highly regarded, and often highly paid American lawyers clamoring to defend them. At Nuremberg the defendants had lawyers, but they were all Germans, often Nazis, paid a stipend by the U.S. Army. They did not have either prestigious law firms or powerful human rights organizations behind them. Indeed there was no human rights machinery in Nuremberg—or anywhere else in the world in 1945. Apart, that is, from one institution: the U.S. Armed Forces and their democratic partners.

The U.S. military was then, and has remained, the greatest defender of human rights that the world has ever seen. Think only of the millions rescued from tyranny by the American soldiers, sailors, marines, and airmen in Europe and Asia through the three-and-a-half years the U.S. fought in the Second World War. America's allies played vital roles, but without the extraordinary courage and sacrifice of American fighting forces and their leaders, fascism could never have been conquered, nor the postwar world rebuilt, nor the tragedy of communist dictatorship faced down and finally defeated. More recently, in former Yugoslavia, Albania, Iraq, Afghanistan, and elsewhere, American treasure has been spent and much American blood has been spilled in promoting more just governments and defending Muslims against sectarian fundamentalists, in many cases promoted by Al Qaeda.*

---

* In a Memorial Day 2011 essay, the classicist and historian Victor Davis Hanson wrote, "For nearly a century, the American soldier has often been the last, indeed the only, impediment to butchery, enslavement, and autocracy.

It was the custom of great leaders from Pericles to Napoleon to declare that the graves of their soldiers in far-off foreign soils were testaments to their nations' grandeur, power, and reach; yet our white crosses in American cemeteries from Epinal, St.-Mihiel, and Normandy to Manila, Tunisia, and Sicily are tributes to American military courage and competency—and a willingness to see an end to wars that brutal men started and might have won had our youth not crossed the seas.

We should remember all that in the present age of cynicism and nihilism, recalling that nothing has really changed, as some Americans this Memorial Day seek to foster something better than Saddam Hussein, the Taliban, and Moammar Qaddafi. Behind every American soldier, dozens of their countrymen tonight sleep soundly—and hundreds more in their shadow abroad will wake up alive and safe." [*National Review* online, May 30, 2011.]

❖ ◎ ❖

Since 1945, the international human rights movement has come of age and done great good. The responses to the Second World War—Nuremberg itself, the creation of the United Nations, the rewriting of the Geneva Conventions, and the establishment of the International Court of Justice were all designed to help the rise of an international rules-based system. Through the next half-century that system fostered the rise of national and international human rights organizations. Groups like Amnesty International, originally founded in Britain in the 1960s to defend prisoners of conscience around the world, the American-based Human Rights Watch, and myriad smaller organizations have won great victories in the defense of specific and general rights around the world. For this they deserve unmitigated praise. But in recent years, as they have grown in influence and in political power (and grown more critical of the United States), they have attracted more controversy. Since Vietnam, civil liberties and human rights activists have moved more and more into the domain of national security affairs, all over the world. The new concept of "lawfare"—meaning the use (and sometimes misuse) of law as an asymmetrical weapon of war—has become an increasingly important weapon against governments, above all the United States.

Abroad, U.S. diplomats and military personnel have become more vulnerable to the newly popular doctrine of universal jurisdiction, which insists that courts anywhere can issue arrest warrants for people alleged to have committed crimes against international law. It is an irony, but America is particularly susceptible to such judicial activism in the very core of the free world that its soldiers have died to liberate and served to sustain.

Thus in 2003 a court in Belgium named General Tommy Franks for his role in the Iraq war under a 1990s law giving Belgian courts the power to try war crimes and genocide wherever in the world they are committed.

Donald Rumsfeld pointed out that alleged violations of international law were "sometimes nothing other than the assertion of a hostile foreign critic, perched on a judicial bench or at a university, or within an activist political organization." He argued that the law was more likely to be used against Americans than against real dictators actually guilty of war crimes. Belgium had never moved against Saddam Hussein, for example. [5]

Brussels is the home of NATO headquarters and Rumsfeld feared that under the new law, all American officials and soldiers serving there would be vulnerable to political show trials. "Belgium's power to do this infringed on American democracy, by subordinating our government—our officials and our country's policies—to a foreign government or organization that is unaccountable to the American people. The more I considered the Belgian law, the angrier I became." In his memoirs Rumsfeld recounts that he warned the Belgian Defense Minister that NATO's headquarters would be relocated from Brussels unless the Belgian government changed the law. It did so, quickly. [6]

Within the United States, a general dislike of war coupled with the specific, awful abuses at Abu Ghraib prison in Iraq (quickly stopped by the Pentagon and punished under law), the dilemmas of Guantanamo, and other aspects of the War on Terror encouraged much of the human rights community to be fiercely critical of the U.S. government. As we have already seen, it was effective in using the law and Al Qaeda defendants had a powerful legal lobby, which its critics nicknamed the Gitmo Bar.

One of the powerhouses of that bar has been the Center for Constitutional Rights. Far from supporting the status quo, as its name might suggest, this is a radical organization. It was founded in 1966 by the left-wing lawyer William Kunstler, who once described his work as that of a "double agent . . . working within the system to bring down the system." [7]

The president of the Center at the time of 9/11 was Michael Ratner, a veteran of lawfare with clear views. He accused Alberto Gonzalez, President Bush's White House counsel and then attorney general (2005–2007) of having "his hand deep in the blood of the conspiracy of torture. "[8] He described Guantanamo as "a human rights abomination" and "an offshore Devil's Island [which] has no place in a country that claims it abides by the rule of law."[9] The Nazis, he said, "used the Reichstag fire the same way Bush used 9/11.... [T]hat's really the beginning of the coup d'etat in America."[10]

That so-called coup was good business for the Center, which came into the judicial mainstream after 9/11 by taking up the cases of detainees at Guantanamo. Its income doubled to almost five million dollars and it also benefited from thousands of hours of work provided free by pro bono lawyers, many of whom worked for some of America's most prestigious white shoe law firms. Apart from litigation on behalf of detainees, the Center also campaigned, both in the U.S. and Europe, for the indictment of senior officials of the Bush administration for war crimes.

Representation of anyone accused of a crime is a sine qua non—all those facing trial need proper representation, whether they are detained in Guantanamo or a civilian prison, accused of acts of terror or shoplifting. Moreover, the essential, principled American legal tradition of providing counsel for unpopular clients is as old as John Adams' representation of British soldiers charged in the Boston massacre. The War on Terror raised a whole host of new, important, and complex questions, involving both national security and liberty. Detention alone raised all sorts of complicated issues and effective defense counsel, in both civilian and military courts, was crucial to resolving them.

But to critics of the Gitmo Bar, particularly amongst American conservatives, the zeal with which some liberal lawyers espoused the cause of Islamists who wish to destroy Western society and all its values went beyond legal representation. And on this the conservatives had a point. Some of the lawyers, at times, seemed more concerned about the alleged injustices done to the detained terrorists than they did to those perpetrated by them.[11]

The lawyers thus criticized would no doubt retort that even those accused of the worst terrorist crimes must still be represented, that when Guantanamo was opened it was filled with men who had been rounded up indiscriminately, and that without sustained defense, the innocent could never have been freed and the real suspects could never have been adequately defended. Those are proper arguments. It is also true, however, that some of the defense lawyers seemed to embrace their clients' causes in ways that abused the traditional client-attorney relationship.*

---

* Lawyers working under the umbrella of the John Adams Project, which was set up to assist defenses in Guantanamo, were accused in 2009 of having surreptitiously taken photographs of C.I.A. officers in the Washington area and then shown them to detainees in order to identify those who might have been involved in "enhanced interrogations." The attorneys' intention appeared to have been to prepare the way for lawsuits against individual C.I.A. officers whose identities were protected by law. The Justice Department was reported to be investigating whether laws, including the Intelligence Identities Protection Act, had been broken.

In 2005, one attorney, Lynne Stewart, who had no links to the John Adams Project or the Gitmo Bar, was convicted and sentenced to twenty-eight months, later increased to ten years, for her overindulgent representation of "the blind Sheikh," Omar Abdel-Rahman. Under the guise of seeking better prison conditions for her client, she helped him send instructions to his Egypt–based terror group, al-Gama'a al-Islamiyya, to commit acts of violence.

Stewart's supporters in the academic and legal communities complained that she was the victim of "classic McCarthy era tactics: fearmongering and guilt by association." By contrast, the author Gabriel Schoenfeld argued that "Stewart's story, and the sympathy and support she has garnered, exemplify the new intensity with which some in America's legal elite defend terrorists bent on America's destruction. In this sense, her case is a marker of a profoundly altered legal culture—one that is, in turn, reflected in sweeping changes of a different sort to the national-security apparatus itself." [Gabriel Schoenfeld, *Legalism in Wartime*, National Affairs, Spring 2011.]

One thing is certain. The quality and scope of legal representation for detainees in Guantanamo dramatically surpasses what any German or Japanese defendant could have expected after World War II. When the Al Qaeda suspects in Guantanamo came to trial, they did not want for first-class representation.

❖ ◎ ❖

One of President Obama's first executive orders, signed on January 22, 2009, was dramatic and ambitious: a commitment to close Guantanamo within twelve months. President Bush had wanted to do the same thing and although he had not succeeded, he had managed to remove all but around 250 of the nearly 800 people who had at one time or another been detained in the camp in Cuba. In this he had enjoyed very little help from America's allies; they were eager to criticize U.S. detention methods but much less willing to help resolve the issue by taking former detainees.

Obama's promise to close Guantanamo resonated not only with those on the political left who hoped that it meant the end of non-criminal detention and a return to the law enforcement model of counterterrorism. There was also a hope that the move would restore harmony between the U.S. and the rest of the democratic world. But as the legal scholar Benjamin Wittes has pointed out, Obama was only talking about America's most public detention facility. He made no mention of closing Bagram in Afghanistan; many more suspects were held there and with much less monitoring by the international human rights community. Moreover, after the Obama administration conducted a review of the detainees, it acknowledged that there were at least forty-eight detainees at Guantanamo who could neither be released nor tried because, in Wittes's words, "they have not committed crimes cognizable under American law, because evidence against them was collected in the rough and tumble of warfare and would be excluded under various evidentiary rules, or because the evidence is tainted by coercion."[12] Add to that

number some sixty Yemenis who could not be sent home because the political situation there was too chaotic, others slated for release for whom the
administration could find no new home, and a few who, for reasons of their
own safety, were not to be sent back into the world. As of this writing in the
summer of 2011, approximately 170 detainees remained in Guantanamo
and most of them could not easily be removed, above all because of conditions in their home country, Yemen.

Immediately after his inauguration, the President Obama halted the
military trial in Guantanamo of Khalid Sheikh Mohammed and his 9/11
co-conspirators. All other plans for military trials in Guantanamo were
put on hold.

President Obama also made big changes to the C.I.A., appointing Leon
Panetta as director, shutting down the agency's program of "enhanced
interrogation," and directing that in the future all interrogations by U.S.
personnel must be carried out only according to the instructions laid out
in the Army Field Manual.

Shortly afterwards he ordered the publication of four Justice Department memoranda written after 9/11 that detailed the "enhanced
interrogation techniques" permitted for use by the C.I.A. These documents became known as "the torture memos" and were released despite protests from Panetta, five previous directors of the C.I.A. and
several serving clandestine officers. Former Vice President Cheney demanded that Obama also release other C.I.A. memos that proved, he
believed, that "enhanced interrogation techniques" had saved American lives by detecting and stopping attacks. The White House ini-
tially refused to do this. The *Washington Post* columnist Richard Cohen,
not a predictable Cheney supporter, observed, "In effect Cheney poses
a hard, hard question: Is it more immoral to torture than it is to fail
to protect the deaths of thousands?" It was not a matter of ideology,

thought Cohen, but of people throwing themselves from burning towers. "If Cheney is right, then let the debate begin: What to do about enhanced interrogation methods? Should they be banned across the board, always and forever? Can we talk about what is, and not just what ought to be?" [13] It was the dilemma of the lesser evil again, and it did indeed require rational debate.

Instead, the new administration changed the language of government. President Bush's phrase "the War on Terror" was abjured; "terrorist attacks" became "man-made disasters"; wars were transformed into "overseas contingency operations." Concerns about the threat from radical Islam were downplayed in public. The new president made it clear that he wished to try and establish a much closer relationship between the United States and what he called the "Muslim world," he even instructed Charles Bolden, the new head of N.A.S.A., to reach out to that world. [14]

However, President Obama failed to live up to all the expectations of his supporters. Despite his anti-Bush rhetoric, he continued many of the former president's counterterrorism policies. He accepted the Bush administration's "war paradigm" and, though he reaffirmed the Geneva Conventions, he did not start to treat detainees as P.O.W.s. After long debate, he approved a time-limited surge of troops in Afghanistan, he opposed the extension of habeas corpus rights to terrorist suspects held in Bagram airbase and other military sites in Afghanistan, and he extended the killing of terrorist suspects in Afghanistan and Pakistan by high-altitude unmanned drones. The implications of this policy—a shift away from detention and interrogation for the sake of intelligence towards killing with no questions asked—was momentous. He also dropped his pre-election promise to foreswear all military commissions for terrorists. Instead he reformed them in the Military Commissions Act of 2009. This retained most of the procedures of Bush's 2006 Act, while giving defendants some extra protections.

❖ ◉ ❖

Eric Holder was an old friend of President Obama who had served as deputy attorney general under President Clinton. In January 2001, he had attracted unfavorable publicity for his role in enabling Clinton to grant a controversial pardon to the fugitive financier, Marc Rich, and for recommending clemency to Puerto Rican terrorists. Holder had most recently been an attorney at Covington and Burling. He was not directly involved in the firm's pro bono work for Guantanamo detainees, but he appointed to senior Justice Department positions several prominent members of the so-called Gitmo Bar. This excited continued criticism from commentators on the political right, but it is important to note that the lawyers were recused from matters on which they had previously worked.

On November 13, 2009—the eighth anniversary of President Bush's publication of "Military Order: Terrorism"—Eric Holder announced that Khalid Sheikh Mohammed and his four alleged co-conspirators of 9/11 would be flown from Guantanamo to New York to be tried in the federal courthouse in Foley Square, Manhattan—only a few blocks from the site of the World Trade Center.

To preserve the independence of the attorney general's office, Holder never mentioned asking for President Obama's advice or consent before he made the decision. However, he said he had specifically cleared the proposal with New York's mayor, Michael Bloomberg; with the governor of New York State, David Paterson; and with Senator Charles Schumer of New York. These officials seemed less certain that they had really given informed consent. [15]

Holder's announcement of the trial was emotional. He said that "after eight years of delay, those allegedly responsible for the attacks of September 11 will finally face justice. They will be brought to New York—to *New York*—to answer for their alleged crimes in a courthouse just blocks away from where the Twin Towers once stood." He declared that this would be "the trial of the century." Subsequently, he said that it would be "the defining event of my time as attorney general." [16]

But he did not intend to send all Guantanamo detainees to federal court. In his November 13 press conference, Holder invoked a protocol released by the Justice Department in July 2009, the "Determination of Guantanamo Cases Referred for Prosecution." This stated that where feasible, federal courts should be used unless other compelling factors suggested that prosecution in "a reformed military commission" was more appropriate. The decision depended *inter alia* on the gravity of the offenses alleged, the identity of the victims, and the location in which the offenses occurred. Other considerations included the need to protect intelligence sources and methods, foreign policy concerns, and legal or evidentiary problems.

The attorney general did not fully explain how these criteria had been exercised in relation to Khalid Sheikh Mohammed and his colleagues. But it seemed evident that if the attack occurred on U.S. soil and its victims were Americans, and particularly American civilians, then a civilian trial would be favored. On the other hand, attacks on American military personnel abroad—as in the case of the U.S.S. *Cole*—would still be dealt with by military commissions.

But why should those who killed American civilians inside America be given more protections than those who murdered American servicemen and women abroad? [17] Did this not create a perverse incentive for more attacks like 9/11? That was precisely the opposite of what the Geneva Conventions intended by giving protection to both regular soldiers and civilians. (It is also worth noting that Holder's decision on Khalid Sheikh

Mohammed and his co-conspirators was exactly the opposite of President Roosevelt's response in the case of the German saboteurs in *Ex Parte Quirin* in 1942. The Nazis were immediately arraigned before a specially created military commission.)

Echoing Obama, Holder lauded his government's commitment to giving the 9/11 plotters their "day in court." He further argued that it would "teach the entire world about who we are but also the basic principles of rule of law…"[18]

The effect of this virtuous rhetoric was somewhat spoiled when first Holder and then the president insisted that Khalid Sheikh Mohammed would be found guilty and that death, very probably, would be the sentence. Holder had always claimed that Justice Jackson was his legal hero and, indeed, he hung Jackson's portrait in his office. He had perhaps forgotten one of Jackson's important warnings that you must never put a man on trial unless you are prepared to see him walk free.

Holder's announcement excited both praise and criticism from professionals and lay people alike. Alan Dershowitz, professor of law at Harvard University, argued that it was undoubtedly the right decision because "only civilian courts can assure 'the most exacting demands of justice.'" He went further: "In this case, the United States will be on trial as surely as Mr. Mohammed." [19] That seemed an exaggeration but around the world, perhaps particularly in Europe, it was a widespread point of view.

Such notions of moral equivalence enraged others. The economist and political philosopher Thomas Sowell thought it "sheer insanity" to try foreign terrorists in American courts as if they were American citizens accused of day-to-day crimes. Terrorists were not even entitled to the protections of the Geneva Conventions, much less the Constitution of the United States. Proceedings in open court give information to the enemy.

Why take such risks to please "world opinion"? Sowell asked, "Just who are these saintly nations whose favor we must curry, at the risk of American lives and the national security of the United States?" [20]

Michael Mukasey raised other concerns. The former attorney general thought it regrettable that both the president and his chief law officer trumpeted the virtues of a fair trial for KSM while also assuring the world that conviction and the death penalty were the ineluctable outcomes. Perhaps even more significant: "[I]n treating unlawful combatants more favorably than lawful ones, we undo more than a century of effort to civilize the rules of warfare, and we undermine our own safety in the process. A world like that, where choices have no consequences, is a world inhabited only by children and then only in their fantasies. If we try to live in it, we do so at peril to ourselves and our children." [21]

❖ ◎ ❖

There are many obvious reasons for preferring a civil, federal trial over a military commission or tribunal. The first, already stated, is that the United States is a democracy, indeed the world's most vital democracy, founded upon the rule of law. It is the leader of the free world, the center that has always held. One can argue that on the integrity of its institutions, real and perceived, Western civilization depends. It must be seen to abide by its values. But how far the U.S. should tailor its national security policies to the perceptions of the world beyond the oceans is a continuing argument.

The American Bar Association made this point: "No matter how heinous the charges, the long-awaited trials of these alleged terrorists must be both fair and perceived as fair, or the resulting verdicts will not be recognized as legitimate."[22]

Put another way, the bar association argued that military trials damage America's reputation in the world, whereas federal trials are a symbolic, legal retort to the barbarity and tyranny the terrorists celebrate. This was certainly demonstrated in the federal trial of Richard Reid, the British would-be shoe bomber who tried to blow up an American Airlines flight from Paris to Miami in December 2001.[23] In court, after he was convicted and sentenced to eighty years in prison, Reid declared his "allegiance to Osama bin Laden, to Islam, and to the religion of Allah." He told the court "I am at war with your country."[24] This provoked the presiding federal judge, William Young, to make impassioned final comments to Reid and the court. "We are not afraid of any of your terrorist co-conspirators, Mr. Reid. We are Americans. We have been through the fire before. . . . You are not an enemy combatant. You are a terrorist. You are not a soldier in any war, you are a terrorist. . . . And we do not negotiate with terrorists. We do not treat with terrorists. We do not sign documents with terrorists. We hunt them down one by one and bring them to justice."

Judge Young said he had tried to grapple with the question of why Reid had tried to murder so many people and could only conclude that it was because "You hate our freedom. Our individual freedom. . . . It is for freedom's sake that that your lawyers are striving so vigorously on your behalf. . . . We care about it because we all know that the way we treat you, Mr. Reid, is the measure of our own liberties. . . . See that flag, Mr. Reid. That's the flag of the United States of America. That flag will fly there long after this is all forgotten. That flag still stands for freedom. You know it always will. Custody, Mr. Officer. Stand him down."[25] Reid's imprisonment in a maximum security jail has been uncontroversial since.

There are many other things that critics do not like about military tribunals. Under the 2009 Military Commissions Act, the definition of "unprivileged enemy belligerent" was expanded to include those who have "purposefully and materially" supported hostilities against the United States, even if they have not taken part in the hostilities themselves, and even if they are arrested far from the battlefield. This, it is argued, could turn ordinary civilians—such as a mother giving food to her combatant son, or an individual who donates money to a charity linked to a terrorist cause—into "combatants" who could be arrested and tried.

On the other hand, if an Al Qaeda terrorist wearing a suicide vest is clearly a combatant, surely so is the person who made the vest and strapped it on? What about the financier whose money laundering paid for the suicide operation? Or the religious leader who deliberately inspired the murderer? Are they not also a crucial part of the enemy's force? Some European governments consider the U.S. definition of a combatant too broad. But, the operations of the financier may pose an even greater threat than the specific bomber, and as John Bellinger, former legal advisor for the U.S. State Department, has pointed out, the detention of these operatives is lawful. "The laws of war have long permitted the detention of supporters of hostile forces during armed conflict. . . . Article 42 of the Fourth Geneva Convention clearly contemplates security internment of protected persons 'where the security of the Detaining Power makes it absolutely necessary.' [26] And such people need to be released only on the cessation of active hostilities. The Allies would never have released German prisoners to return to the fight before V.E. Day in May 1945.

Between 9/11 and 2010, military commissions completed only five terrorism-related cases, (Hicks, Hamdan, Bahlul, Khadr, and Qosi) and two of the three convicted prisoners have already been released. David Hicks was an Australian captured in Afghanistan; he was the first person convicted in a military commission when he entered into a plea agreement on material support for terrorism charges in March 2007. But this trial took place only as the result of a negotiation between Dick Cheney and the then-prime minister (and close U.S. supporter) of Australia, John Howard. The agreement was that Hicks be given a nine-month sentence, most of which he served back at home in Australia. By contrast, John Walker Lindh, an American captured fighting with the Taliban in 2001, was given a sentence of twenty years without parole by a federal court. Even if all of the time Hicks served prior to his plea bargain is counted, his total time in custody was only six years, less than one-third of the sentence Lindh received.

In the same time period, the ACLU and other groups claim, criminal courts had convicted more than two hundred individuals on terrorism charges, with none of the uncertainty that still plagued the military commissions system. But this is an unfair comparison. Some of the defendants in these cases were significant, but the majority of them faced relatively minor charges and were arrested inside the United States where U.S. criminal law applied. Only a few of them (Jose Padilla, Ali Saleh al Marri, Richard Reid, and Zacarias Moussaoui) involved significant Al Qaeda operatives and they were not seized abroad, either on a battlefield or in a secret safe house.

The Center for Constitutional Rights and other critics complain that in military processes the accused is denied the right to be informed promptly, at the time of his detention, of the nature and cause of the charges against him. There is no right to a speedy trial (and they certainly will not be speedy if the opponents of military commissions have their way), and the court is not independent because the procedure for appointing military judges is left to the discretion of the secretary of defense. The Military Commissions Act denies the accused full access to exculpatory evidence known to the government, and allows for the introduction of certain coerced evidence. It permits the introduction of evidence obtained without a warrant or probable cause, and even hearsay if a judge considers it reliable and probative.

In sum, the critics complain that even the 2009 Military Commissions Act does not adequately fulfill America's requirements under the Geneva Conventions to provide trial by a "regularly constituted court."

They have threatened that any move to try Khalid Sheikh Mohammed before a military commission would be met with fierce legal resistance that would go all the way to the Supreme Court.

What the critics rarely mention is that every single case before a military court can be appealed all the way through the federal courts to the Supreme Court. And so the ultimate safeguard exists for Khalid Sheikh Mohammed and any other detainee whose trial might begin in a military commission in Guantanamo. This is crucial and, in the view of many lawyers, it renders almost meaningless many of the complaints made against specific details of the military commissions.

❖ ◉ ❖

America remains in a state of war; it is important to recall that President Bush received on September 18, 2001, and President Obama retained, sweeping Congressional approval for the conduct of this war. That Authorization for the Use of Military Force (AUMF) provides the legal justification for all military action against Al Qaeda and its associates.

If one accepts that terrorists like Khalid Sheikh Mohammed have deliberately eschewed the protections of the Geneva Conventions by refusing to act according to the laws of war, then there is an argument that they should be treated as criminals rather than as prisoners of war.

But there has been one basic legal problem for many suspected terrorists in detention. United States criminal law did not always apply to actions by non-U.S. nationals outside the United States that did not involve killing

Americans. Khalid Sheikh Mohammed himself could be prosecuted under U.S. criminal law for planning and executing terrorist attacks within the United States, but many detainees have committed no violations of U.S. law.

For those whose offenses do fall under United States criminal law, consider the implications of trials in federal courts. Such courts must insist on strict rules requiring certain and specific treatment of those arrested and charged with crimes. It starts at the beginning. Indeed, most importantly of all, everyone arrested on suspicion of committing a crime has to be warned of his or her right to remain silent. In America suspects have to be read their Miranda rights to protect themselves against self-incrimination. The precise words differ from one U.S. jurisdiction to another, but a fairly typical warning that an arresting officer is required to give a suspect is:

> "You have the right to remain silent. Anything you say can and will be used against you in a court of law. You have the right to speak to an attorney. If you cannot afford an attorney, one will be appointed to you. Do you understand these rights as they have been read to you?"

That is not all. The courts have ruled that this warning must be "meaningful," and the suspect must answer "Yes." This is difficult enough in a stressful situation after a resisted arrest in an urban crime scene. It is impossible on the battlefield. Soldiers in a combat zone cannot be expected to read captured enemy combatants, lawful or unlawful, their rights. Nor can they protect the chain of custody of evidence gathered at the scene of a potential "crime." Nor can the punctiliousness sought from police at home be duplicated in moments of extreme danger abroad. On the night that Khalid Sheikh Mohammed was discovered in a safe house in Rawalpindi, the building was surrounded and stormed. His guards were overcome and he was dragged, disheveled, from his bed by C.IA. officers, and Pakistani forces and police. Miranda was not on their agenda.

The irregular nature of his arrest is only the first of the problems that would be aroused by the arrival of Khalid Sheikh Mohammed in a criminal court. In such courts, rights are prescribed and of course demanded. The U.S. government would move with difficulty from the rules of counterterrorism in Pakistan and Afghanistan to the strict procedures of a U.S. courtroom. In theory, the Miranda rule illustrates this serious problem. However, in recent years the courts have come to recognize the reality of the concerns; it is now not true that breach of Miranda would be a prohibitive bar to the federal court trial of a suspect detained in a military context.

There are other precedents that must worry prosecutors. The cases of O.J. Simpson and of El Sayyid Nosair, the killer of Rabbi Meir Kahane, the head of the Jewish Defense League, come to mind. Each was found not guilty in jury trials despite overwhelming evidence. Jurors can do strange things in a media circus. Moreover, jurors sitting in a prominent terrorist trial in a federal court might need special protection both during and after any trial. The jurors on a military commission are all serving officers with extensive military training. They would not require protection.

Any federal judge would also have to consider whether the pre-trial publicity had been so great that Khalid Sheikh Mohammed could not receive a fair trial. Statements by senior members of the administration can hardly have helped. When President Obama was asked whether Americans would find it offensive that Khalid Sheikh Mohammed would be granted constitutional rights, he replied, "I don't think it will be offensive at all when he's convicted and the death penalty is applied to him." [27] One can argue that in all such statements the president was merely stating his faith in the ability of the federal courts to secure a conviction. However, one can expect scores of defense motions claiming that the president's prejudicial announcement violates due process and the Sixth Amendment and that the charges should be dropped forthwith.

After all the reforms made to the original 2002 Military Commissions Order, one of the major remaining differences between military and civilian trials is that even under the 2009 Military Commissions Act, hearsay evidence is allowed. Hearsay allows the prosecution to overcome gaps in the evidence chain of custody, especially from the point of capture on the battlefield or elsewhere until it reaches the hands of law enforcement. Military judges are likely to understand this process, and must be convinced by the prosecution that the evidence offered is reliable. And it is worth remembering that the International Criminal Court, a new institution that is widely approved by international lawyers, also allows hearsay if it is "relevant and necessary."

Among the statutory procedures that give the government most trouble in federal trials of terrorists is the *Brady* rule, which comes from a 1963 Supreme Court judgment, *Brady v. Maryland*. This holds that the government must provide any defendant with all evidence that might prove exculpatory. The defense even has the right to know how much a witness was paid for travel expenses. *Brady* is a valuable tool for defense lawyers and is a constitutionally-based requirement. *Brady* questions are usually played out in pre-trial hearings where the defense requests specific witnesses and documents and where the court has to decide whether the requests are merely opportunistic or should be granted. If not precisely followed, it often leads to reversals of convictions. [28]

*Brady* figured large in one of the most important post-9/11 federal trials of Islamist terrorists—that of Zacarias Moussaoui, the so-called twentieth 9/11 hijacker who was arrested a few weeks before the attack because of his suspicious behavior at a flying school in Minnesota. Although he ultimately pleaded guilty, his trial has been described as "—a three and a half year legal nightmare for the prosecution." [29] Moussaoui insisted on defending himself and an Alice in Wonderland process began.

In court Moussaoui filed threats against public officials, ranted and declared that he prayed for "the destruction of the Jewish people." Using *Brady* with enthusiasm, he demanded to depose a large number of detained enemy combatant witnesses. The judge gave him access to three of them. The government was, obviously, not keen on the idea of one terrorist suspect interrogating another and declined to comply with Moussaoui's demands. As a result, the court insisted that the government drop any pursuit of the death penalty.

Moussaoui also used *Brady* to demand thousands of pages of classified documents via the Classified Information Procedure Act (CIPA). This usually means that the government sanitizes documents and prepares a classified summary for a security-cleared defense counsel. However Moussaoui, who never pretended he was not a member of the 9/11 gang, insisted that he personally would review the classified summaries.

While the government was considering how best to refuse to furnish a self-confessed terrorist summaries of classified documents, Moussaoui decided—over the objection of his court-appointed "stand-by" lawyers—to plead guilty. He was given a life sentence without parole. [30]

But that infuriated Moussaoui. Like Khalid Sheikh Mohammed, he sought the death penalty—so he could die as "a martyr." So he appealed, arguing that because *Brady* and CIPA were violated, he had been forced to plead guilty and his rights to execution had been denied him. The Appeals Court eventually published a seventy-eight-page ruling that denied him relief on the grounds that because he had pleaded guilty he had waived the right to object. It is uncertain what would have happened if Moussaoui had pleaded not guilty and gone to full trial. Like the case of O.J. Simpson, his trial would have been spectacular, but whether it would have delivered justice is less certain.

Eric Holder had committed himself to proving Khalid Sheikh Mohammed's guilt beyond a reasonable doubt in a court of law, while also guaranteeing the constitutional rights of a non-American citizen captured and held (kidnapped, some would say) outside the United States and treated harshly (tortured, many said) while in U.S. custody. Holder had made a promise that seemed almost impossible to keep.

It is the mantra of those who practice criminal justice that "it is better for ten guilty men to go free than to have one innocent man convicted." Fair enough. But is it also fair and proper to ask whether that generous principle must always be extended to those who have boasted that their principal ambition is to murder their way to a destruction of the rule of law and its replacement by a sectarian dictatorship?

The very fact that 9/11 happened at all spelled failure for the law enforcement approach to terrorism. Criminal justice is fundamental to civil society, but it is not always appropriate to warfare, especially not to a war such as that fought after 9/11, in which intelligence-gathering is a vital prerequisite for victory. Criminal justice is reactive, fighting terrorism is proactive. Intelligence—information—is the most important goal.

The dilemmas were clear when Holder was asked by Senator Lindsey Graham, a Republican from South Carolina and former military lawyer, at a hearing of the Senate Judiciary Committee, what the Obama administration planned to do if and when Osama bin Laden was captured. Holder's reply—"It depends"—did not carry great conviction. Graham asked why he would not be sent to federal court like Khalid Sheikh Mohammed. And when would he be read his Miranda rights and provided with an attorney? Again Holder replied, "it depends." In a later exchange, he also tried to render the question moot by surmising that bin Laden would never be captured alive. With some prescience, he said, "You're talking about a hypothetical that will never occur. The reality is that we will be reading Miranda rights to the corpse of Osama bin Laden. . . . He will be killed by us or he will be killed by his own people so that he is not captured alive." [31]

❖ ◉ ❖

The underlying question that the trial or trials of Khalid Sheikh Mohammed raises is how far the judiciary should be involved in, let alone come to dominate, foreign and defense policy. Justice Jackson was clear. In the case of *Johnson v. Eisentrager* (1950), which I cited above, Jackson warned that judicial intervention in wartime

> would diminish the prestige of our commanders, not only with enemies but with wavering neutrals. It would be difficult to devise more effective fettering of a field commander than to allow the very enemies he is ordered to reduce to submission to call him to account in his own civil courts and divert his efforts and attention from the military offensive abroad to the legal defensive at home. Nor is it unlikely that the result of such enemy litigiousness would be a conflict between judicial and military opinion highly comforting to enemies of the United States.

By the beginning of the twenty-first century much of what Jackson had warned against had come to pass.

*Chapter 6*

# REALITIES

ERIC HOLDER WAS NOT LUCKY. His decision to try Khalid
Sheikh Mohammed in Manhattan was announced just days after the most
murderous terrorist attack on American soil since 9/11. It was more than
that—it was the most bloody example yet of homegrown Islamist terrorism. And it helped show that the centrally-controlled, tightly-focused
terror network that bin Laden had launched upon the world had now
metastasized into a deadly and unpredictable franchise that empowered
even educated and privileged individuals to embark on mass murder in the
name of their God.

On November 5, 2009, Major Nidal Malik Hasan carried out a massacre at Fort Hood, Texas. Shouting the Arabic phrase, *"Allahu Akhbar"*
("God is great"), Hassan sprayed his fellow soldiers with gunfire, killing
thirteen and wounding thirty.

Michelle Harper, a civilian Army employee, later described how she hid
behind a desk and made a 911 call as Hasan continued his rampage. "Oh
my God, everybody is shot," she told the 911 operator. [1]

Staff Sergeant Patrick Zeigler had just come unscathed through a tour in
Iraq when he was shot four times by Hasan; one bullet went through his
skull and destroyed about a fifth of his brain. His family and his fiancée, Jessica Hansen, were warned that he might never recover. But thanks to astonishing willpower on his own part, the devotion of Jessica, and the skill of
the surgeons, in July 2010, after eight operations on his brain, he walked out
of the Mayo Clinic in Minnesota and then he and Jessica were married. [2]

The attacker, Nidal Hasan, was a Muslim, born in Virginia to Palestinian immigrants from Jordan. Hasan joined the army after graduating from college and became a psychiatrist at Fort Hood. Part of his work was to counsel soldiers who had returned from combat in Iraq and Afghanistan. In 2009, Hasan feared deployment to Afghanistan himself. Both his superior officers and the F.B.I. were aware that he had expressed extremist views. But nothing had been done about this, for fear of causing offense, both to Hasan and to other Muslim soldiers. [3]

Such fears dominated early public responses to his act of mass murder. Polls showed that most Americans believed that the shootings should have been investigated by the military as a terrorist act. But "opinion formers" debated as to whether Hasan could be called a "terrorist," and his Islamist beliefs and connections were either ignored or played down. President Obama declared, "We cannot fully know what leads a man to do such a thing," while a writer at *Newsweek* dismissed Hasan as "a nut case." Army Chief of Staff George W. Casey Jr. cautioned that speculation about Hasan's motives "could cause a backlash against some of our Muslim soldiers," while Attorney General Eric Holder declined to state that radical Islam was the major motive for Hasan's attack. Similar sentiments were expressed in much of the media. [4]

*The Nation* magazine, a reliable barometer of left-wing opinion, asserted that even to mention that Hasan was a Palestinian Muslim was "Islamophobic." The *Huffington Post* declared, "there is no concrete reporting as to whether Nidal Malik Hasan was in fact a Muslim or an Arab." Others tried to depict Hasan as a victim not a killer: he had been so shaken by the stories he heard from soldiers returning from combat in Iraq and Afghanistan that he himself had been infected by the virulent disease of post-traumatic stress disorder. Amongst American commentators it was, as often, Christopher Hitchens who pointed out that this was all self-deluding nonsense, or "Multicultural Masochism."[5]

Then the shocking detail emerged of just how much the army knew about Hasan's radical Islamist sympathies before he embarked on his killing spree. When, as a student, Hasan was required to present a paper on a psychiatric theme, he produced a draft which consisted of quotes from the Koran praising the abuse and killing of non-Muslims. Asked to revise it, he made minor changes and was allowed to graduate. In June 2007, he had given a lecture at Walter Reed Medical Center that had troubled his classmates because he defended Osama bin Laden and suicide bombers and warned that "adverse events" could occur if the Pentagon did not allow Muslim soldiers to become "conscientious objectors" in the War on Terror. There were many other occasions in which Hasan made clear to others at Walter Reed the strength of his religious fervor. [6]

Moreover, Hasan's computer had been monitored by the F.B.I., which was aware that he had visited radical Islamist websites and exchanged emails with an increasingly influential new guru of jihadism, Anwar al-Awlaki, an American imam now based in Yemen who unfortunately plays an increasingly large part in the story to come.

Hasan had asked al-Awlaki via email when jihad tactics were justified, and in what circumstances the killing of innocent bystanders was allowed. Hasan also wrote that he looked forward to the time when he and al-Awlaki would be united in paradise. Following this disturbing exchange, al-Awlaki posted a ruling online that bullets discharged at American soldiers were fired in a holy cause. After Hasan's massacre, al-Awlaki blessed the action and Al Qaeda spokesman Adam Gadahn praised his "*Mujahid* brother" as a "pioneer, a trailblazer, and a role-model." [7]

It seems remarkable and deplorable that knowledge of Hasan's activities and attitudes should not have driven the military authorities to restrain him before he could kill so many people. The hobgoblin of political correctness had played its part, but so did the law. The F.B.I. had interpreted his emails to Anwar al-Awlaki as "consistent with research being conducted by Major Hasan in his position as a psychiatrist at the Walter Reed Medical Center." The F.B.I. investigators were evidently influenced by the evaluation reports of Hasan's superiors—they described him as an authority on Islam, and one described his work as having "an extraordinary potential to inform national policy and military strategy." [8] He was described as a "star officer" dedicated to "illuminating the role of culture and Islamic faith within the global War on Terrorism." [9]

Three months after Major Hasan committed his mass murder, the Pentagon published an investigation into his conduct that seemed unable to address the disaster. After discussing the way in which alcohol and drug abuse and sexual violence "may trigger suicide in those who are already vulnerable," the report gingerly approached the subject of religion. It stated, "religious fundamentalism alone is not a risk factor; most fundamentalist groups are not violent, and religious-based violence is not confined to members of fundamentalist groups." That may be true, but it was irrelevant. Major Hasan's fundamentalism was specifically devoted to violence. [10]

A much more honest and substantial report was published in early 2011 by the Senate Homeland Security and Governmental Affairs Committee, chaired by Senator Joseph Lieberman. Entitled "A Ticking Time Bomb," this concluded that the Defense Department and the F.B.I. should have recognized that Hasan had become an adherent of "violent Islamist extremism" long before he went on his rampage. The report called for better military training to identify early signs of Islamist extremism and for policies to root it out. It argued that the underlying problem—for all government departments—is that First Amendment rights to freedom of speech often prevent the government from intervening to thwart radical behavior. [11] Officials supervising Hasan—just like members of the public—were nervous lest they be accused of racism. They were also keen to promote the dream of multiculturalism to which so many institutions, American and European, subscribe.

Commenting on Senator Lieberman's report, Dorothy Rabinowitz suggested that the enthusiastic testaments to Major Hasan were probably genuine. A non-Muslim who had exhibited such worrying traits as Hasan would have faced serious consequences, but he was untouchable. "He was a star not simply because he was a Muslim, but because he was a special kind—the sort who posed, in his flaunting of jihadist sympathies, the most extreme test of liberal toleration." [12]

The consequences of tolerating Hasan were catastrophic for the victims at Fort Hood. Sergeant Zeigler's fiancée and then wife, Jessica, wrote in her blog: "November 5th *was* an act of war . . . it wasn't one man, it is a global war we are fighting." [13] Not only that, but the war has become decentralized. The Al Qaeda leadership was now inspiring rather than specifically directing individuals to undertake attacks. Terrorists were more diffused and self-starting and thus even less susceptible to detection and prevention.

❖ ◎ ❖

The horror of Major Hasan's religious rampage undoubtedly increased public disquiet over Eric Holder's plan to bring Khalid Sheikh Mohammed and his colleagues to New York City for trial. On December 5, 2009, a group of several hundred protestors braved pouring rain to hold a two-hour protest rally outside the courthouse in Foley Square. People denounced Holder as "traitor," "Marxist mole," and "arrogant bastard." [14]

An important part in the rally was played by Debra Burlingame, whose brother Charles had been the pilot of the plane crashed by terrorists into the Pentagon and who now ran Keep America Safe, an advocacy group critical of the Obama administration's national security policies. [15] The group saw no reason to give terrorist suspects the full rights of American citizens. Andrew McCarthy, who had led the prosecution of the 1993 World Trade Center bombers, and who was now a fierce critic of using federal courts to deal with terrorists, insisted that this was no time "to wrap our enemies in our Bill of Rights." Edith Lutnick, whose brother Gary was killed on 9/11, said that he and all the other victims "were murdered by the terrorist Khalid Sheikh Mohammed, and we do not want him and his fellow terrorists tried in that building." [16]

Events immediately conspired to reinforce such views.

On Christmas Day 2009, a young Nigerian man, Umar Farouk Abdulmutallab, tried to blow up a Northwest Airlines flight from Amsterdam over Detroit by exploding a bomb concealed in his underpants. The chemical explosive he used was PETN, the same substance used by "shoe bomber" Richard Reid in 2001, which does not show up on airport body scanners. Since a detonator might have been detected at check-in, Abdulmutallab also carried a syringe filled with acid that, when injected into the PETN, was supposed to create the explosion.

Abdulmutallab's background did not follow the conventional wisdom that poverty and deprivation lead to radicalization. Far from it—he was the son of a prominent Nigerian banker and had studied at University College, London (UCL), where he lived well and had become president of the Islamic Society.

If one hoped that the presidents of such academic organizations would be above violence and interested only in philosophy, one would be disappointed. In recent decades, Britain has become an increasingly dangerous breeding ground for Islamist extremism among young Muslims. The Muslim population is growing fast in Britain, as in other European countries, and many authorities have shown themselves incapable of dealing with the demands of young Islamist radicals. British universities have been at best complacent about the seriousness of the threat of radicalization, and at worst complicit in the spread of this pathology on campus. Under the cloak of freedom of speech, incitement against Jews and other "infidels" has become common.*

Umar Farouk Abdulmutallab was one of many who were radicalized. It emerged after his arrest that he was the fourth president of a London student Islamic society to face terrorist charges in three years. Another was facing retrial on charges that he was involved in the 2006 liquid bomb plot to blow up airliners. The independent think tank The Quilliam Foundation later published a damning study of the intellectual progress made by terrorism through British society. In particular it looked at the Islamic Society at City University, which had already graduated one terrorist and was constantly encouraging others. According to Quilliam, the Society promoted the writings of some of the most bloody Al Qaeda killers and held regular Friday prayer meetings that disdained "man-made law," cheered the murder of infidels and homosexuals, and endorsed marital rape and wife-beating.[17]

Prime Minister Tony Blair was well aware of the internal threat to

---

* The authorities at University College, London were, like many others, reluctant to accept the reality of Islamist extremism on campus. When Abdulmutallab was arrested, the UCL president declared that the school was not a fertile recruitment for terrorists and claimed that even to allege such a thing was evidence of "Islamophobia." The college's eventual report on Abdulmutallab found "no evidence to suggest either that . . . Abdulmutallab was radicalized while a student at UCL, or that conditions at UCL during that time or subsequently were conducive to the radicalization of students." All of this was predictable in London but it was quite unrealistic. The security service, MI6, has published its estimate that some 2,000 young Islamic men in Britain pose a terrorist threat. [Alexander Meleagrou-Hitchens and Michael Weiss, "Terrorism and the British Academy," *Weekly Standard*, October 22, 2010.]

Britain and other European societies from homegrown terrorists, but the prevailing attitude of many others in his Labour party and amongst the British cultural establishment was complacency and toleration in the name of multiculturalism. Not for nothing did London become known as "Londonistan."

At University College, London in early 2007, Abdulmutallab, as president of the Islamic Society, presided over a "War on Terror Week," which could have more accurately been described as a "Blame America" marathon. According to the *New York Times*, the guest speakers included "radical imams, former Guantanamo Bay prisoners, and a cast of mostly left-wing, anti-American British politicians and human rights advocates." The views of the main lecturer, Asim Qureshi, are straightforward. In a speech given in 2006 outside of the U.S. embassy, Qureshi exhorted the crowd, "We know that it is incumbent upon all of us to support the jihad of our brothers and sisters in these countries when they are facing the oppression of the West." At which he and the crowd broke into a chant of *"Allahu Akhbar."* [18]

After London, Abdulmutallab enrolled in a business program in Dubai before leaving in the summer of 2009 for Yemen. There he apparently went to join Al Qaeda in the remote Shabwa mountains. By now his father had become so concerned about his son's growing extremism that he informed the U.S. Embassy in Abuja, Nigeria. This was a difficult, not to say enormous, decision for a parent to make. The United States government took no action.

In the last quarter of 2009, the young man's radicalization seems to have been completed in Yemen under the tutelage of the mellifluous Anwar al-Awlaki, who had twice been hosted by the East London mosque that Abdulmutallab had attended. The mosque has denied published reports that in a 2003 sermon to the mosque, al-Awlaki instructed his audience never to co-operate with the British police or security authorities.

The real concern is that such a dangerous jihadist should have been invited to speak in London anyway.

In Yemen the young man was fitted with explosive underpants and given the instructions on how to use them. According to one account, al-Awlaki convinced his young protégé that undertaking his mission would make him "the tip of the spear of the Muslim nation." [19]

Thus inspired and trained, Abdulmutallab traveled home to Nigeria and then flew on to Amsterdam. Despite his father's warning to the U.S., he was not on any No-Fly list. His behavior—buying a one way ticket to Detroit and traveling without luggage—should have aroused suspicion. But it did not. He had no problem boarding the flight on December 25, 2009. [20]

Shortly before landing, Abdulmutallab did as he was trained to do. The bomb in his pants ignited but mercifully failed to explode. Thanks to that and to the bravery of fellow passengers who extinguished the fire and overpowered their would-be murderer, the plane landed safely and he was arrested.

That Christmas afternoon, the U.S. Department of Justice had three options. It could read Abdulmutallab his Miranda rights and charge him in federal court. It could detain him as an enemy belligerent. Or it could hold him for extensive questioning under the "public safety exception" to the Miranda requirement, and subsequently indict him, ensuring that nothing he had said during questioning that might amount to self-incrimination was used against him in court.

Under the "public safety exception," local F.B.I. agents—who knew nothing of Abdulmutallab and little of Al Qaeda in the Arabian Peninsula—were allowed to question him for fifty minutes. The intelligence community's existing dossier on him—including information from both his father and from intercepts—was not available to them. [21]

Nonetheless, in that first fifty minutes, Abdulmutallab is said to have shared important intelligence about his training by Al Qaeda in Yemen. Then the Justice Department decided he should be read his Miranda rights, and he was provided with an attorney. He promptly stopped talking.

The government could have paused. It could have taken more time to consider whether to treat him as an enemy combatant or a criminal suspect, in light of the substantial information suggesting links to Al Qaeda in the Arabian Peninsula, with whom the United States is legally at war. Instead, the Justice Department instantly charged him with a federal crime, which meant that he was at once given the protections of the U.S. Constitution. Neither the director of the F.B.I., nor the director of National Intelligence, nor the secretary of Homeland Security, nor the director of the National Counterterrorism Center, were consulted before the decision was made by the Justice Department. [22]

When President Obama had suspended the Bush administration's detention and interrogation practices at the beginning of his presidency, he convened a task force to recommend new procedures. In August 2009 the Justice Department responded by announcing the creation of the High-Value Detainee Interrogation Group (HIG), a mobile team of experienced interrogators, linguists, Al Qaeda experts, and others who would immediately swing into action to question captured suspects. They were not called on to assist in Detroit.

The treatment of Abdulmutallab aroused a storm and not just among Republican critics of President Obama. Senators Joseph Lieberman and Susan Collins, the leaders of the Homeland Security and Governmental Affairs Committee, insisted, in a letter to Eric Holder, that Abdulmutallab was "an enemy combatant and should be detained, interrogated, and ultimately charged as such." They thought the conduct of the Justice Department had been very poor and they urged that the Nigerian terrorist should be transferred at once to the Defense Department for interrogation and trial. [23] Even Dennis Blair, Obama's director of national intelligence, later acknowledged that he had not been consulted and that the decision to Mirandize the Nigerian so swiftly was a "mistake." The *Washington Post*, no enthusiast for the Bush administration's War on Terror policies, called the decision "myopic, irresponsible, and potentially dangerous . . . a knee-jerk default to a crime-and-punishment model." [24]

Michael Mukasey, Eric Holder's predecessor, recalled the Nazi saboteurs of 1942 (the case of *Ex Parte Quirin*), pointing out that they, like Abdulmutallab, were originally arrested and questioned by the F.B.I., but were subsequently treated as enemy combatants at the insistence of President Roosevelt. In 1942, the F.B.I. was more of a domestic crime-fighting organization, whereas after 9/11 tasks included more intelligence-gathering, helping to prevent and combat threats to national security, and furthering U.S. foreign policy goals.

Mukasey also emphasized that, although the Supreme Court had held, in the case of *Hamdi v. Rumsfeld*, that while "indefinite detention for the purpose of interrogation is not authorized," detention for the purpose of neutralizing an unlawful enemy combatant was permissible. Moreover, the Court had held that the only right of such a combatant—even if he was an American citizen—was to challenge his classification in a habeas corpus proceeding. The precedent of Richard Reid, who was warned of his Miranda rights and prosecuted in a civilian court, was not relevant. His attempt to blow up an airliner occurred in December 2001, before the procedures were developed to allow for the exploitation of a suspect's intelligence value.

Mukasey believed that the decision on how to deal with Abdulmutallab should have involved the C.I.A. and national intelligence directors "and ultimately the president" as well as the Justice Department. "I like to think the default setting would have been toward gathering intelligence rather than worrying about whether a man who did his crime in front of 285 witnesses could be convicted without using his confession." The war against Islamist extremism, he said, was "unlike any other war we have fought" and the only way to prevail was "to gather intelligence on who is doing what where and to take the initiative to stop it." [25]

Instead, Miranda induced sullen silence.

Weeks later, Abdulmutallab's distraught parents were flown to visit him in prison in the United States; they persuaded him to start talking again. But by this point, much of their son's knowledge was out-of-date, because his trainers in Yemen had been given time to change their disposition and procedures.

In their January 2010 letter, Senators Joseph Lieberman and Susan Collins wrote to Eric Holder and to the president's counterterrorism adviser, John Brennan, urging them to treat Abdulmutallab as an "unprivileged enemy belligerent" and not a criminal vested with the constitutional rights of an American citizen, so that he could be "questioned and charged accordingly." They noted that President Obama's repeated assertions that "we are at war" did not appear "to be reflected in the actions of some in the Executive Branch." Eric Holder did not agree. [26]

The renewed fear aroused by the young Nigerian Islamist led more and more people to question the wisdom of any terrorist trial in Manhattan. In early January 2010, Scott Brown, the Republican candidate in the special Massachusetts election that followed the death of Edward Kennedy, seemed to catch the new mood of anxiety. He broadcasted a television spot, which showed a picture of him in his National Guard fatigues, declaring, "Some people believe our Constitution exists to grant rights to terrorists who want to harm us. I disagree." Brown also declared his support for waterboarding terrorists, which the Obama administration had defined as torture. [27] Exit polls showed that Brown's tough stance contributed to his remarkable victory in a Democratic stronghold.

As criticism of the plan to try Khalid Sheikh Mohammed in Manhattan grew, Dianne Feinstein, the Democratic chair of the Senate Intelligence Committee, pointed out that "the trial of the most significant terrorist in custody would add to the threat" of terrorist attacks in New York City. The mayor of New York City, Michael Bloomberg, abandoned his previous lukewarm support, and the city's police commissioner, Raymond Kelly, made ever more dramatic assessments of the security threat and the costs that any trial would impose on the city. [28]

The administration wavered. In March 2010, President Obama's senior adviser David Axelrod reported that the administration still had not made a final decision and anonymous White House sources were quoted saying that the trial would not take place in New York after all. On March 16, Eric Holder claimed before Congress that a decision was "weeks away." [29]

It was no surprise that the American Civil Liberties Union and other such organizations became alarmed. Ben Wizner, one of its senior attorneys, made a spirited criticism of a military trial for KSM. "This is the most important criminal case, probably in the history of the United States. And the idea that we're going to bring a case like that into an untested system, where the rules are pretty much being made up as we go along, there are going to be massive legal and constitutional challenges brought to this. I just don't understand why any government would want to do that." [30]

Wizner criticized Senators Lindsey Graham, Joseph Lieberman, and John McCain and other proponents of military courts. "They want to see themselves as warriors, for them the idea that you would bring these cases into time-tested civilian courts is some sign of weakness, that we're not tough enough, that we see this as just a law enforcement issue and not the war that it is. This is the worst kind of identity politics." [31]

There were many lawyers in Holder's Justice Department who agreed with such sentiments. Holder complained that his proposal for a criminal trial had been politicized, asking, "Why can't we use a great criminal justice system that has proven effective . . . in a wide range of cases over the past two hundred years?" He also asked that Congress appropriate the money to move Guantanamo detainees to an under-used prison in Thomson, Illinois. "There is no reason to believe that people held in Guantanamo cannot be held wherever we put them in the United States . . . very safely and very effectively." [32]

❖ ◉ ❖

The new reality of Al Qaeda forced itself once again into the debate. On May Day (May 1), 2010, another young Islamist tried to conduct mass murder in America. This time, the would-be killer, an American citizen named Faisal Shahzad, sought to attack people in Times Square with a bomb he had been taught how to build by the Pakistani Taliban.

The United States had been good to Faisal Shahzad, a naturalized Pakistani-American who had lived there for the past ten years. Having obtained a university degree, he was sponsored by two American companies and became a naturalized U.S. citizen in April 2009. He married, had two children, and seemed to be living a quiet, happy life in Connecticut. [33]

But that same year, having publicly sworn allegiance to the United States, Shahzad secretly became a radical Muslim, traveled to Pakistan, and spent forty days with the Pakistani Taliban (TTP) in Waziristan. There he was instructed in the construction of bombs and made a video about his plan to attack America. In this he declared that his intention was to "incite the Muslims to get up and fight against the enemy of Islam." He declared, "Jihad is one of the pillars upon which Islam stands" and "I have been trying to join my brothers in jihad ever since 9/11 happened. I am planning to wage an attack inside America." It was not difficult to do, he boasted, urging other Muslim men, "Get up and learn from me and make an effort. Nothing is impossible if you just keep in mind that Allah is with you." [34]

His Taliban controllers gave Shahzad $5000 to buy the materials for a bomb and installed software on his computer that enabled him to communicate easily with them. Back in Connecticut, Shahzad bought fertilizer, propane, gasoline, other components, and a secondhand Nissan Pathfinder.

On May Day afternoon, he loaded the homemade bomb into the Nissan and drove to Times Square, parked on Forty-fifth Street and Seventh Avenue, and lit the fuse. Expecting the bomb to explode a few minutes later, he walked away, carrying a semiautomatic rifle in a computer bag—he intended to shoot any policeman who tried to apprehend him. Mercifully, the bomb failed to detonate; street vendors noticed smoke coming from the car and alerted the police, who emptied the area of people and disarmed the device.

Back home in Connecticut, Shahzad watched the television accounts of his failure; on May 3, believing that he was about to be arrested, he bought a one-way ticket on Emirates Airline to Pakistan. Although the F.B.I. had traced his name and he was now on a "No-Fly" list, he was allowed to board the flight; his plane was already taxiing towards the runway before it was halted and he was arrested.

Unlike Farouk Abdulmutallab, Shahzad was a U.S. citizen and the fact that he was read his Miranda rights aroused scant comment. He seemed eager, even proud, to tell his story and in court on June 21, 2010, he announced, "I want to plead guilty and I'm going to plead guilty a hundred times forward, because—until the hour the U.S. pulls its forces from Iraq and Afghanistan and stops the drone strikes in Somalia and Yemen and in Pakistan and stops the occupation of Muslim lands and stops killing the Muslims and stops reporting the Muslims to its government—we will be attacking [the] U.S., and I plead guilty to that." [35]

He asserted, "I am part of the answer to the U.S. terrorizing [of] the Muslim nations and the Muslim people, and on behalf of that, I'm avenging the attacks," adding, "we Muslims are one community." His motive was clear: "One has to understand where I'm coming from. I consider myself a Mujahid, a Muslim soldier." [36]

When the judge pointed out that pedestrians strolling around Times Square on the early evening of May 1 were not attacking Muslims, Shahzad replied, "Well, the [American] people select the government. We consider them all the same." This statement reflects the radical Islamist view that by definition, infidels cannot be innocents. Faisal Shahzad's defiance was not comforting. But it showed that whatever euphemism the administration chose to use for terrorist attacks, they are motivated by a persistent and powerful Islamist ideology. [37]

At the end of September 2010, federal prosecutors filed a memorandum in support of the government's recommendation of life imprisonment. They pointed out that although Shahzad was living a life with his wife and two young children that was full of promise, he had "knowingly and deliberately chosen a different path—a nihilistic path that celebrated conflict and death, cloaked in the rhetoric of a distorted interpretation of Islam."

The prosecutors argued, "there are few threats to the national security and the way of life in this country greater than a citizen who chooses to serve as an operative for a foreign terrorist organization and attempts to wage an attack inside the United States." Perhaps most perplexing and shocking to the prosecutors, "far from expressing remorse or contrition Shahzad has only evinced a lasting sense of pride in his actions." [38]

On the same day that Shahzad testified in court, the Supreme Court made a unanimous ruling upholding a law criminalizing "material support" to groups that assist people like Shahzad. At that time, around fifty such organizations were officially designated "terrorist groups" by the State Department, although the Pakistani Taliban, which trained and financed Shahzad, was not on the list. The

Court also ruled that material support was illegal even if it was intended to bolster "non-violent" elements of terrorist factions purporting to further their "humanitarian" or "peaceful" efforts. Moreover, by a vote of six to three the Court found that there is "no distinction between the violent and non-violent wings of terrorist groups." Chief Justice Roberts, who wrote the majority opinion, concluded that efforts to help such groups deliver humanitarian aid—as Hamas does in Gaza and Hezbollah does in Lebanon—only serve to legitimize them, at a time when "the government's interest in combating terrorism is an urgent objective of the highest order."

❖ ◉ ❖

By the middle of 2010, after the Major Hasan, Abdulmutallab, and Faisal Shahzad attacks in the United States—let alone other such attacks as the devastating assault by a tiny group of Pakistani Islamist extremists on Mumbai in December 2008—it was becoming clear that the centrally controlled terror network that bin Laden had launched upon the world was now a franchise.

In some ways this development outpaced President Obama's chosen policy of "reaching out to the Muslim world." The subtext of this approach was that President Bush had failed to do any such thing, though Bush had, from the moment of the 9/11 attacks on, always stated that America was not at war with Islam but with a small group of fanatics. That was an essential truth which both men recognized. Where Obama differed, however, was in his optimistic conviction that, unlike Bush, he could persuade regimes and peoples in Muslim nations that, with him as president, there were no longer real reasons for enmity with the United States.

What appeared to President Obama as a hand of friendship often appeared to his critics as a reluctance to speak truth to murder. Thus, in October 2009, on the twenty-sixth anniversary of the terrorist truck bomb attack on the U.S. marine barracks in Beirut, in which 241 U.S. marines, soldiers, and sailors were killed, Obama issued a statement which made no mention of the murderers—Hezbollah terrorists under the control of Syria and Iran—let alone the fact that such people were still targeting Americans today.

He declared the bombing "a senseless tragedy." But it was no such thing—on the contrary, it was a deliberate part of the Iranian–led campaign to drive the U.S. out of Lebanon. It succeeded, Lebanon suffered, and by October 2009, Hezbollah and Iran were even more powerful enemies of the United States than they had been twenty-six years before. Yet they escaped mention in the president's recollection of the mass murder. [39]

Similarly, on May 17, 2010, President Obama spoke about the murdered *Wall Street Journal* reporter, Daniel Pearl—in the presence of Pearl's family—on signing the "Daniel Pearl Freedom of the Press Act." He said, "Obviously, the loss of Daniel Pearl was one of those moments that captured the world's imagination because it reminded us of how valuable a free press is." [40]

This was at best a euphemism. Pearl had not been "lost." He was deliberately murdered by Islamist terrorists who were delighted to record their horrific act on video and release it on the Internet. The man actually convicted of Pearl's murder was Omar Sheikh, a British subject who had studied at the London School of Economics, certainly no victim of deprivation. As we have seen, credit for the killing was also claimed by Khalid Sheikh Mohammed. His boastful confession bears repeating: "I decapitated with my blessed right hand the head of the American Jew Daniel Pearl, in the city of Karachi." [41]

At the time Mohammed made this claim, it could not be proven, but in early 2011 a three-year investigation at Georgetown University, supported by the Pearl Project, reported that Khalid Sheikh Mohammed was almost certainly the killer. The report said that U.S. investigators had used a technique called "vein matching," which showed that the veins in the wrist of the masked man filmed wielding a knife over Daniel Pearl matched those of Mohammed. [42] *

There were other such elisions, notably Eric Holder's inability to state at a Congressional hearing that there was anything in common between the murderer at Fort Hood, the Christmas underpants bomber over Detroit, and the Times Square would-be bomber. Congressman Lamar Smith asked the attorney general, "Do you feel that these individuals might have been incited to take the actions that they did because of radical Islam?" This is the exchange that in fact followed:

---

\* The investigation into the murder was carried out by a group of journalism students at Georgetown University, led by Asra Nomai—a friend of Pearl and his wife—with whom he was staying in Karachi when he was abducted in January 2002. She described the inquiry as "a labor of love" and said that "The thing I found the most shocking was that so many people were involved and so many remain free." Amongst the most horrific conclusions in the inquiry was that when Pearl's throat was cut, the murderers' video was not working and so the act was carried out a second time. On that occasion the reporter was decapitated and his head help up to the camera.

The inquiry found that some twenty-seven men were connected to the killing and half of them remained at large. "The Pearl Project reveals that justice was not served for Danny. We couldn't save him, but we have uncovered the truth left behind," said Asra Nomani. "Through his death, Danny teaches us important lessons about the reality on the ground in Pakistan regarding militancy, Islamic extremism, and terrorism." [Andrew Buncombe, *The Independent*, April 2, 2011; *Commentary*, January 20, 2011.]

"Because of . . . ?" asked Holder.

"Radical Islam."

"There are a variety of reasons why I think people have taken these actions," replied the attorney general. "I think you have to look at each individual case." [43]

The congressman offered him another chance. "But radical Islam could have been one of the reasons?"

"There are a variety of reasons why people . . . "

"But was radical Islam one of them?"

"There are a variety of reasons why people do these things. Some of them are potentially religious."

"Okay," replied Congressman Smith. "But all I'm asking is if you think, among those variety of reasons, radical Islam might have been one of the reasons that the individuals took the steps that they did."

"You see, you say 'radical Islam,'" interjected Holder. "I mean, I think those people who espouse a, a version of Islam that is not. . . . "

"Are you uncomfortable attributing any of these actions to radical Islam?" the congressman asked. [44]

In a similar vein, Senator Joseph Lieberman concluded in June 2010 that the Obama administration simply refused to face the fact that the U.S. was at war not just with Al Qaeda but with violent Islamist extremism. Lieberman was direct about the problem: "This war will not end when Al Qaeda has been vanquished—though that, of course, is a critical goal—but only when the ideology of violent Islamist extremism that inspires and predates it is decisively rejected." [45]

The senator quoted Dean Acheson: "No people in history have ever survived who thought they could protect their freedom by making themselves inoffensive to their enemies." [46]

❖ ◎ ❖

The most important terrorist trial in the context of the fate of Khalid Sheikh Mohammed began in September 2010 in the Southern District of New York. Ahmed Khalfan Ghailani was the first Guantanamo prisoner to have been brought into the United States to be tried in a federal court. The Justice Department saw this trial as a rehearsal that would show that Khalid Sheikh Mohammed and his alleged 9/11 co-conspirators could also be tried in a criminal court.

Ghailani, a Tanzanian national, was accused of having been part of Al Qaeda's deadly bombings of the U.S. embassies in Dar es Salaam and Nairobi in 1998. Over two hundred people—mostly Africans but including a dozen Americans—died that day, and thousands more Africans were seriously injured. Ghailani had flown out of Dar es Salaam to Karachi before the bombs exploded. When he eventually arrived in Afghanistan, he was treated as a hero by Al Qaeda; he became a bodyguard and cook to Osama bin Laden, was trained to forge documents (which he did very well), and was reported to have met some of the 9/11 hijackers before they embarked on their own mission.

Four of Ghailani's accomplices in the embassy bombings were successfully prosecuted in 2001, but Ghailani was still at large, and he was placed on the F.B.I.'s "Most Wanted List." In May 2004, the U.S. government announced that he was one of seven Al Qaeda terrorists suspected of planning an imminent attack. In July 2004, Ghailani was captured in a joint operation by Pakistani and U.S. officials. He was subsequently held at a C.I.A. "black site"—as a "high value" detainee, where he was subjected to "enhanced interrogation techniques" short of waterboarding.[47]

According to the C.I.A., the information he provided was helpful. An agency memo, "Detainee Reporting Pivotal for the War Against Al Qaeda," of June 3, 2005 stated that Ghailani "has provided new insights into Al Qaeda's skills and networks. As a facilitator and one of Al

Qaeda's top document forgers since the September 11 attacks, with access to individuals across the organizations until his arrest in July 2004, he has reported on how he forged passports and to whom he supplied them." [48]

In 2006, Ghailani was transferred to Guantanamo, where the Bush administration planned to put him on trial before a military commission to face nine war crimes charges, six of which carried the death penalty. But the Obama administration decided that his guilt was so obvious that he could safely be brought to New York to stand trial in a federal court.

The trial opened on Tuesday, October 11, 2010 to immediate problems. To begin with, much of the evidence that had been used in the earlier embassy bombing trials was no longer available. For instance, the owner of the truck that Ghailani had used in the Tanzanian attack, and who had established Ghailani's role back in 2001, had died. Just before the trial began, the presiding judge, Lewis A. Kaplan, created a crisis for the prosecution by barring the testimony of its most important witness, Hussein Abebe. He would have testified that he had sold Ghailani the TNT used to blow up the embassy in Dar es Salaam. But the government had first heard his name from Ghailani himself when he was being subjected to the C.I.A.'s "coercive questioning." The judge therefore ruled that his testimony was "part of the poisonous tree" and would be disallowed. One should note that much the same might have happened in a military commission. [49]

By making his decision at the last minute, when witnesses were already gathered, Judge Kaplan effectively denied the government the opportunity to appeal. He gave an eloquent justification for his ruling, writing that although he was "acutely aware of the perilous nature of the world in which we live . . . the Constitution is the rock upon which our nation rests. We must follow it not only when it is convenient, but when fear and danger beckon in a different direction." This was a noble sentiment, but Kaplan went on to say that even if Ghailani was acquitted, his status as an "enemy combatant" would allow the government to hold him until the end of hostilities. [50]

Ghailani had been interviewed by a psychiatrist, Dr. Saathoff, whose task was to determine whether he was competent to stand trial given his allegation that he had been tortured by the C.I.A. Dr. Saathoff found that Ghailani was more than competent—perhaps because he had become an enthusiastic reader of John Grisham's legal thrillers. He offered a well-informed view of the differences between military and civilian courts from the point of view of an Al Qaeda detainee: "When I was at Gitmo, they were able to use hearsay evidence," he said. "Here, they have constitutional rights." He understood the charges. "They make sense to me," he told his psychiatrist. "There will be a jury who will listen to the crime itself. The jury will make the decision, guilty or not guilty." [51]

The prosecution claimed that Ghailani was "committed to Al Qaeda's overriding goal of killing Americans" but his defense insisted that he was a "dupe" of Al Qaeda, and had merely been running errands for friends he believed to be genuine businessmen, not terrorists. His lawyer claimed that Ghailani had never been to Al Qaeda terrorist training camps and was never indoctrinated: "It is not his hatred. He is neither a member of Al Qaeda nor does he share their goals. . . . He was with them but he was not one of them." [52]

There was much that both the defense and prosecution knew that the jury did not hear, quite apart from the disallowed testimony from the man who claimed to have sold him the explosives. They were not told about the confession he had made during his time in Guantanamo or at the secret C.I.A. "black site" in which his lawyers alleged that he had been tortured. Such admissions were disallowed as evidence tainted by coercive interrogation practices. In his confession he had said that he knew the embassy was the target. The jury also did not hear that during his six years as a fugitive after the bombing, he trained with Al Qaeda in Afghanistan and was a bodyguard for bin Laden. [53] These facts might also have been excluded in a military commission in Guantanamo.

Even without such evidence, the defense's claim that Ghailani was an "innocent, naïve boy [who] was fooled by his friends" was absurd. Judge Kaplan certainly did not believe it. "Ghailani continued to be of intelligence value throughout his time in C.I.A. custody," he acknowledged. [54]

The judge also pointed out that "Ghailani's counsel have had access to extensive classified materials related to his interrogation, yet they have pointed to no evidence to the contrary." [55] In other words they knew that their claim that he was a dupe was demonstrably false. Nonetheless they made it, over and over again. Skillfully, they developed the notion of Ghailani as a charming young man who just ran errands and helped out people he liked. [56]

On the other side, the government was able to produce substantial evidence, including his purchase of the truck used in the bombing, his giving a cell phone to the suicide bombers, his being in the company of the Al Qaeda cells that executed the attacks, and his having in his apartment a detonator that the F.B.I. claimed was "exactly like those used in the bombings." [57]

The fear of conservatives that Ghailani's trial would be turned into an anti-American circus was not realized, but neither were the hopes of those on the left that the trial would draw harsh criticism of the Bush administration's detention and interrogation policies. Indeed, Judge Kaplan rejected a defense request that he dismiss the indictment because of the allegations that Mr. Ghailani had been treated harshly, and he also ruled that the long delays in bringing him into court had not violated his right to a speedy trial.

Subsequent reports from the jurors revealed that as they deliberated, one of their number (inevitably described as the "rogue juror" of legend) held out to acquit on all charges. On November 16, the jury asked the judge whether Ghailani needed to know the specific objectives of the conspiracy to be convicted. The next morning, the judge told them, "Yes" and later that day the jury reached a decision—one that the "rogue" amongst them was prepared to accept. It was shocking.

When the charges for the murder of the 284 embassy victims were read out one by one, the jury foreman announced the verdict to each: "Not Guilty . . . Not Guilty . . . Not Guilty." Ghailani was convicted of only one charge out of 285: conspiring to destroy the U.S. government buildings in which those victims died.

Judge Kaplan praised the jury as "people who are not beholden to any government, including this one." But the verdict was dismaying, especially to the families of all those murdered—to them justice had clearly been denied. The Department of Justice made the best of the situation: "We respect the jury's verdict and are pleased that Ahmed Ghailani now faces a minimum of twenty years in prison and a potential life sentence." [58] But the case was a serious setback to Eric Holder's hopes of using the civilian courts to try terrorists.

During the trial, Judge Kaplan had noted that Ghailani's "status as an 'enemy combatant' would probably permit his detention as something akin to a prisoner of war until hostilities between the United States and Al Qaeda and the Taliban end, even if he were not found guilty in this case." This raised a vital question: would federal trials really showcase American justice if the government insisted on its right to imprison indefinitely even those who had been acquitted? [59]

In January 2011 Judge Kaplan announced that he had gone for the maximum sentence—life, thus rejecting the defense's plea for leniency because of the jury's verdict and because of Ghailani's alleged mistreatment during his interrogation. Kaplan said that whatever Ghailani had suffered "pales in comparison to the suffering and the horror he and his confederates caused." He dismissed the defense's claim that Ghailani was an innocent abroad who had no idea of the consequences of his actions; the judge said that he knew and intended that people would be killed in the attack. "This crime was so horrible," said Kaplan. "It was a cold-blooded killing and maiming of innocent people on an enormous scale." The defense immediately said they would appeal the sentence.

❖ ◉ ❖

There will be no consensus on the Ghailani trial and verdict. The most vitriolic reaction came from the Center for Constitutional Rights (CCR), which issued a statement that began, "CCR questions the ability of anyone who is Muslim to receive a truly fair trial in any American judicial forum post 9/11. . . . If anyone is unsatisfied with Ghailani's acquittal on 284 counts, they should blame the C.I.A. agents who tortured him." [60]

These were shocking words; according to CCR, the whole panoply of American justice, whether civilian or military, should be dismissed because of the racism of the system. This was worse than nonsense—it was a deliberate anti-American smear from a powerful left wing organization that always claims the high ground in defending America's great legal traditions.*

---

* The national security analyst Thomas Joscelyn wrote: "CCR is denouncing the entire American legal system and, in fact, America herself. Why is this important? Well, CCR has organized much of the legal opposition to America's counter-terrorism policies. CCR was instrumental in getting the right for Guantanamo detainees to challenge their detention in federal courts. That has gone so well that one D.C. district judge even ruled that a top Al Qaeda recruiter who assisted the 9/11 hijackers should be released. The D.C. Circuit Court, thankfully, overturned that decision." Joscelyn recalled the debate about the role of the "Gitmo Bar" in the War on Terror: "Some have argued that by representing 'unpopular' clients, they are merely adhering to a noble legal tradition in the same manner as John Adams, who defended British soldiers years prior to the Revolutionary War. Granted, some lawyers probably are compelled by their own notions of legal principle, but not all of them are. John Adams sought to create a free society in which all faiths can be practiced and none are enforced by the state. He succeeded. This nation's second president probably would not appreciate CCR's smear of the nation he helped found." [Thomas Joscelyn, "Smearing America in Defense of a Terrorist," *Weekly Standard*, November 18, 2010.]

In *Commentary* magazine, John Podhoretz decried the "astounding and vicious vulgarity" of CCR's comments. CCR was, said Podhoretz, an "evil organization. In the guise of protecting civil liberties, it uses the American legal system to attack the American political system and the American way of life. Its approach is to offer aggressively self-righteous defenses of the morally indefensible—i.e. the logic that says a waterboard is worse than a killing—in a classic bait-and-switch according to which any form of state action against anyone is unacceptable unless that person happens to be a cop, a soldier, or an official of the U.S. government, in which case he is guilty until proven innocent." [61]

Other commentators argued that the Ghailani case showed the innate superiority of the criminal courts. Diane Marie Amann, professor of law at the University of California, argued that traditional and unquestionably legitimate methods of criminal adjudication had succeeded. Ghailani "was not tried before a novel military commission sitting at some unreachable site, but rather before a jury convened in an open courtroom in America's largest city." The judge had handled the torture claims with care, refusing to dismiss the prosecution "on account of outrageous government misconduct" but excluding "illegally obtained information." The trial, she concluded, "confirmed the capacity of federal criminal courts to protect both individual rights and public safety." [62]

These points can all be argued, but the fact remains that the Ghailani jury came perilously close to acquitting him altogether, which would have been a catastrophe for the U.S. government, let alone the families of the victims. Either the government would have had to let him go, which would have been a political humiliation at home and abroad with immense strategic consequences; or they would have had to detain him despite the verdict of innocence. Quite apart from the damage that would have done to America's reputation, such an action would have raised the question that Senator Grassley had asked of Eric Holder a year before: If prisoners are going to remain incarcerated even if declared innocent, what is the point of putting them on trial at all? Indeed, would this not completely undermine the concept of a fair trial in the civilian court system, not only for accused terrorists but for all defendants? Remember Justice Jackson's stricture that prosecutors should never put a suspect on trial unless they understand he could walk free. That same warning applies to military commissions as to federal courts.

Michael Hayden, the former C.I.A. director, said after the verdict that "the first priority must be intelligence gathering. . . . Intelligence should not be placed in a law enforcement model. To adopt this policy would be at our own peril." Hayden thought the choice should be either to hold detainees indefinitely as enemy combatants or, if that was deemed unethical, then to try them before military commissions. [63]

Similarly, former attorney general Michael Mukasey argued that "to take someone who helped to kill 285 people and to convict him of conspiring to destroy government property is a cruel travesty. . . . A different outcome could have been expected at Guantanamo because of the different rules that pertain there. . . . There is no question that valuable information was gotten from him that led to evidence that could have been used against him in a military commission." [64]

But that is not certain. Indeed, in his order rejecting the witness whom he described as "fruit of the poisonous tree," Judge Kaplan pointed to restrictions against the use of evidence obtained by "enhanced interrogations" in military trials, and suggested that a military court would have done the same.

Weighing such uncertainties, Benjamin Wittes concluded, "It is easy to assert that things would have been different in a commission but there is scant support for that in either the rules of the commissions themselves or in the constitutional law that lies beneath them." [65]

The tendency to think that only a federal trial can deliver real justice is widespread but not, in the case of the United States in 2011, justified. The safeguards that have been built into the military commissions and successive judgments of the Supreme Court since 2001 guaranteed that defendants had ultimate rights of appeal almost identical to those convicted in federal court. Al Qaeda defendants were all presumed innocent, their guilt had to be proved beyond reasonable doubt, and each had the right of appeal all the way to the Supreme Court. Apart from the differences in the composition of the jury, the biggest remaining distinctions between the two systems were that the military commissions would allow hearsay evidence to be produced, and classified information would be more strictly protected.

There are strong arguments for both federal and military trials. One C.I.A. officer, himself involved in the interrogation of Al Qaeda detainees, said to me, "Certainly Al Qaeda required a military response. But in the United States, criminal tools were the only ones we should have used. The two battlefields are different. . . . We are winning this campaign, slowly degrading Al Qaeda, its affiliates, and its now-debunked message. One of its main goals is to be seen as an opponent on a military field with us. By trying them in military tribunals, we play up to this self-image. I'd like to see them portrayed not as terrorists, which glorifies them, but as common murderers, which they hate (and against which they have little defense). Some view criminal proceedings as weak; I view them as exactly the opposite, our treating a common criminal with only the merit he deserves." [66]

By complete contrast, one senior military lawyer, a judge advocate general who prosecuted detainees at Guantanamo in 2010, insisted to me that "Terrorists such as Khalid Sheikh Mohammed should be tried by professional warriors precisely because they are fanatics who illegally presume to be warriors. The laws of war have been developed over time to minimize the disastrous effects of war on civilization.

"Men such as KSM who are openly contemptuous of the laws of war must be anathemized while at the same time those laws are maintained. Far from enjoying exalted status as warriors at a military commission, KSM and his co-conspirators will be tried by professional warriors and found wanting."

❖ ◎ ❖

There is a simple truth. Military and federal courts are both needed. Michael Walzer, the philosopher whom I quoted earlier on torture, made the wise point that the anguished debate over whether 9/11 was an act of war or a crime was foolish. It was not one or the other—it was both.

"The struggle with Al Qaeda is police work wherever police work is possible—in West European countries, for example, which constitute a zone of peace, where Islamist terrorists are rightly regarded as criminals. . . . In Afghanistan in 2001, however, the struggle with Al Qaeda required a war—because the Taliban regime provided Al Qaeda with all the benefits of sovereignty. That war is still going on. . . . For Al Qaeda and for the United States, Pakistan is not a zone of peace. . . . Even if we acted in accordance with the crime paradigm, we have enemies who are committed to the war paradigm. And that requires that we be committed to it, too, some of the time." [67]

There was an irony to such continuing discussion at the beginning of President Obama's third year in office. The Bush administration had sought to capture, detain, and interrogate terrorist suspects—harshly sometimes—and then send them to military trial. The Obama administration had condemned such policies but it had failed to devise an alternative framework that was politically viable. However, the administration was proving, in one sense, more ruthless than its predecessor. Rather than chasing and detaining Al Qaeda suspects for the intelligence they could offer, it was killing more and more of them outright by targeting them with high-altitude drones over Pakistan, Afghanistan, and other countries. Which is the more moral solution? That is now the question.

*Chapter 7*

# VERDICTS

IN 2010 THE OBAMA ADMINISTRATION ORDERED the targeted killing, by unmanned Predator drone aircraft, of a U.S. citizen, Anwar al-Awlaki, then residing in Yemen. This one man—and the decision to try and kill him—showed most graphically how the continuing war against Al Qaeda and other terrorist groups had changed. (The Bush administration was not known ever to have targeted an American citizen for killing.[1] But then it had never confronted a major Al Qaeda operational leader who was a U.S. citizen.)

President Obama had quietly changed U.S. priorities in what was no longer called the global War on Terror. Guantanamo, rendition, and enhanced interrogation had earned the opprobrium of much of the world, including the U.S.'s European allies—though official European protests were often hypocritical: allied governments knew how serious the threats to them from jihadists (some their own citizens) remained and how much they depended on American reach and intelligence.

President Obama announced in January 2009 that he would close Guantanamo within a year. (The Bush administration had also diminished its role—only two new detainees had been sent there since September 2006.) Bagram, in Afghanistan, was still open for the detention of men caught in Afghanistan and Pakistan. But efforts to capture major Al Qaeda figures almost ceased. Instead, Obama killed them; he made targeting by drones, Unmanned Aerial Vehicles (UAVs), the centerpiece of U.S. counterterrorism operations. There were not many alternatives—

large numbers of Al Qaeda had moved into the tribal areas of Pakistan, where the United States had almost no access on the ground.

The UAVs, originally observation birds, hover at ten thousand feet. Controlled from afar—often from within the United States—they are equipped with remarkable long-range cameras and other sensors, which can detect even the movement of specific individuals two miles below. Operated by the C.I.A. and the U.S. military, they were used first for surveillance over Afghanistan and Pakistan.

Drones had been developed into missile platforms under the Bush administration but Bush used them relatively rarely as attack weapons until the last months of his presidency. He feared civilian casualties and the resultant accusations of war crimes by those who, in the United States and around the world, had demonized him and his administration. [2]

Barack Obama faced no such problem either in his 2008 campaign or when he became president in January 2009. The worldwide admiration (sometimes adulation) for the new president was so strong that his war plans were not dismissed as evil or risible. In the case of drones, this was remarkable because while improper interrogation is an abuse of a person's rights, an attack by drones is, in a phrase used in Vietnam, "termination with extreme prejudice." The widespread public acquiescence (in both the U.S. and Europe) to aerial killing by President Obama was a powerful demonstration of the way in which political and "moral" judgments can be driven by perceptions of personality and politics.

Throughout 2009 and 2010 a growing number of Taliban and Al Qaeda suspects in Afghanistan, Pakistan, Somalia, and Yemen were targeted. In September and October 2010, there were more drone attacks in the tribal areas of Pakistan than in all of 2008, President Bush's last year in office. This particular spike was reported to be an attempt to disrupt Islamist plans to repeat in Europe the horrifically successful terrorist attack on Mumbai at the end of November 2008. On that occasion a small group of young men from the Pakistani terrorist group Lashkar-e-Taiba, armed with automatic rifles and grenades, were able to terrorize the city as they carried out a string of murders in hotels, cafés, a railway station, and other targets. True to the vicious anti-Semitism of Islamism, they also sought out an almost unknown Jewish hostel in the city and murdered the young couple in charge of it. Their "success" in causing hundreds of deaths and incalculable economic damage showed how much havoc lightly-armed terrorists can create.

At the end of 2010 there were intelligence indications of similar attacks on European cities being planned in the border areas of Pakistan and Afghanistan. German security forces were placed in a state of emergency after intelligence suggested a jihadist attack on the Reichstag in Berlin.[3] U.S. defense of its allies increased. On October 4, 2010, drones struck a mosque in Mir Ali, a town in North Waziristan, and eight German Muslims were reported killed. There were now so many Germans training as terrorists that there were whole "German Taliban villages" in Waziristan.

British Islamists were also targeted. Britain's laxity in dealing with radical Islamists had, as we have seen, earned the capital the name Londonistan amongst security services. Many of the most violent British jihadists had families in Pakistan and trained there.* Indeed, Prime Minister Gordon Brown said that three quarters of Islamist terrorist plots in Britain originated in Pakistan.[4]

---

* *Londonistan* was the title of a 2006 book by Melanie Phillips; it was one of the first attempts to analyze the effects of massive immigration into Britain and the threat that Islamists pose to social democracy. It was a courageous work—Phillips was much attacked for her efforts by commentators and politicians on the left. Subsequently, Prime Minister David Cameron and German Chancellor Angela Merkel both acknowledged that multiculturalism had "failed."

American human rights organizations such as the ACLU and the Center for Constitutional Rights, already dismayed by Obama's failure to disengage America *totally* from Bush's military missions, began a campaign to delegitimize targeted attacks. They and others on the left characterized the use of drones as the cowardly, secretive C.I.A. committing illegal assassination, "unlawful killing," from the skies.

International law allows countries to target individuals or groups that threaten them. In the case of the United States, specific authority for such targeting derives from Congress's original Authorization for the Use of Military Force of September 18, 2001. Any act of self-defense must, of course, meet the basic legal requirements of necessity and proportionality and that raises questions of "collateral damage," the number of innocent civilians killed in a targeted attack upon a terrorist. International legal standards on proportionality are deliberately vague; the customary rule is only that the harms expected from any attack must not be "excessive" in relation to the expected benefits. The law requires that commanders act in good faith, not according to some magic formula.

When the Iraq war began in 2003 the U.S. had only a few dozen, relatively simple drones. By 2011 there were over seven thousand and they were far more advanced. Some had a wingspan of forty-eight feet and needed runways to take off, while others could be carried by a soldier in his backpack and launched by hand. There has also been great progress in sensor technology, which has dramatically increased the U.S.'s ability to track and target enemy forces. The Pentagon is now experimenting with drones the size of small birds, even insects like dragonflies. Such technical wizardry seems extraordinary but, according to Dr. P. W. Singer, a senior fellow at the Brookings Institution and an expert on robotics in warfare, the drones of 2011 were still like Model-T Fords. Robotics, he argued, would in the next few years have a revolutionary effect on war and society.[5]

America's monopoly on drones is already a thing of the past. Over forty countries are now developing or buying them and they are already in the hands not only of rivals to the West such as Russia and China, but also enemies like Iran and Hezbollah. Iran regularly flies small drones over and alongside U.S. warships in the Persian Gulf in order to monitor all U.S. naval activity and personnel. The U.S. has made a strategic decision not to fire upon them for fear of adverse international reactions.

The implications of this leaping technology are revolutionary—and frightening. The Luftwaffe could not fly across the Atlantic in World War II but a seventy-seven-year-old, legally blind, model plane enthusiast man has already managed to dispatch his own handmade drone over that three-thousand-mile moat. [6] There is every reason to fear that Al Qaeda or its associates will be able to do the same thing. Indeed, in September 2011, a twenty-six-year-old American Muslim, Rezwan Ferdaus, was arrested by the FBI and indicted for allegedly supporting Al Qaeda and plotting to attack the Pentagon and the Capitol with model airplanes filled with plastic explosives.

The ever-expanding range, intelligence, and firepower of drones raises myriad new questions of law and morality. They bring to the fore once again the Geneva Conventions whose interpretation has so dominated the waging of the War on Terror. Dr. Singer has pointed out, "The prevailing laws of war, the Geneva Conventions, were written in a year [1929] in which people listened to Al Jolson on 78 rpm records and the average house cost 7,400 dollars. Is it too much to ask them to regulate a twenty-first-century technology like a MQ-9 Reaper that is being used to target a modern-day insurgent who is intentionally violating those laws by hiding out in a civilian house?" [7]

To which the answer is Yes—it is indeed too much to expect Geneva, as written, to cope. The Conventions have been under immense strain in recent decades, particularly since bin Laden declared war on America. The development and proliferation of drones will provide yet another reason to revisit and rewrite them.

For their own reasons, the ACLU and the Center for Constitutional Rights raised many such questions as they tried to issue injunctions against what they denounced as the "unlawful" use of drones. They also went to the law to protect the terrorist Anwar al-Awlaki from being attacked from the sky above Yemen.

❖ ◎ ❖

Al-Awlaki featured in the last chapter as the imam who inspired Major Hasan on his murderous rampage in Fort Hood, who personally instructed Farouk Abdulmutallab to blow up an airliner over Detroit, and who motivated Faisal Shahzad to attempt carnage in Times Square.

Al-Awlaki was an American citizen born of Yemeni parents in New Mexico in 1971. He lived with his parents in the U.S. until he was seven, moved to Yemen, and then returned to America and obtained degrees at both Colorado State and San Diego State universities. Not only well-educated, he was soft spoken and persuasive, and he quickly became an effective and radical preacher, working in Colorado, California, and the Dar al-Hijrah mosque in Falls Church, Virginia. In 2001 he was in contact with two of the 9/11 hijackers as they prepared for their assault on America.

Shortly after 9/11, the *New York Times*, ever optimistic in such matters, described al-Awlaki as part of "a new generation of Muslim leader capable of merging East and West."[8] This confidence was misplaced. Indeed, questions were later raised as to whether he was not "an overlooked key player" in the 9/11 plot.[9] In 2004 al-Awlaki moved, no doubt wisely from his point of view, to Yemen, an impoverished and divided tribal country of some 24 million directly south of Saudi Arabia and commanding the sea route from the Gulf to the Suez Canal. The country's longtime president, Ali Abdullah Saleh, was seen in Washington as a crucial ally in the war against Al Qaeda but the government's writ did not reach far into the wild provinces where Al Qaeda in the Arabian Peninsula (AQAP), a merger of the groups from Saudi Arabia and Yemen, had become one of the fastest growing Islamist groups in the world. Throughout the first decade of the new century, Yemen spiraled towards the grim vortex of failed statehood, even before the massive popular uprisings that swept the region in early 2011.

Al-Awlaki became an important member of AQAP. At the request of the United States, he was arrested in 2006 but was released later that year. During his time in prison, he claimed later, he was not allowed to read Islamic texts; instead he dived into the novels of Charles Dickens and, unusually for an Islamist terrorist, became a literary critic. "What fascinated me with these novels," he wrote later, "were the amazing characters Dickens created and the similarity of some of them to some people today. . . . For example: the thick and boastful Mr. Josiah Bounderby of Coketown was similar to George W. Bush; Lucy's father, Mr. Gradgrind, was similar to some Muslim parents who are programmed to think that only Medicine and Engineering are worthy professions for their children . . . and Uriah Heep was similar to some pitiful Muslims today." [10]

From his Yemeni base, al-Awlaki became the most successful Internet evangelist of the jihadi age. He could speak not only of Dickens but also of Michael Jackson and other heroes of popular culture. His lectures promoting hatred of infidels ("kuffar") and especially his fellow Americans have been found in the computers of more and more terrorist suspects around the world. In his talks he expressed cleverly the call for a new global strategy for jihadism made by the Al Qaeda strategist, Abu Musab al-Suri, who had argued that in the post–9/11 era Al Qaeda should become a much more diffuse movement where individuals waged their personal jihads against the Great Satan. [11]*

That is what has come to pass. After 9/11 the U.S. succeeded in containing the original tight-knit hierarchy dominated by bin Laden. But his following grew and spread to include many affiliates including Al Qaeda in the Arabian Peninsula (AQAP), LeT in Pakistan, al Shabaab in Somalia (another failed state) and more. (Al Qaeda in Iraq murdered thousands of people after the overthrow of Saddam Hussein in 2003 and came close to defeating the United States and reducing Iraq to bloody chaos. But, as I have mentioned, U.S. counterterrorism and counterinsurgency policies devised by General Jack Keane, General David Petraeus, and analysts such as Fred Kagan, and accepted by President Bush, eventually dealt the group a severe blow.)

Then there was the third tier of freelance cells and individuals, inspired and sometimes guided by the layers above them. By 2010 there were thousands, probably tens of thousands of such self-starting, "lone wolf" terrorists who imbibed their hatred from the Internet, made contacts who reinforced their prejudices, and awaited propitious moments to attack.

In early 2010, the Internet's chat rooms, YouTube videos, and social networking sites gave great impetus to the wave of popular demonstrations against autocratic governments in North Africa and the Middle East. Not for noth-

---

\* The 1,600-page manifesto of Abu Musab al-Suri, a Syrian–born militant with
   Spanish citizenship, was published in 2004; it examined the failures of Islamist
   terrorist groups and called for "secret bands of disconnected cells that are both varied
   and abundant" to cooperate so loosely with each other that they would be almost
   impossible to penetrate. Decentralization was almost total—the only thing
   connecting the different groups would be "the common aim, a common name, the
   common doctrinal jihadi program, and a comprehensive educational program." [Rick
   Nelson & Thomas Sanderson, "A Threat Transformed: Al Qaeda and Associated
   Movements in 2011," Center for Strategic and International Studies, February 2011.]

ing was the upheaval in Egypt sometimes called the Facebook Revolution. But these same virtual meeting places were also fecund breeding grounds that inspired Islamic radicalism in individuals at their computers all over the world.*

Almost no one was more skilled at arousing such people than al-Awlaki. In 2008, Charles Allen, then the chief intelligence official at the U.S. Department of Homeland Security, cited him as an example of Al Qaeda's "reach into the United States." [12] But, as we have seen, no alarm bells were raised by his email correspondence with Major Nidal Hasan before that man's murderous assault on his comrades at Fort Hood in November 2009. Subsequently al-Awlaki mocked the U.S.: "I wondered how the American security agencies, who claim to be able to read car license plate numbers from space, everywhere in the world, I wondered how [they did not reveal this]." [13] He was correct: the F.B.I. and other agencies bungled all attempts to monitor and understand Hasan and thus allowed him to commit his terrible murders. Al-Awlaki also expressed his regret that his other disciple, Farouk Abdulmutallab, the "underpants bomber," had failed to blow up over three hundred people on board Flight 253 to Detroit. "Those who might be killed in a plane are merely a drop of water in a sea." [14]

He and his comrades in Yemen published online a stylish English-language magazine called *Inspire*, designed to incite individual Muslims to kill more "kuffar." (This was edited by a Saudi-American jihadist in

---

* Thus Ahmed Abdullah Minni, an American Muslim from northern Virginia, spent large amounts of time on YouTube watching videos of Taliban and Al Qaeda attacks on the U.S.–led coalition in Afghanistan. He posted praise for such attacks on YouTube's comment section and this attracted the attention of a Taliban recruiter called "Saifullah." This man then started an email correspondence with Minni, encouraging him and a group of friends to come to Pakistan. They were arrested before they could commit harm but the incident was yet another illustration of the power of the Internet. [Scott Shane, "Web Post Began Tale of Detained Americans," *New York Times*, December 13, 2009.]

Yemen, Samir Khan. [15]) One of its recurrent themes was that attacks did not have to be large-scale to be successful—they just had to make an impact and inspire other Muslims. In 2009 al-Awlaki wrote in *Inspire*, "Today the world turns upside down when one Muslim performs a martyrdom operation. Can you imagine what would happen if that is done by seven hundred Muslims on the same day?!"

In a typical sermon, "Forty-Four Ways to Support Jihad," al-Awlaki instructed his listeners that "the hatred of kuffar is a central element of our military creed. We need to realize that Allah will not grant us victory as long as we still have some love towards his enemies in our hearts.... Jihad must be practiced by the child even if the parents refuse; by the wife even if the husband objects; and by the one in debt even if the lender disagrees.... The point needs to be stressed: Jihad today is obligatory on every capable Muslim." [16]

In a talk broadcast from Yemen on the Internet in April 2010, al-Awlaki's message to Muslims in America was stark: "How can your conscience allow you to live in peaceful co-existence with the nation that is responsible for the tyranny and crimes committed against your own brothers and sisters? How can you have your loyalty to a government that is leading the war against Islam and Muslims ... the war between Muslims and the West is escalating." [17] He was determined to do everything to hasten that process.*

The deadly threat from "lone-wolf" jihadists was brutally demonstrated in London in May 2010. A British member of Parliament, Stephen Timms, was stabbed in the stomach by a female constituent armed with a kitchen knife; he was fortunate not to die. His assailant, Roshonara Choudhry, a British

---

* Al-Awlaki also met with and inspired as many traveling jihadists as possible in Yemen. A German jihadist of Moroccan origin, Abu Ibrahim al Almani, described how he spent valuable time with al-Awlaki in Yemen. "During an indescribable adventure in Yemen we had the honor of meeting one of the true scholars of our time, the Sheikh and the missionary Imam Anwar al-Awlaki.

Muslim, was an intelligent young woman of Bangladeshi heritage, studying at King's College, London, one of Britain's finest colleges. She had shown neither her parents nor her friends any signs of radicalization. After she was arrested, she claimed that watching over one hundred hours of al-Awlaki's videos had inspired her to kill her MP because he had voted in favor of the war in Iraq. She was tried, found guilty of attempted murder, and jailed for life. *Inspire* magazine described her as model for Western Muslims for the way she "rushed to her obligation of jihad and answered the call of Allah." [18]

Similarly in Baltimore, one Antonio Martinez was arrested after he concocted a one-man plan to commit murder outside a military recruitment center in Maryland. On his Facebook page he wrote, "I love Sheikh Anwar al-Awalki [sic] for the sake of ALLAH. A real insperation [sic] for the Ummah, I don't care if he is on the terrorist list!" Al-Awlaki was also linked to a group of Canadian Muslims charged with plotting attacks on the Parliament building in Ottawa, to six men convicted of plotting to attack Fort Dix in New Jersey, and to the 2005 London subway bombers. [19]

A February 2011 report by the Center for Strategic and International Studies in Washington described the dangerous process of individual radicalization. "For 'wannabe' terrorists living in the United States and other Western coun-

---

We could benefit much from him and spent precious hours with him." He claimed that Al-Awlaki "was active in honey sales, [and] had joined forces with some virtuous, big businessmen in order to finance the jihad in Somalia and to send to the brothers in Iraq, Somalia, and Afghanistan." Abu Ibrahim also described how Al Qaeda and its affiliates maintained safehouses across Europe and the Middle East for travelers en route to war zones to wage jihad. His journey to Afghanistan "lasted exactly one month and was very professionally organized. In the various countries, there were intermediate stations at which they were cared for, we got new travel documents, and, at a particular point in time, a mujahid who was working with the field service accompanied us to the ground of jihad." [Bill Roggio, *Long War Journal*, February 15, 2011.]

tries, online content like an al-Awlaki lecture must very often supplant the counsel of a living, breathing cleric."The Internet can radicalize and forge links between terrorists and recruits thousands of miles apart. "With radicalization, recruitment, and planning now possible in a virtual realm, Islamist extremists no longer must meet in person to enact their agenda." [20]

Al-Awlaki's rhetoric was dangerous but alone it would not have been enough for the administration to try to kill him. Officials told the *New York Times* that he had "shifted from encouraging attacks on the United States to directly participating in them." [21] His role in grooming the underpants bomber was one case in point.

Another, which became public only later, was the case of Rajib Karim, a Bangladeshi-born computer expert working for British Airways in Newcastle, England. To appear innocuous, Karim shaved his beard, played soccer, and never discussed politics. But he was a secret member of a terrorist organization, Jamaat ul Mujahideen Bangladesh (JMB). In early 2010—just after the failure of Abdulmutallab's Christmas Day bombing—he began to exchange highly encrypted email messages with al-Awlaki in Yemen and told him how much he hated living amongst the "kuffar."

Al-Awlaki asked him about his access to airports and his knowledge of "the limitations and cracks" in airport security systems. Karim replied that he could disrupt British Airways' computer systems and he knew "two brothers"—one was a baggage handler at Heathrow and the other worked in airport security. "Both are good practicing brothers and sympathise towards the cause of the mujahideen and do not slander them." [22]

Al-Awlaki urged Karim to transfer to British Airways' flight crew: his new pupil applied to do just that but was turned down. "Our highest priority is the U.S.," wrote al-Awlaki. "Anything there, even on a smaller scale compared with what we may do in the UK, would be our choice. So the question is: with the people you have, is it possible to get a package or a person with a package on board a flight heading to the U.S.?" Karim replied that he would "work with the bros to find out the possibilities."

Discovered only by chance by British intelligence, Karim was arrested in February 2010. Months were needed before the sophisticated encryption of his exchanges with al-Awlaki could be deciphered. He was tried on terrorism charges, convicted, and, in March 2011, sentenced to thirty years in prison. [23]

Al-Awlaki was at the heart of another such airline bombing plot at the end of 2010 when Al Qaeda in the Arabian Peninsula almost succeeded in sending two printers, their ink cartridges filled with PETN explosive, on flights into the United States. After a warning from Saudi intelligence, which had a double agent in the plot, the bombs were discovered (with difficulty) and disarmed at Dubai and at East Midlands airport in Britain. They were addressed to Jewish organizations in Chicago—this was apparently a morbid joke—and it seemed that they were intended to explode over North American cities. As another "joke," al-Awlaki had included a copy of Dickens's *Great Expectations* in one parcel.

An explosion on either or both planes would have been catastrophic. Even without that, AQAP claimed success: "The operation was to be based on two factors: The first is that the packages pass through the latest security equipment. The second, the spread of fear that would cause the West to invest billions of dollars in new security procedures." [24] By contrast, *Inspire* claimed, the plot had cost only $4,200 to mount; it was part of a new "strategy of a thousand cuts" designed to bleed the Western economies to death. [25]

The violence and intimidation of Islamism takes many forms. Consider the endless plight of the Danish cartoonists who drew pictures of Mohammed in 2005. (Some of the *hadiths* (sayings of and about Mohammed) forbid depictions of him, but the Koran does not.) Islamic anger at these representations of the Prophet (one of them had him with a bomb in his turban) was manufactured and manipulated by extremists around the world, in particular by Yusuf al Qaradawi, the most influential Islamic cleric in the Muslim Brotherhood. Danish embassies and other interests were attacked and over 100 people were killed in riots. The lives of the cartoonists were from then on under constant threat. In January 2010 a Somali terrorist almost succeeded in murdering one of them, Kurt Westergaard, by breaking into his Copenhagen home armed with an axe and a knife. Fortunately, he had already built himself a "safe room" into which he locked himself—this saved his life. His assailant was arrested.

The intimidation never ended. Yale University commissioned a book on the whole controversy—but was frightened to reprint the cartoons in it, thereby rendering its publication somewhat pointless, and in 2010 the Metropolitan Museum of Art took down any representation of Mohammed from its walls, including precious Persian miniatures which had been on display for years, for fear of Islamist violence.

Particularly poignant was the case of Molly Norris. In April 2010, Ms. Norris, a cartoonist on the *Seattle Weekly*, was appalled by the worldwide self censorship over images of Mohammed. She drew a poster advertising an event—"Everybody Draw Mohammed Day"—on May 20, 2011. [26] Her intention was not to abuse Islam but to create safety in numbers and to defend freedom of speech. This was honorable but rash.

To her horror, her idea went viral on Facebook with thousands of different sorts of drawings of Mohammed submitted. As worldwide arguments over her initiative began, she disassociated herself from it. Too late. Like some ghastly mythical fury lurking in faraway mountains, Anwar al-Awlaki immediately issued from his eyrie in Yemen a fatwa demanding the death of Molly Norris and everyone else who had drawn Mohammed. "The medicine prescribed by the Messenger of Allah is the execution of those involved," he said in *Inspire* magazine. "The large number of participants makes it easier for us because there are more targets to choose from." He said it would be difficult for the authorities to protect them all. And there were indeed more than enough radicalized American Muslims to pose a real and perpetual threat to Molly Norris. The F.B.I. declared it would not defend her and the *Seattle Weekly* announced "there is no more Molly." She became a non person, hiding in Washington State—or somewhere else.

Molly Norris's entire life, not just her freedom of speech, was ruined in the land of the First Amendment by a threat from an Islamist terrorist demanding the murder of yet more Americans. [27] This is the route down which freedom dies. We make fun of Christianity, mock (or malign) the Jews, laugh at the Dalai Lama, but we often maintain a respectful silence about Islam. Why is one religion being accorded so much more deference than all the others?

The existential threats were first made manifest in the horrific case of Salman Rushdie. The renowned British novelist was sentenced to death in a fatwa, issued by Ayatollah Khomeini in 1989, for allegedly committing "blasphemy against Islam" in his book *The Satanic Verses*. The fatwa sparked violence by Muslims, ostensibly directed against Rushdie and his book, around the world. Several people associated with the book were attacked (one was murdered) and many more died in riots around the world. Rushdie himself had to live under police protection for many years thereafter. The anxiety not to cause offense has increased as the concept of "Islamophobia" has become more powerful and has had the effect of inhibiting discussion.* During the

---

\* "Islamophobia" is a new concept. In 1997, the British Runnymede Trust defined it as the "dread or hatred of Islam and therefore, to the fear and dislike of all Muslims." It has had the effect of creating a new "thought crime." The French philosopher, Pascal Bruckner, pointed out that Islamophobia is unique from racism or anti-Semitism, saying, "Racism attacks people for what they are: black, Arab, Jewish, white. The critical mind on the other hand undermines revealed truths and subjects the scriptures to exegesis and transformation. To confuse the two is to shift religious questions from the intellectual to a judicial level. *(continues)*

course of 2010, the U.S. Treasury Department decided that it had enough evidence to designate al-Awlaki publicly as a terrorist, asserting that he had "involved himself in every aspect of the supply chain of terrorism—fundraising for terrorist groups, recruiting and training operatives, and planning and ordering attacks on innocents." The National Security Council considered the case and agreed that al-Awlaki could be targeted.[28]

When they discovered this, the American Civil Liberties Union and the Center for Constitutional Rights attempted to come to the terrorist's aid.*

❖ ◉ ❖

---

(continued from previous page)

Every objection, every joke becomes a crime." The notion of Islamophobia is dangerous because "contesting a form of obedience, rejecting ideas one considers false or dangerous, is the very foundation of intellectual life... The invention of Islamophobia fulfills several functions: to deny the reality of an Islamist offensive in Europe the better to legitimate it, but especially to silence Muslims who dare to criticise their faith... We are seeing the fabrication on a global scale of a new crime of opinion analogous to the crime that used to be committed by 'enemies of the people' in the Soviet Union." [Pascal Bruckner. *The Tyranny of Guilt*, Princeton, 2010, pp. 47–53.]

According to the F.B.I.'s hate crime statistics, from 1996-2009 not one Muslim was killed in an anti-Islamic or Islamophobic incident in the United States. By contrast, in recent years Christians have come under increasingly brutal assault from Islamist extremists in many Muslim countries, including Iraq and Egypt. [*New York Times*, December 13, 2010; and *Wall Street Journal*, December 14, 2010.]

* The ACLU's view was put forth by Scott Fenstermaker in a short debate with Bill O'Reilly on his program, "The O'Reilly Factor," on Fox News. Fenstermaker, a criminal defense attorney with the ACLU, declared that drone attacks on Al Qaeda suspects like Anwar al-Awlaki were illegal. He stated that al-Awlaki was not the enemy, there was no proof he was part of Al Qaeda and anyway, Al Qaeda is

In November 2010, al-Awlaki released a video in which he stated "Don't consult with anybody in killing the Americans; fighting the devil doesn't require consultation or prayers or seeking divine guidance." [29] By coincidence on that same day, the human rights groups went to the District Court in Washington, D.C. to argue that that al-Awlaki could not instruct counsel to seek an injunction to prevent the C.I.A. targeting him since he was unreachable in the ungoverned parts of Yemen. So they had invited his father to file a lawsuit as his son's "next friend," to stop any such thing happening. [30]

In other words, the groups claimed that the nature of al-Awlaki's work—plotting in Yemen how best to kill Americans—made it impossible for him to defend himself in court in Washington. They seemed to be asserting a constitutional right not to be caught while conspiring to commit murder. * Benjamin Wittes of the Brookings Institution wrote on his perceptive *Lawfare Blog* that this argument

---

posing any threat to us now." Asked by O'Reilly whether he might be targeted by Al Qaeda just because he was an American, he replied, "I'm a bad example: I'm probably quite a hero to Al Qaeda." He told O'Reilly that so far as Al Qaeda was concerned, "I don't think you have the first idea of what you're talking about." [www.mediaite.com, August 4, 2010.]

* The ACLU/CCR suit claimed that Yemen was not a foreign battlefield and so al-Awlaki should be entitled to due process. It asked the District Court to grant an injunction and subject Defense and C.I.A. drone strikes to judicial review. A preliminary injunction to enjoin the government from killing a U.S. citizen outside of armed conflict in violation of the Constitution and international law will not "substantially harm" the U.S., the ACLU argued since the Pentagon could still pursue al-Awlaki "with constitutional law enforcement tools." To which the *Wall Street Journal* added this comment, "Except of course for the innocent U.S. civilians who may be killed in the meantime if the ACLU prevails." ["The Lawfare Wars," *Wall Street Journal*, September 2, 2010.]

was "maddening. . . . It essentially asserts al-Awlaki's right to avail himself of the justice system without submitting to it." [31]

The case came before Judge John Bates of the District Court in Washington, D.C.; he seemed equally skeptical and asked, "What is it that should lead me to believe that he [Anwar al-Awlaki] wants to bring this case?[32]

Good question: there was no evidence at all. Indeed, al-Awlaki, like Khalid Sheikh Mohammed and other Islamists, had often made clear his contempt for U.S. law and said that only the law of Allah, sharia law, counted for anything. Muslims must not be forced to accept the rulings of Western courts, and to abide by Western laws was "to live as sheep, as pleasantly as a flock of tame, peaceful and obedient sheep. One billion and a quarter Muslims with no say on the world stage, stripped of their right to live as Muslims under the law of Islam, directly and indirectly occupied by the West, are asked to live as sheep." He rejected totally the proposal of moderate Muslim clerics that Muslims, Christians, and Jews should try to coexist peacefully in the modern nation state. [33]

Despite al-Awlaki's contempt for Western jurisprudence and society, and despite his avowed ambition to kill many more Americans, the ACLU and CCR still tried to show that the U.S. government had no authority to stop him by whatever measures were possible.*

---

* The dilemma the human rights argument ignored was this: if al-Awlaki, or anyone else, was launching attacks against the U.S. from an ungoverned space where U.S. law enforcement could not reach, then surely the U.S. must have other legal ways of stopping him? If targeted killing was made illegal, then the only alternative would be a major military operation—an invasion of U.S. troops. But often the location—deep in Yemen or Waziristan—makes that impossible. [*Foreign Policy*, November 2010; and Lawfare Blog, October 13, 2010.]

In January 2011, Judge Bates released a strong judgment rejecting the ACLU/CCR plea. He not only ruled that al-Awlaki's father lacked standing to bring the case but also ruled that the case presented a non-justiciable political question. The judge acknowledged that his conclusion was "somewhat unsettling" but nonetheless argued that "there are circumstances in which the Executive's unilateral decision to kill a U.S. citizen overseas is 'constitutionally committed to the political branches' and judicially unreviewable."[34]

The ACLU and the Center for Constitutional Rights both denounced Judge Bates's decision in no uncertain terms. They had even worse news to come.

❖ ◉ ❖

On March 7, 2011, President Obama signed an Executive Order lifting the freeze on military trials that he himself had imposed in January 2009, and effectively acknowledging that Guantanamo would remain open for the foreseeable future. Thus he had abandoned two of the signature policies on which he had campaigned and which he had promulgated with great fanfare in January 2009.

Obama was bowing to both the political realities that he had created and the practical realities he had ignored. He and many of his supporters, near and far, had disdained George W. Bush and rebuked him for his policies in the War on Terror. But by the spring of 2011 he appears to have realized that his promises of "hope and change" were not easy to effect in the war against Al Qaeda. Having claimed in 2008 that President Bush's policies undermined "our Constitution and our freedom," Obama had since traced their history back to George Washington and declared, "They are an appropriate venue for trying detainees for violations of the laws of war. They allow for the protection of sensitive sources, and methods of intelligence-gathering, they allow for the safety and security of participants, and for the presentation of evidence gathered from the battlefield, that cannot always be presented effectively in federal courts." [35] The *Wall Street Journal* pointed out, "The killers at Guantanamo will now be brought to justice via a process that the president once depicted as akin to the Ministry of Love in '1984.'" [36]

It was now clear that Guantanamo would remain open, perhaps indefinitely. That was a serious reversal for Obama himself and a shock to many of his supporters. But it is important to stress that the Guantanamo of 2011 was very different from the prison site hastily created by the Bush administration soon after 9/11, a place that was depicted by America's enemies as an illegal black hole filled with tortured suspects clad in orange suits and locked in wire cages.

By now Guantanamo was unique for the opposite reasons. The Bush administration had chosen it because it lay beyond the reach of U.S. courts. Now, by complete contrast, it was the only detention site used by the military in the War on Terror that was supervised by the federal courts and by lawyers pursuing habeas corpus cases on behalf of the inmates. Detainees at Guantanamo had more access to lawyers than in any other detention center, and press visits to the center were more frequent. In 2010 there had been over 1,400 legal visits to some 200 detainees. As Benjamin Wittes pointed out, Guantanamo had "evolved into a facility that offers a far more attractive model of how long-term counterterrorism detention can proceed than do the other sites the U.S. has used." Wittes advised Obama to "embrace" Guantanamo. [37]

If its reputation was nonetheless still awful, that was partly because President Obama and other like-minded people in the elite

American and other media still excoriated it instead of acknowledging the changes that both Republican and Democrat administrations had brought about. The Obama administration had now recognized that detention in wartime was both legal and necessary and that Guantanamo, for all its shortcomings, played an important part in America's self-defense. It had not been created after 9/11 because the Bush administration was uniquely malevolent, but because a detention facility was needed quickly after the start of the U.S.–led war against the Taliban and Al Qaeda. Not for nothing did Secretary Rumsfeld call Gitmo "the least worst place." But that was an almost impossible idea to convey. The tendency amongst "opinion formers" was always to believe the worst of American motives and behavior in Guantanamo.*

Both Bush and Obama had sought to release as many detainees as possible—each administration wished to close Guantanamo, meet the concerns of European allies, put trust in the Saudi government's rehabilitation program for jihadists, and take risks.

---

\* In May 2011, the American Society of Magazine Editors awarded their National Magazine Award for Reporting to Scott Horton for an article published in *Harpers* magazine in January 2010. The article alleged that three detainees who had committed suicide at Guantanamo in June 2006 had in fact "most likely" been tortured to death by U.S. personnel at the camp. According to Cully Stimson, former head of detainee policy at the Pentagon, the author not only accused U.S. military personnel of homicide, he accused senior lawyers in both the Obama and Bush administrations of lying to federal judges about the affair. As Benjamin Wittes put it, the story was "nothing more than a set of wholly unfounded accusations of murder and conspiracy directed against our men and women in uniform dressed up as investigative journalism." Wittes was "speechless" that Horton should have been honored by the Society of Magazine Editors. [Lawfare Blog, May 25, 2011.]

But there were many problems, including finding safe destinations for many of those deemed no threat to the United States. There was also a high rate of recidivism—of released detainees returning to war. By the end of 2010, according to U.S. intelligence, 25 percent of the 598 detainees who had been set free were now confirmed or suspected of returning to the fight against America.[38]

A few examples. As this book went to press in the summer of 2011, the State Department named Othman al Ghamdi, commander of Al Qaeda in the Arabian Peninsula (AQAP) as a Specially Designated Global Terrorist. The Department did not mention that he had been one of the earliest detainees sent to Guantanamo in early 2002, after being captured by the Pakistani police near the Afghan border. At first he tried to hide his identity by pretending to be a Yemeni, but eventually it transpired that he had been a former Saudi soldier who had joined the jihad and was trained in Al Qaeda's al Farouq camp in Afghanistan. He cooperated very little with interrogators in Guantanamo and was assessed as a "medium" rather than "high" threat. In 2005 the Bush administration's Joint Task Force approved him for transfer back to Saudi Arabia, so long as the Saudis retained "control" over him and others like him. This meant a jihadist "rehabilitation" program and then release into Saudi Arabia. His "rehabilitation" was clearly not very successful, since by 2009 he was one of eleven former Guantanamo detainees on Saudi Arabia's most wanted list and in 2010 he became more of a public leader of AQAP, denouncing America's "crusade" against the Muslim world, and celebrating the triumph of 9/11.[39]

Classified documents released by WikiLeaks in 2011 revealed that amongst those who were released, one Yemeni returned home to serve as al-Awlaki's deputy, another became a Taliban commander, and many were trained as suicide bombers. Another, Ayman Batarfi, a confidante of bin Laden who was deeply involved in Al Qaeda's anthrax program, was released even though he was deemed "likely to pose a threat to the U.S., its interests, and its allies." [40]

Yet another was Abdul Hafiz, who had been held at Guantanamo because he was implicated in the murder of a Red Cross worker in Afghanistan. After he was given his freedom, he became a Taliban commander "who hunts charity workers in Afghanistan." [41]

Then there was a Libyan detainee, Sufyan Ben Qumu, who was transferred from Guantanamo back home to Libya in 2007. In spring 2011 he was reported to be fighting against Colonel Gaddafi along with other jihadist veterans of Afghanistan. Declassified documents from Guantanamo showed him to have been close to the top Al Qaeda leadership and noted, "The Libyan government considers detainee a dangerous man with no qualms about committing terrorist acts. He was known as one of the extremist commanders of the Afghan Arabs." In other words, like other Libyan jihadists fighting to overthrow Gaddafi in 2011, he was unlikely to be a real ally to the NATO attempt to replace the colonel with a more democratic regime. [42]

In Spring 2011, there were 172 prisoners still in Guantanamo, of whom the administration said nearly fifty could not be put on trial because, amongst other reasons, their evidence might be tainted by their treatment during "enhanced interrogations." The other 124 could now be tried in either military or civilian courts or, in theory, resettled abroad.

Few of the cases were simple. Take the group of Chinese Uighurs who had been there since the camp opened in early 2002. As the analyst Thomas Joscelyn has pointed out, they were not "the worst of the worst," but they were not innocent goatherds either. [43] They were members of the Eastern Turkistan Islamic Party, an Al Qaeda affiliate, and they had been trained to fight alongside the Taliban and Al Qaeda by Abdul Haq, whom the Obama administration had designated a high-ranking Al Qaeda terrorist and had killed with a drone attack in northern Pakistan. Nonetheless both Bush and Obama were prepared to release them.

They could not, for their own safety, be returned to China; seventeen of them accepted resettlement to various places, some of them to the Pacific island of Palau. The last five preferred to stay in Guantanamo "because they have no connection to the island" of Palau, according to their American lawyers. They had no connection to the United States either, but that was where their lawyers argued they should be resettled. That option had in fact been considered and rejected by the Obama administration's own Guantanamo Review Task Force. Nonetheless, their case against the government progressed through the court system until it was eventually turned down.

The *New York Times* was indignant on their behalf. Ignoring their admission that they were trained by Abdul Haq, the paper claimed that they "are not enemies, let alone enemy combatants" and their appeal "in no way threatens national security." [44]

The forty-eight hard core detainees presented a real problem. (By July 2011, two deaths had reduced the number to forty-six.) If they could neither be tried nor released, then it appeared that they might remain in Guantanamo in perpetuity. This was not a pleasant prospect, but the administration was now prepared to argue that it had the legal authority to hold all of the detainees at Guantanamo under the laws of war. The courts had upheld that view, while finding that some detainees should be released for lack of evidence against them. All detainees would still have the right to petition the federal courts under the doctrine of habeas corpus. And under Obama's new proposals their status would be constantly reviewed.*

Obama's announcement did not please human rights groups. "With the stroke of a pen," said Tom Parker of Amnesty International, "President

---

* These reviews would be conducted by officials from the Departments of State, Defense, Justice, Homeland Security, and intelligence officers. Detainees would be allowed attorneys to represent them to challenge the government's decisions. There

Obama extinguished any lingering hope that his administration would return the United States to the rule of law by referring detainee cases from Guantanamo Bay to federal courts rather than the widely discredited military commissions." Anthony D. Romero, executive director of the American Civil Liberties Union, said "providing more process to Guantanamo detainees is just window dressing for the reality that today's executive order institutionalized indefinite detention, which is unlawful, unwise, and un-American." [45] Those charges were partisan, but undoubtedly true was Romero's complaint that "in a little over two years, the Obama administration has done a complete about-face." Similarly, Clive Stafford-Smith, British lawyer, founder of the human rights group Reprieve, and attorney for fifteen detainees at Guantanamo, asserted that in some ways Obama's new system was worse than that of President Bush. The "kangaroo court," he said, was back.[46] David Remes, an American attorney who represented sixteen Yemeni detainees, said that the review process was no better than that of George W. Bush and there was merely "a new cast of characters" on review boards. It certainly would not do any of his Yemeni clients any good; the administration was not planning to send home any Yemeni detainees because Yemen lacked the ability to reintegrate and monitor them. [47]

Also expressing shock was the *New York Times*, which called Obama's decisions "a stain on American justice." [48] And in the online magazine *Slate*, the legal analyst Dahlia Lithwick maintained that the decision was "cowardly, stupid, and tragically wrong." In her view, the administration had "surrendered to the bullying, fear-mongering, and demagoguery of those seeking to create two kinds of American law."[49] From the opposite

---

would be full reviews every three years and interim reviews every six months to determine whether there was any additional information on any detainee. The Obama administration insisted all this was new, and to some extent it was; but the Bush administration had "administrative review boards" intended to do the same thing, albeit with a less elaborate process.

end of the spectrum, the *Washington Times* approved of Obama's change of heart and wondered how long it would be before "the distraught workers in the peace movement" felt compelled "to mutter the words 'Obama' and 'war criminal' in the same breath." The paper also maintained that President Obama owed his predecessor an apology for smearing him and his policies so thoroughly.[50] That is certainly correct.

The United States is, alas, likely to be involved in future conflicts that resemble that against Al Qaeda. Detention facilities will be needed again.

Swift intelligence gathering will, as after 9/11, be deemed a priority in any future conflict, and the United States will almost certainly continue to disagree with its European allies on the need to treat terrorists as honorable prisoners of war. By the same token, the Europeans will continue to leave the disagreeable and costly parts of the defense of the West to the United States. (As we have seen, German, British, and other European jihadists training in secret camps in Pakistan and Afghanistan were amongst the targets of U.S. drones in 2010 and 2011.)

In a future conflict, dangerous people will be detained as they were in Afghanistan after 9/11 but, in the fog of war, "innocent goat herders" will also be seized in error. All of them will need to be detained somewhere, and now that Guantanamo is under the supervision of the U.S. federal courts, the administration of the day will be more likely to choose somewhere close to the theater of war—like Bagram, where national security anxieties still precede judicial concerns. Then the criticism will start all over again. And thus, as Benjamin Wittes points out, "we will have recreated Guantanamo . . . the real Guantanamo—which is not the facility itself but the problems that gave rise to the facility, the problems that closing the facility will do nothing to address." [51]

❖ ◉ ❖

Given his other recent shifts towards the policies of President Bush, it was no surprise that on April 5, 2011, President Obama added to the anguish of many of his old supporters and new critics on the left by performing another painful somersault. He announced the start of his campaign for re-election in 2012, and on that same day he had his attorney general, Eric Holder, reverse himself on the trial of Khalid Sheikh Mohammed and his co-conspirators. In November 2009 Holder had promised "the trial of the century" in federal court in Manhattan, but now he announced that the trial of the Al Qaeda men would take place before a military commission in Guantanamo after all. In his statement the attorney general blamed Congress for denying the administration the right to transfer terrorists to federal courts in the United States. He was right—in December of 2010, after the near disaster of the Ghailani trial, Congress had indeed legislated to limit the executive's ability in this regard. But Holder made it sound as if he had lost a partisan battle; in fact many Democrats, like Senator Charles Schumer of New York, had taken the lead, insisting that the terrorists should not enjoy all the constitutional protections of American citizens.[52] (There were echoes here of Justice Jackson's *Eisentrager* opinion that foreign combatants arrayed against America should not enjoy all the legal privileges of American citizens.) Obama had no alternative but to sign the legislation, and to accept its consequences.

The families of victims of the 9/11 attacks, still seeking justice, could be forgiven for feeling that the Obama administration had squandered more than two years. At the end of 2008 the defendants had announced their intention to plead guilty before a military commission in Guantanamo. President Obama cancelled that opportunity. Alexander Santora, the father of firefighter Christopher Santora, who died on 9/11, complained that the U.S. government should have reached the sentencing stage by now. Instead "here we are, starting from square one. It just boggles my mind."[53]

The reversal of Eric Holder's original plan to have the trial in Manhattan of course appalled organizations like the Center for Constitutional Rights and the American Civil Liberties Union for reasons that are well known. There was a more widespread fear that military commissions in Guantanamo would not play well in the Middle East. That may well be true, but it is also important to remember that Islamists and their followers will denounce any form of trial of their members. For them there is no law but sharia.

As I hope I have shown in earlier chapters, it is simply not true in the United States today that only a federal, civil trial can deliver real justice. The safeguards that have been built into the military commissions and successive judgments of the Supreme Court since 2001 guarantee that defendants in military tribunals have ultimate rights of appeal almost identical to those convicted in federal court.

The proceedings in Guantanamo will take place in public view, although there is still room for improvements in access for the press. Khalid Sheikh Mohammed and other Al Qaeda defendants will all be presumed innocent, they will be entitled to both military and civilian counsel who will cross-examine all witnesses against them and see all mitigating evidence in the prosecution's hands. Their guilt must be proved beyond reasonable doubt, and each will have the right of appeal all the way to the Supreme Court. The death penalty cannot be imposed unless there is a unanimous guilty verdict amongst the members of the commission and the government cannot appeal a verdict of not guilty. The accused will have, as I have said above, far greater rights than the Nazis were given at Nuremberg.

The answers to the questions raised in this book are not clear-cut or simple. Many of the relevant Supreme Court decisions since 9/11 have been made by slim majorities, one way or the other. In such complicated areas of law it is rare to find unanimity. This is not surprising. Indeed, such debate is a token of the vitality of American jurisprudence—and that debate was continuing when, at the beginning of May 2011, the U.S. achieved its greatest single success so far in the War on Terror.

*Chapter 8*

# JUSTICE

ON THE NIGHT OF MAY 1–2, 2011, two teams of America's finest Special Forces, the SEALs (Sea, Air, and Land), swooped by helicopter out of Afghanistan and into the compound of a house in Abbottabad, Pakistan. From intelligence collected painstakingly over many years, the U.S. had good reason to believe, but no certainty, that Osama bin Laden was living in this garrison town, which was at the heart of Pakistan's military establishment. The intelligence proved correct.

The SEALs, based in Virginia, are all very highly trained, but some are even more so. The top group used to be known as SEAL Team Six, and is now called both Development Group (DevGru) and Dam Neck. It is split into four squadrons of forty men each: Silver, Red, Gold, and Blue. For this bin Laden mission, Red Squadron was chosen and its members were summoned to base several weeks before the attack was expected. Once on the base, they were locked down and allowed no contact with the outside world. They were put into intense training for the specifics of this assault. Shortly before the planned date, they were flown across the world to Jalalabad and soon afterwards they were in helicopters heading for the suspect compound in Abbottabad. Politically, this was probably the most important mission the DevGru had ever undertaken, but in military terms it was not the most difficult. Often they land about seven kilometers away and have to hike to the target. On this occasion, they landed on the target. The only mishap was that one of the two quietened helicopters crashed on landing and had to be destroyed.

The Al Qaeda leader was found in an upstairs room. He did not clearly surrender and he was shot dead. His corpse was flown, together with a mass of computer drives, USB sticks, and other Al Qaeda documentation gathered by the SEALs, to Jalalabad. Within hours his body had been positively identified from DNA samples and flown to a U.S. carrier in the Gulf of Arabia, where it was washed, wrapped in a white shroud, prayed over in Arabic and English, and buried at sea. In Washington, President Obama went on television and, with understandable satisfaction, announced "Justice has been done."*

Outside the White House, at Ground Zero, and all across America there were scenes of jubilation, and the president was praised for his courage in authorizing a dangerous mission that had no guarantee of success. The SEALs, too, were lauded across the political spectrum. It was about time they had such impartial recognition—in another example of the disproportionate abuse which the Bush administration had endured, on the wilder shores of the left, the SEAL Team Six had sometimes been described as "Cheney's Death Squad." [1]

---

* One legal finality came on Friday, June 17, 2011, when U.S. District Judge Lewis A. Kaplan in New York granted a request from prosecutors to drop the terrorism counts against bin Laden. The government filing listed bin Laden's alleged crimes back to 1998, and then stated: "On or about May 1, 2011, while this case was still pending, defendant Osama bin Laden was killed in Abbottabad, Pakistan, in the course of an operation conducted by the United States." George Z. Toscas, deputy assistant attorney general for counterterrorism and counterespionage in the Justice Department's National Security Division, certified that the C.I.A. and U.S. military personnel confirmed bin Laden's death through DNA tests, facial recognition analysis, and an identification of the body by one of his wives. The *Washington Post* commented, "the dismissal marked a quiet end to one phase of a long-standing debate over whether bin Laden and other terrorism suspects should be tried in federal courts or before the military." [Jerry Markon, "Bin Laden court case dismissed," *Washington Post*, June 17, 2011.]

Despite the widespread relief across America that the godfather of 9/11 was gone, bin Laden's death led to fierce arguments about the provenance of the intelligence that led to his discovery and about the law governing such killings. (Not to mention searching questions into the degree and level of Pakistani official collusion in bin Laden's residential arrangements in the heart of Pakistan's military establishment.) A key question was how vital to his eventual discovery was the information derived from the "enhanced interrogation" of Khalid Sheikh Mohammed and other Al Qaeda detainees. Senator John McCain, who was tortured as a prisoner of war in Hanoi, and had been a principled opponent of any form of abusive or "enhanced" interrogation techniques ever since, claimed that none of the crucial information that led to bin Laden came from coercive interrogation.

The opposite opinion was expressed by Michael Mukasey, former attorney general who, at his confirmation hearings in 2007, had refused to agree that waterboarding was "torture." He now insisted that the intelligence that led to bin Laden "began with a disclosure from Khalid Sheikh Mohammed, who broke like a dam under the pressure of harsh interrogation techniques that included waterboarding. He loosed a torrent of information—including eventually the nickname of a trusted courier of bin Laden." [2] *

McCain called upon Mukasey to correct this "misstatement." But in a letter to the senator, the director of the C.I.A., Leon Panetta, wrote that the trail to Abbottabad was the result of intensive intelligence work over ten years. He left open the utility of enhanced interrogation, saying that some of the detainees who had provided useful information had

---

* John Brennan, Obama's chief counterterrorism adviser, had stated in 2008 that there had been "a lot of information that has come out from these interrogation procedures that the agency has in fact used against the real hardcore terrorists. It has saved lives. And let's not forget, these are hardened terrorists who have been responsible for 9/11, who have shown no remorse at all for the deaths of 3,000 innocents."

been subjected to enhanced interrogation techniques. "Whether those techniques were the 'only timely and effective way' to obtain such information is a matter of debate and cannot be established definitively." [3]

John Yoo, the deputy assistant attorney general under Bush, who had written the guidelines for the "enhanced interrogation techniques" (and therefore was dubbed by the left as the "author of the torture memos"), wrote in the *Wall Street Journal* that the discovery of bin Laden "vindicates the Bush administration, whose intelligence architecture marked the path to bin Laden's door. According to current and former administration officials, C.I.A. interrogators gathered the initial information that ultimately led to bin Laden's death. The United States located Al Qaeda's leader by learning the identity of a trusted courier from the tough interrogations of Khalid Sheikh Mohammed, the architect of the 9/11 attacks, and his successor, Abu Faraj al-Libi." Mr. Yoo gave Obama credit but suggested "he should also recognize that he succeeded despite his urge to disavow Bush administration policies. Perhaps one day he will acknowledge his predecessor's role in making this week's dramatic success possible. More important, he should end the criminal investigation of C.I.A. agents and restart the interrogation program that helped lead us to bin Laden." [4] At the end of June 2011 the investigation was in large part dropped.*

---

\* In August 2009, Attorney General Eric Holder had appointed John Durham, a Connecticut prosecutor, to examine the C.I.A.'s treatment of more than 100 detainees held in overseas "black sites," despite the objections of seven former C.I.A. directors. They pointed out that they had already been cleared by the previous administration and it would place the officers in double jeopardy. On June 30, 2011, Holder announced that except in the case of two detainees who had died in custody, further "investigation of the remaining matters is not warranted." This decision was welcomed by the C.I.A. and its supporters and condemned by the American Civil Liberties Union.
["Vindicating the C.I.A., Ending a Disgraceful Investigation," *Wall Street Journal*, July 2, 2011; "Justice Ends 2nd review of C.I.A. questioners," *Washington Times*, June 30, 2011.)

Michael Hayden, director of the C.I.A. from 2006 to 2009, thought no debate was necessary. Writing in the *Wall Street Journal*, he said that when he was first briefed on the prospects of finding bin Laden, "a crucial component of the briefing was information provided by three C.I.A. detainees, all of whom had been subjected to some form of enhanced interrogation." He went further:

> So that there is no ambiguity, let me be doubly clear: It is nearly impossible for me to imagine any operation like the May 2 assault on bin Laden's compound in Abbottabad, Pakistan, that would not have made substantial use of the trove of information derived from C.I.A. detainees, including those on whom enhanced techniques had been used.[5]

Hayden's testimony was given added weight by the fact that when he took over the C.I.A., he suspended waterboarding and some other "enhanced techniques" of interrogation "because American law had changed, our understanding of the threat had deepened, and we were now blessed with additional sources of information." As for the appropriateness of waterboarding, he now said he recognized "the immense challenge of balancing harsh treatment with saving innocent lives." He, too, understood the dilemma of the lesser evil.[6]

❖ ◉ ❖

Parallel to the debate over methods of interrogation, questions about the legality of the killing were raised.

The U.S. government made unnecessary problems for itself by allowing officials to brief reporters with different versions of bin Laden's death. Early accounts said he was armed and that he used one of his wives as a human shield. These versions were incorrect and were soon denied. Eric Holder stated that American forces would have captured him alive if he had clearly surrendered. As always, threat assessments had been made before the mission. These would have certainly included the risk that bin Laden would be wearing a suicide vest and would seek martyrdom. If so, the pair of SEALs entering his room would have had approximately one-tenth of a second to pre-empt him. With suspected suicide bombers, anything less than complete surrender (hands above the head and open) can be reason enough to attack in self-defense.* International law allows killing if the quarry does not clearly surrender.

The U.S. also had legal cover for the killing from the "Authorization for the Military Use of Force" of September 18, 2001, which gave the president the right to use "all necessary and appropriate force" against those who organized the 9/11 attacks. There was the question of whether

---

* Amongst many disturbing precedents, in 2004 Islamic suspects in the Madrid train bombing that killed 191 people booby-trapped their hideout. When the police converged upon them, they blew it up, killing themselves and a Spanish special forces agent. Moreover, U.S. personnel had been particularly aware of the threat of suicide bombings aimed at themselves since the catastrophic attack by a Jordanian double agent on C.I.A. officers in Khost, Afghanistan. Jordanian intelligence , the General Intelligence Department (GID), has been a crucial ally to the C.I.A. for many decades, has a record of successful penetration of jihadist groups, and has provided the U.S. with invaluable information on many occasions. The GID had recruited Humam Khalil Abu-Mulal al-Balawi as a source on the Al Qaeda leadership. He claimed to know the whereabouts of bin Laden's deputy (and successor) Ayman al-Zawahiri and was brought to the C.I.A. base in Khost on December 30, 2009. He was, in fact, working for Al Qaeda. Although C.I.A. officers had been warned that his loyalty was in question, inexplicable lapses of security allowed him onto the base without being searched, and he then detonated his suicide vest, killing five C.I.A. officers, two C.I.A. security contractors, a Jordanian officer, and the Afghan driver who had brought him to the base. Six other C.I.A. officers were wounded. It was the deadliest attack on the C.I.A. in decades. [Kristen Chick, "C.I.A. ignored Jordanian intelligence before suicide bombing in Khost, Afghanistan," *Christian Science Monitor*, October 20, 2010.]

bin Laden could be lawfully targeted outside of any recognized battle-grounds—in suburban Pakistan rather than in Afghanistan or the un-governed tribal territories of Pakistan. However, Pakistan was already an important battlefront in the global War on Terror—and by allowing U.S. drone strikes and other military actions inside the country, it could be argued that Pakistan's leaders had already consented to such an attack as that in which bin Laden was killed.

Moreover, targeting individual enemy combatants in war is accepted as both legal and moral. Two obvious precedents were the May 1942 killing, organized by British intelligence, of S.S. General Reinhard Heydrich, who had committed numerous atrocities as the ruler of Nazi-occupied Czechoslovakia, and the U.S. targeting of Admiral Isoroku Yamamoto, the commander of the Japanese fleet, in April 1943. Yamamoto had not committed war crimes; he was killed because he was considered a highly effective commander and his death would be a blow to the Japanese war effort. If uniformed military officers can be legitimate targets, then surely so can terrorist leaders. [7]

The Obama administration's legal position was expressed by Harold Koh, the State Department's legal advisor. "Given bin Laden's unquestioned leadership position within Al Qaeda and his clear continuing operational role, there can be no question that he was the leader of an enemy force and a legitimate target in our armed conflict with Al Qaeda." Moreover, he posed an "imminent threat" to the United States "that engaged our right to use force, a threat that materials seized during the raid have only further documented. Under these circumstances, there is no question that he presented a lawful target for the use of lethal force." As for whether he should have been taken alive, Koh stated that the SEALs "were prepared to capture bin Laden if he had surrendered in a way that they could safely accept. The laws of armed conflict require acceptance of a genuine offer of surrender that is clearly communicated by the surrendering party and received by the opposing force, under circumstances where it is feasible for the opposing force to accept that offer of surrender. But where that is not the case, those laws authorize use of lethal force against an enemy belligerent, under the circumstances presented here."[8]

Some academics and human rights groups disagreed. Noam Chomsky—one of the Americans, along with Jimmy Carter, whom bin Laden liked to quote with approval—added the terrorist to the list of monsters whom he has excused over many decades of attacks on U.S. policies. He denounced bin Laden's killing as the "political assassination" of an "unarmed victim" and questioned whether the Al Qaeda leader had anything to do with 9/11. Chomsky demanded to know "how we would be reacting if Iraqi commandos landed at George W. Bush's compound, assassinated him, and dumped his body in the Atlantic. Uncontroversially, his crimes vastly exceed bin Laden's."[9]

Kenneth Roth, the executive director of Human Rights Watch, wrote on his Twitter page that bin Laden's death was not justice because there had been "no trial" or "conviction."[10] This was, as we have seen, not an isolated view, but Human Rights Watch went on to use the death of bin Laden as an event to criticize the U.S. and its allies. The U.S. and other countries, said the organization, "should mark this moment as a new chapter—one in which they no longer resort to torture, ill-treatment, and other violations of basic rights in their understandable quest to prevent further strikes." The organization's deputy executive director for programs, Iain Levine, said that bin Laden's death "should also bring to an end a horrific chapter of human rights abuses in the name of counterterrorism." Following criticism, Human Rights Watch removed these statements from its website. Gerald Steinberg, president of NGO Monitor, commented that they showed the organization's "central role in exploiting moral principles for immoral objectives. This is another illustration of HRW's record of highly misleading analyses on terrorism and responses, and the centrality of its political and ideological bias."[11]

In Europe many reactions were, predictably, equally unenthusiastic. Some of those who had loathed George W. Bush suddenly found their onetime hero, President Obama, wanting. After German Chancellor Angela Merkel said she was "glad it was successful, the killing of bin Laden," she was immediately attacked across the German political spectrum. Siegfried Kauder, a member of her own conservative Christian Democrat party, claimed that her words were "a vengeful way of thinking that one shouldn't have; that's medieval." He demanded that the United Nations create "binding laws" to determine "what can be done and what cannot." Claus Kress, a professor of international law at Cologne University, told the leading German news magazine, *Der Spiegel*, that justice could only be done through the legal process and he doubted that bin Laden any longer "commanded an organization that was conducting an armed conflict either in or from Pakistan." *Der Spiegel* agreed, saying that Obama should have put bin Laden "into the dock of an international court" if he had wanted right to be on America's side.

The *Wall Street Journal* commented, "[W]e can only say it's a pity Germany's elite morality squads weren't in Abbottabad sometime before Sunday to make that courageous arrest."[12]

Geoffrey Robertson, an eminent human rights lawyer in Britain now defending Julian Assange, the WikiLeaks founder, asserted on BBC TV that Obama's statement that "justice was done" was "a total misuse of language." He added, "This is the justice of the Red Queen: sentence first, trial later."[13] A constant newspaper and television commentator, Yasmin Alibhai-Brown, declared on BBC TV's "Question Time" program that she had been almost in love with President Obama, but he had now shown himself to be "an Ugly American." On the same program, a distinguished Liberal Democrat, Lord Ashdown, opined that he was proud that Britain was a country of laws, unlike the United States. It was left to Douglas Murray, a young conservative writer and activist, to defend America. (A member of the studio audience said that of all the panelists only Murray was speaking for the victims of Al Qaeda killings.) Murray was the associate director of the Henry Jackson Society, which had become one of the principal intellectual critics of Islamist intolerance and brutality in Britain, and of the delegitimization of Israel abroad.

In the comments on bin Laden's death, a nadir of sorts was reached by Cageprisoners, the pressure group linked to the venerable human rights organization, Amnesty International. After the death of bin Laden, Cageprisoners released a faux news story headlined "Barack Obama is Dead." The story showed a picture of "American War Criminal" Obama's corpse, mocked up to look like the hoax pictures of bin Laden's body that had circulated on the Internet. The story described how Obama had been killed by Pakistani security forces and how he was cremated after a Christian service on an aircraft carrier. Cageprisoners said that it was trying "to highlight the immorality of extrajudicial killings" and was not "promoting the killing of Obama."[14]

One might expect protest in Britain at the spectacle of a "human rights organization" having to clarify that it was not actually calling for the murder of the president of the United States. Amnesty made no such protest about its associate. One of the few people to draw attention to the spectacle was Robin Simcox of the Henry Jackson Society, who pointed out that Cageprisoners' "joke" and the acquiescence that greeted it demonstrated "the moral and intellectual breakdown of the human rights industry in the United Kingdom." Simcox argued that if the fact of

Cageprisoners "writing snuff pieces about President Obama being assassinated does not wake up human rights groups to this, it is hard to know what will."[15]

Amnesty, like Human Rights Watch, did vital work defending the oppressed in many places around the world, but at least in the matter of counterterrorism they were criticized for becoming increasingly partisan. It often seemed that they were more concerned about the way in which the United States and Israel responded to terror than about the crimes of the Islamist terrorists and the abuses of the Arab dictatorships.*

At the U.N.'s Human Rights Council, an organization replete with countries that abuse human rights as a matter of routine, Commissioner Navanethem Pillay demanded to know "the precise facts" of bin Laden's death. She asserted that under international law "you're not allowed . . . to commit extra-judicial killings." Two professors and U.N. consultants, Christof Heyns and Martin Scheinin, issued a statement insisting that all "terrorists should be dealt with as criminals, through legal processes of arrest, trial and judicially-decided punishment." They, too, insisted that the U.N. be given "more facts." In other words, these

---

* The extent to which Human Rights Watch now excited controversy was demonstrated powerfully when, in October 2009, its founder and former chairman, Robert Bernstein, criticized the organization in an article in the *New York Times*. Bernstein's principal concern, in which he was not alone, was that the organization had abandoned fairness in the Middle East and was seeking to turn Israel into a pariah state.

Human Rights Watch was formed in 1988 by the grouping of several regional human rights committees, dealing with the Soviet Union, the Americas, and *(continues)*

U.N. officials were asserting that the U.S. would be criminally at fault in killing bin Laden unless the U.N.'s interpretation of standards had been met.*

The opposite view was expressed by Christopher Hitchens, the British born writer, who became a citizen of the United States after 9/11 and

---

*(continued from previous page)* other areas under the global Human Rights Watch umbrella. In the next twenty years it grew enormously in prestige and effectiveness. By 2010 it had a budget of $44 million and conducted research in some ninety countries, publishing scores of reports every year.

Amongst its most valuable reports were those documenting the abuses of Saddam Hussein's regime. But between 2000 and 2010 it published more reports on abuses of human rights in Israel than in Iran, Libya, Saudi Arabia, Syria, and Algeria. There were roughly as many reports on Israel as on the dictatorships of Iran, Libya, and Syria combined. Bernstein's concern about its bias against Israel was given weight by the revelation that Human Rights Watch had tried to raise money in Saudi Arabia (a dictatorship) by emphasizing its criticisms of Israel (the only democracy in the region). [ Ben Birnbaum, "Minority Report: Human Rights Watch Fights a Civil War Over Israel," *New Republic,* April 27, 2010.]

\* But the organization would have difficulties in reaching any sensible conclusions on such matters. It had not even been able to agree on a definition of terrorism. This was because of opposition by the twenty-two members of the Arab League and the fifty-seven members of the Organization of the Islamic Conference, neither of whom was prepared to recognize the reality of Islamist extremism. Thus the Arab Terrorism Convention exempts from its definition of terrorism any suicide bombing or slitting of children's throats (for example) under the umbrella of "all cases of struggle by whatever means ... against foreign occupation and aggression for liberation and self-determination." The U.N. Human Rights Council preferred to concentrate on "the conditions conducive to the spread of terrorism," by which they meant "youth unemployment ... marginalization and the subsequent sense of victimization," rather than on "anti-Semitic hate speech or nihilist acts of vicious cruelty conducted by Al Qaeda and other terrorists." [Anne Bayevsky, UN Watch, May 2011.]

has been one of the most clear-eyed and consistent critics of America's Islamist and despotic enemies. Hitchens found himself hoping that "Bin Laden had a few moments at the end to realize who it was who had found him and to wonder who the traitor had been. That would be something. Not much, but something." Hitchens pointed out that in the years since 9/11 the principal military triumphs of bin Laden and his fellow psychopaths had been "against such targets as Afghan schoolgirls, Shiite Muslim civilians, and defenseless synagogues in Tunisia and Turkey. Has there ever been a more contemptible leader from behind, or a commander who authorized more blanket death sentences on bystanders?" [16]

Michael Walzer, author of *Just and Unjust Wars*, had no doubt about the propriety of killing bin Laden. It was an act of war, he wrote, and "He was certainly a legitimate target, as the head of an organization that had declared itself to be at war with the United States—and delivered a devastating attack. . . . Killing Osama did him no injustice. But was it a violation of our own values to have killed rather than arrested him? Should he have been treated as a criminal rather than an enemy—brought back to the United States and put on trial?" Walzer argued that "He was indeed both a criminal and an enemy, but I don't see the justice or the morality of asking U.S. Commandos to act like policemen when they were clearly not operating in a zone of peace and when arresting Osama might have made their mission much more dangerous than it already was." [17]

Let us return again to Justice Robert Jackson. He knew that the laws of warfare are not static and that new forms of attack justify new forms of defense. Despite his belief in international law, Jackson was open to precisely the sort of justice that was visited upon Osama bin Laden. In late April 1945, as Soviet forces were closing in on Hitler in his bunker, Jackson agreed with President Truman that it was for the executive to decide which Nazi war criminals should be submitted to trial. He did not want any kind of show trial, but he acknowledged that there might be some criminals whom the administration would wish to execute forthwith. Justice Jackson had no problem with that. He said, "I have no purpose to enter into any controversy as to what shall be done with war criminals either high or humble. If it is considered good policy for the future peace of the world, if it is believed that the example will outweigh the tendency to create among their own countrymen a myth of martyrdom, then let them be executed. But in that case let the decision to execute them be made as a military or political decision. We must not use the forms of judicial proceedings to carry out or rationalize previously settled political or military policy." [18]

Justice Jackson, chief U.S. prosecutor at the Nuremberg Military Tribunal, would have accepted both the killing of bin Laden and the arraignment before a military court of Khalid Sheikh Mohammed.

# Epilogue

GEORGE ORWELL IS USUALLY A FOOTSURE GUIDE across political battlegrounds. In late 1943, when the tide had turned in the Allies' favor, he wrote about post-war trials.[1] Oddly, he advocated Hitler and Mussolini slipping away. His verdict for them would not be death unless the Germans and Italians themselves carried out summary executions (as they eventually did in Mussolini's case).

He wanted "no martyrizing, no St. Helena business." Above all, he disdained the idea of a "solemn hypocritical 'trial of war criminals,' with all the slow cruel pageantry of the law, which after a lapse of time has so strange a way of focusing a romantic light on the accused and turning a scoundrel into a hero."[2]

For once Orwell missed his step. Nuremberg did none of those things. As we have seen, the trial had flaws. To some it will always seem to be "victors' justice" and it can be called hypocritical in that the Soviet Union, guilty of many of its own crimes against humanity, was an equal partner with the democratic prosecutors and judges.

But, overall, it succeeded. It was solemn, as it should have been, and what Orwell called "the pageantry of the law" was neither cruel nor slow. Orwell's fear that the defendants would later be cast in a romantic light and turned from scoundrels into heroes has not been realized. They are still seen as mass murderers. Nuremberg not only dispatched justice swiftly, it also created a historical narrative that has survived. (By contrast, the 1946–1948 trials of Japanese war criminals were less of a success and no common memory or consensus was created by judgment at Tokyo.)

My father, whom I quoted at the beginning of this book, was asked in 1977 to respond to an anti-Semitic pamphlet entitled "Did Six Million Really Die?" which questioned the validity of the judgments at Nuremberg. He dismissed the publication, saying, "I do not feel called upon to defend the legal status of the International Military Tribunal at Nuremberg nor to justify its conclusions, based as they were upon a mass of incontrovertible evidence, including very extensive official documentation obtained from Nazi sources, the authenticity of which was undeniable."

He recalled that the defendant Hans Frank, the Nazi governor general of Poland, told the Tribunal, "A thousand years will pass and this guilt of Germany will not be erased."[3] My father disagreed. He came to marvel at the postwar rehabilitation of West Germany under the guidance of the United States and its Western allies. He pointed out, "Since the war, the German people have made a notable contribution to the peace of the world and the welfare of all races. It is certainly not their wish to conceal, still less to 'erase' the guilt of the Nazi leaders whose then-conspiracy dominated, dragooned, and deluded the ordinary people of their country."[4]

In the recreation of a Germany reflecting its own genius, not the horrific distortions of Nazism, Nuremberg played an important role. That was in part because of the close cultural affinities between most of the victors (not the Soviet Union) and the vanquished. German expectations of justice were similar to those of the Western allies. In his closing speech to the Tribunal, my father said that the effects of the trial "will reach out far beyond the punishment of a score or so of guilty men. Issues are at stake far greater than their fate, although upon their fate those issues, in some measure, depend. In the pages of history it will count for nothing whether this trial lasted for two months or for ten. But it will count for much that by just and patient examination the truth has been established about deeds so terrible that their mark may never be erased, and it will count for much that law and justice have been vindicated in the end."

The trial of Khalid Sheikh Mohammed and his co-conspirators will create only a partial record of the way in which Islamist extremism seeks to brutalize and suborn the Muslim parts of the world and conquer the rest. It will not have the same educative effect as did Nuremberg. This is above all because Nuremberg took place only after the war against fascism had ended in unconditional surrender. There has been no such victory over the forces of Islamist terrorism. This trial will not be conclusive.

Nor will it alter the paranoid fantasies of those in the Muslim world who are convinced that 9/11 was inflicted on America by the U.S. government and that all Jews stayed away from the World Trade Center on that day. No kind of American justice (federal or military) will ever be accepted by Islamists and their sympathizers.* Nonetheless, the trial will

---

\* The trial of Aafia Siddiqui, dubbed by the press "Lady Al Qaeda," is instructive in this regard. Highly educated as a neuroscientist in America, married to Khalid Sheikh Mohammed's nephew, Siddiqui was caught in Afghanistan in 2008 with poisonous chemicals, bomb-making instructions, notes about dirty bombs, and a list of New York landmarks. While being questioned by Afghan police she seized a rifle and shot at U.S. soldiers, translators, F.B.I. agents, and others. She was put on trial in the courtroom that Eric Holder had wanted to use for Khalid Sheikh Mohammed and she turned the proceedings into a circus by screaming abuse at America and Jews. (She even demanded that the jury take DNA tests to make sure they were not Jews.) In 2010 she was convicted of trying to kill U.S. soldiers and sentenced to eighty-six years. But by now she had become a heroine and a martyr in Pakistan where millions believed anti-American lies about her being tortured for years in Bagram before her capture in 2008. Ayman al-Zawahiri, bin Laden's successor, demanded that Pakistanis take "the only available path, that of jihad" to liberate her, and the prime minister, Yousuf Raza Gilani, demanded her repatriation. The U.S. government made no real effort to combat the myth.

be an important stage in the long and painful process of addressing our generation's most spectacular edition of barbarism.

❖ ◉ ❖

I have not sought to argue in this book that there is one single or simple way for the U.S. to bring justice to captured Islamist terrorists in this long war. Instead, I have tried to show that the problems the U.S. government has faced since 9/11 in bringing its enemies to court are far more difficult than its critics, at home and abroad, are prepared to acknowledge. Much of the abuse which was hurled at President Bush by his antagonists at home and abroad was disproportionate. But that, too, was a deliberate tactic of "lawfare"—enemies of the use of American power, both domestic and foreign, were constantly trying to move the frontlines in the War on Terrorism from Afghanistan and Iraq to the courtrooms.[5] The wildest exaggerations and lies about U.S. conduct at Guantanamo have been crucial to the propaganda against the United States disseminated around the world, both by released prisoners and by America's enemies.* It is worth repeating that of all the thousands of Al Qaeda suspects detained since 9/11, a total of twenty-eight were subjected to "enhanced interrogation" and three were waterboarded.

---

\* Al Qaeda combatants were instructed always to allege they had been tortured after capture. Ibrahim Shafir Sen, a Turkish detainee, claimed that while detained in Kandahar, female interrogators sexually abused him and desecrated the Koran, that guards beat him with iron bars and had him mauled by dogs. In Guantanamo, he said, "Ninety percent of the soldiers . . . wore skullcaps. They all had Jewish names. There were also fifteen rabbis at Guantanamo that we counted. At least one rabbi was present during interrogations." He was released by the United States in November 2003 and in 2008 was arrested in Turkey and charged with being the leader of an Al Qaeda cell.

"Lawfare" has become an ever more important battleground and the power of the judicial branch over Congress and the president has continued to grow. This has been especially true since 9/11, in particular because of the outrage caused by the abuses at Abu Ghraib and the revelation of harsh interrogations and indefinite detentions at Guantanamo.

There have been several positive effects of lawfare—it minimizes the risk of civilian deaths, accords more legal oversight and greater legitimacy to wartime decisions, and ensures that the rule of law is never suspended. But it also places ever-tighter constraints upon commanders in the field and complicates the U.S.'s ability to protect itself and its allies. As Justice Scalia said in his dissent from the 2008 Supreme Court ruling in *Boumediene v. Bush*, henceforth decisions on "how to handle enemy prisoners in this war will ultimately lie with the branch that knows least about the national security concerns that the subject entails." The framers of the U.S. Constitution did not intend for such judicial power over U.S. foreign policy and security concerns.

As Gabriel Schoenfeld has pointed out, "Lawyers have penetrated every crevice of our defense machinery [there are more than 10,000 attorneys in the Defense Department alone] and they determine the conduct of war to a degree without any precedent." President Obama came to office surrounded by a team of lawyers imbedded in this new legalism to use the law to change the conduct of the war. However, reality intruded and the president has quietly continued many of George W. Bush's policies in the War on Terror. All of which reflects "the perpetual struggle to find an equilibrium between life and liberty—a struggle that every liberal democracy faces acutely in wartime."[6]

In the matter of delivering justice to the Radical Islamist enemy, both federal and military courts have a role to play. The Obama administration was correct when, consistent with the rule of law, it finally agreed to use the specially built court at Guantanamo. It was likely not to be only

KSM and his coconspirators who would be tried there. At the same time, it was incumbent on Congress to allow the administration to bring other detainees to the United States for trial in federal courts. As Robert Chesney, professor of law at the University of Texas School of Law, testified to the Senate Armed Services Committee, sometimes the imperatives of intelligence-gathering through interrogation will suggest that military detention (when legally available and subject to the appropriate constraints as to methods involved) is most suitable. And in other cases, the civilian criminal justice system will be the best way to secure the long-term detention of a dangerous person.[7]

In June 2011 a new chief prosecutor of the military commissions was appointed. Brigadier General Mark Martins, the commander of the Rule of Law Field Force–Afghanistan, was a fine choice to oversee the trial of Khalid Sheikh Mohammed. He was a man with wide experience, a former infantryman who had thought deeply about the history, the virtues, and the drawbacks of military commissions and about the affirmative law operations in which U.S. forces were engaged in Afghanistan. Jack Goldsmith, former government lawyer and author of *The Terror Presidency,* wrote of his appointment, "Some will draw analogies to Robert Jackson's prosecutorial efforts at the Nuremberg Military Tribunal, but in truth Martins faces a more daunting legitimating task than Jackson did."[8]

One problem that he had to overcome before taking up his post in the fall was the difficulty that the media would have in covering the commissions in Guantanamo. A successful trial of Khalid Sheikh Mohammed and his codefendants required not just first-rate lawyering but also open proceedings to convince audiences at home and abroad that justice was being served.

The Pentagon, unlike the federal courts, does not routinely make documents and transcripts of proceedings available promptly. That needed to change, so that the commissions' website would be able to publish real time filings and transcripts of the trial. In an interview with the *Weekly*

*Standard* after his appointment as chief prosecutor, General Martins announced that he would take immediate steps to implement such transparency. There would be video feeds of the Guantanamo courtroom transmitted to at least one site in the United States. They would have a forty-second delay to safeguard national security information. "I am a soldier," he said, "and will certainly do my best to prosecute these cases in a manner that contributes to the legitimacy of all that we undertake in opposing terror networks of global reach." His job was to "rebrand" military commissions as effective, legitimate, and responsible deliverers of justice. General David Petraeus, Martins' former commander in Afghanistan and now the director of the CIA, said there was no one better for the task. "His background is uniquely situated to such a critical mission. . . . Extraordinary. Truly impressive."[9]

Then there was the question of access. The press was already able to cover trials in Guantanamo but geography was a real disincentive. It is easy for journalists to attend trials in American cities, but not many of them would wish to stay for weeks on end in a camp in Cuba. As Benjamin Wittes has pointed out, those who do stay in the camp for long periods will mostly be members of groups (like the ACLU) which "have strong positions against the legitimacy of the commissions; they attend in order to critique."[10]

The ideal way of overcoming this problem would be for the proceedings to be broadcast live on C-SPAN, but the rules of the Manual for Military Commissions seem to prevent this. These rules should be changed, but if that cannot be achieved in time at least there should be closed circuit video feeds to various sites around the United States where reporters and anyone interested could watch the proceedings, as they could a neighborhood federal court. As Wittes said, "if commissions are to have legitimacy, they need to be the sort of thing one presents with pride. . . . Showcasing the trials will, of course, facilitate criticism of them. In this case, however, I suspect the opposite may also be the case. The critics, after all, care enough to be there no matter where commissions take place. It's the rest of us who will see them if the doors swing wide open."[11]

There were other crucial issues to be resolved. First, the original Authorization for the Use of Military Force (AUMF) passed by Congress immediately after the 9/11 attacks is now ten years old. It should be amended.

The original September 2001 legislation authorized "all necessary and appropriate force" against those whom the president determined "planned, authorized, committed, or aided the terrorist attacks... in order to prevent any future acts of international terrorism against the United States by such nations, organizations or persons." The AUMF made no mention of detention but since it was passed, the U.S. has captured terrorist suspects not only in Afghanistan and Pakistan but also in Iraq, Somalia, and Yemen—and elsewhere. The statute has come to apply to a war wider than that which confronted the United States on 9/11 and it needs to reflect the new conditions. In the words of Michael Mukasey, former attorney general, an amended AUMF should "make clear to all involved, from troops to lawyers to judges—and to our enemies—that detention of suspected terrorists is authorized, and to set forth standards for detaining and/or killing terrorists, even those who are affiliated with groups other than those directly responsible for the 9/11 attacks."[12]

Many of the problems, particularly of detention, were explained in a June 2011 testimony to the Senate Armed Services Committee by Vice Admiral William McRaven, who supervised all the U.S. military's special operations, including the SEALs' dispatch of bin Laden. He stated that there was no clear policy on detention. If a suspected terrorist was captured in Yemen or Somalia, for example, he might have to be held on a naval vessel pending a decision to prosecute him in a U.S. court. Failing that he would be transferred "to a third party country." If neither of those options were available, then the suspect would be released.

This was an absurd situation that had come about because the Obama administration had put Guantanamo "off the table" for new detainees—while Congress had legislated to prevent any present detainee in the camp to be brought to the U.S. for federal trial.[13] Each position is too firmly fixed in stone. What is needed now is flexibility. As the new chief prosecutor, General Martins, said, "military commissions and federal courts are both lawful and appropriate forums for trying crimes committed during this long conflict."[14]

◈ ◎ ◈

The trial of Khalid Sheikh Mohammed will address not just a group of thugs but the enduring human phenomenon of evil. Mutable and persistent, evil has not been discouraged by the progress of reason or the taming of nature. No two eras are the same, nor are the threats they face identical. Evil reinvents itself in every age, and is reinvigorated by mankind's inevitable immaturity. Like the fascist ideology that the democratic world fought in the 1940s, the dogma of Al Qaeda and of the Shiite extremist dictators of Iran is despotic, ruthless, anti-Semitic, anti-Christian, and totalitarian.

Since the 1990s, Islamists inspired by bin Laden have been responsible for the murder of thousands and thousands of people all over the world. We are reminded of their war against the world almost daily—from the mass murders on 9/11 itself, through the hideously repetitive suicide bombings which can be plotted almost anywhere, to the recent beheading of United Nations workers in Masar-i-Sharif in Afghanistan as revenge for the public burning of a Koran in Florida. In June 2011 the Pakistani Taliban kidnapped an eight-year old girl, strapped a bomb under her clothes, and tried to get her to carry out a suicide attack. She had the presence of mind to call for help from the soldiers she was supposed to kill along with herself.[15]

Such odious violence should be intolerable. But it has become part of the background noise we believe we have to endure, as we do the imminent danger of Islamist attacks on public places and on the airplanes on which we travel every day. Enemies like this cannot be appeased any more than Hitler could be appeased. They must be fought and defeated. This will never be easy. It is worth recalling Reinhold Niebuhr's warning that "we take and must continue to take, morally hazardous actions to preserve our civilization." [16]

President Bush's global War on Terror—criticized but continued in large part by President Obama—had essential successes. It destroyed the core of Al Qaeda, and bin Laden himself, and no doubt helped prevent another massive attack on the United States. But the war has not ended. In June 2011, the U.S. government confirmed that Al Qaeda remained "the preeminent security threat to the United States." On September 30, 2011, the Obama administration had a resounding success in diminishing that immediate threat. A CIA-controlled drone above Yemen fired a Hellfire missile that killed Anwar al-Awlaki—Al Qaeda's most effective propagandist, whose direct involvement in plots against the United States had led the U.S. government to target him even though he was a U.S. citizen. Killed in the same strike was another American jihadist, Samir Khan, editor of the internet magazine *Inspire*, which encouraged English-speaking Muslims around the world to take up "lone wolf" jihad. As we have seen, each of them had skillfully exploited the internet and played vicious roles in inciting terror against "infidels" throughout the world.*

President Obama said that the successful attack was "further proof Al

---

\* From his base in Yemen, al-Awlaki had become the most influential internet
jihadist in the English-speaking world. However, he remained "an honored guest"
of student Islamic societies and community centers in Britain. In 2003, he had
spoken in person at several events organized by the Muslim Association of Britain

Qaeda and its affiliates will find no safe haven in Yemen or anywhere around the world." He was correct—following only months after the death of bin Laden himself, such attacks demonstrated the success of his intense, high-tech, small-footprint war.

The administration argued, persuasively, that it possessed all the necessary legal authority to act as it did. Al-Awlaki was playing an operational role as part of the enemy forces covered by the September 2001 AUMF legislation; he had long been on notice that he was regarded as such; he had made no attempt to surrender; he was hiding in a country

---

and the Federation of Islamic Societies. At the East London mosque in December 2003, he participated in a "Stop Police Terror" event where he instructed his listeners not to cooperate with the authorities' counterterrorism investigations. In January 2009, he appeared via video link at another East London mosque event called "The End of Time," which featured, inter alia, pictures of New York in flames. After protests from the Henry Jackson Society the mosque issued a statement: "Mr. Awlaki has not been proven guilty in a court of law. Everyone is entitled to their point of view." In April 2009, he was invited to address City University's Islamic Society's annual dinner by video link. This was canceled after protests but he did give a video lecture to a Muslim group at a community center funded by the London borough of Tower Hamlets. In August 2009, he was due to give another video lecture organized by Cageprisoners. Protests from the Henry Jackson Society and others led to the cancellation of this lecture but City University's Islamic Society posted his prerecorded text to its website. The year 2009 was also when al-Awlaki is known to have become active in the secret incitement of specific would-be murderers in the United States, Britain, and elsewhere. [Alexander Meleagrou-Hitchens, "As American as Apple Pie: How Anwar al-Awlaki Became the Face of Western Jihad," The International Centre for the Study of Radicalisation and Political Violence, 2011; http://icsr.info/publications/papers/1315827595ICSRPaperAsAmericanAsApplePieHow AnwaralAwlakiBecametheFaceofWesternJihad.pdf.]

where neither that government nor the U.S. was able to arrest him. As for the idea that al-Awlaki's citizenship should give him protection from U.S. government attack, it is worth recalling that in the 1942 case of *Ex Parte Quirin* (described in Chapter 3), two of the Nazi saboteurs were U.S. citizens. The Supreme Court ruled then that "Citizenship in the United States of an enemy belligerent does not relieve him from the consequences of belligerency."

Obama was praised by his critics. The *Wall Street Journal* called his expansion of the drone campaign "his most significant national security accomplishment. . . . The administration deserves congratulations and thanks."[17] Former vice president Cheney, in an interview with CNN, called the killing "a good strike." He approved of the fact that the Obama administration was "tough and aggressive in defending the nation and using some of the same techniques that the Bush administration did."

Fierce criticisms of Obama's action came from the left and from human rights organizations. In New York, the Center for Constitutional Rights (CCR), which had attempted to use the federal courts to protect al-Awlaki, called it an "assassination" and said it was "the latest of many affronts to domestic and international law." Michael Ratner, the president of CCR, called the killing "extra-judicial murder."

By contrast, Professor Robert Chesney said he believed that the government had the right to target al-Awlaki because they deemed him to be a threat to the United States and lacked the ability to arrest him. But the killing did raise important legal and moral issues. Chesney pointed out that al-Awlaki was an easy case. "What about the next case, in which it's someone we've never heard of and all the government's information is classified? . . . What if they've got the wrong guy?"

In a related vein, John Bellinger III, former legal adviser to the State Department and the National Security Council from 2001–2009, argued that the U.S. must beware losing the support of its allies, none of whom had endorsed the U.S. policy or legal rationale governing the use of drones. Bellinger argued that one of the first Bush administration's biggest mistakes "was adopting novel counterterrorism policies without attempting to explain and secure international support for them." Unless the Obama administration could persuade its allies that its drone policy was responsible, legal, and supportable, it would risk "having its largely successful drone program become as internationally maligned as Guantanamo." This is indeed a danger, and it is another crucial area in which Obama needs to show real leadership.[18]

I have stressed throughout this book that arguments over the proper application of law and the administration of justice are not only inevitable but also healthy in such fraught times as have followed 9/11. John Brennan, the president's chief counterterrorism adviser, said in the summer of 2011 that, "We seek nothing less than the utter destruction of this evil that calls itself Al Qaeda."[19] That is a proper ambition, indeed, the only proper ambition—but to achieve it demands not just courage and skill in the use of American firepower but also self-confidence, courage, and unity in the democratic world. In the twentieth century all totalitarian threats were, in the end, defeated by American leadership of the Western alliance. But in summer 2011 there seemed, for the first time since 1945, a danger that the United States and Europe could lose the will and ability to sustain their united defense of freedom. This was partly because America now had a president who did not always articulate his predecessors' faith in America's power to do great good in the world. The difference was particularly marked between Presidents Reagan and Obama. Reagan's assertions of American exceptionalism, and the power of America to pursue the spread of freedom around the globe, were inspirational to those oppressed by totalitarian regimes—they helped lead directly to the fall of the Berlin Wall. By contrast, Obama refused to offer support for the Iranian protesters gunned down by their clerical masters in 2009. Two years later he seemed uncertain how to respond to the admittedly complicated series of upheavals that were loosely called the Arab Spring. Such apparent ambivalence did not help the U.S. in the Arab world. Indeed, a Zogby poll in July 2011 showed that in many Arab countries, the U.S. under Obama was now even more unpopular than in the last year of the Bush administration.[20]*

In the summer of 2011, this apparent weakening of traditional American leadership, combined with financial emergencies in both Europe and the United States, was leading to strategic defense cuts and reconsideration of Western commitments.

This was dangerous—democracies must be self-confident and strong enough to defend themselves against the forces of tyranny. Many Europeans refuse to acknowledge that without American support, Europe risks repeating the fatal weaknesses of the 1920s and 1930s. If American power is withdrawn, the world will finally realize how much they owe to the most benign hegemony ever created. The French philosopher Pascal Bruckner put it well: "The perpetual peace to which Europe aspires has its source not in Europe but in the United States. . . . If America were to

---

\* President Obama was apparently concerned lest American support should "taint" democratic uprisings. This was not the case. When the U.S. ambassador to Syria visited pro-democracy protestors in the Syrian town of Hama in July of 2011, he was greeted with roses, olive branches, and enthusiasm. It was noteworthy also that there were far fewer disturbances in Iraq which, thanks to the U.S.–led overthrow of Saddam Hussein, already had an elected government. It was not a good government, but the people had been allowed to choose it. [Robert Mackey, "U.S. Ambassador Greeted with Roses by Syrian Protestors in Hama," *New York Times*, July 8, 2011, http: thelede.blogs.nytimes.com/2011/07/08/u-s-ambassador-greeted-with-roses-by-syrian-protesters.]

collapse tomorrow, Europe would fall like a house of cards; it would return to the tergiversation it showed in Munich in 1938 and be reduced to a deluxe sanatorium ready to allow itself to be torn apart, piece by piece, by all sorts of predators."[21]

❖ ◉ ❖

Despite George Orwell's misgivings, at Nuremberg our civilization designed a vehicle to anathemize men imbued with evil. Nuremberg is a precedent on which the United States can build with pride.

As I have noted, the long series of criminal assaults by Al Qaeda and its associates on the world have had their most appalling sustained impact on the Muslim peoples. Many millions of Muslims, from Afghanistan to Nigeria, have suffered the consequences of bin Laden's war. But it is clear from the optimism demonstrated across the Arab world in 2011 that Muslims, like anyone else, seek freedom from despotism—not the sectarian totalitarianism that Al Qaeda imposes.

Evil struck America on September 11, 2011, with vast consequences that are still being played out. The United States held firm in the face of that brutal, reprehensible attack, but it has made mistakes. That is no surprise—as Churchill famously said, "War is a catalogue of blunders. . . . " America's errors in the war that was thrust upon it have been broadcast in endless, unforgiving loops around and around the world.

In his 1973 essay "The Problem of Dirty Hands," which I quoted above, Michael Walzer cites Max Weber's analysis of the fate of the politician who decides he has to authorize torture to save lives. "His choices are hard and painful and he pays a price not only while making them but forever after." A high price is paid by countries, too. Guantanamo and "enhanced interrogation" almost certainly did help the U.S. government save lives in the early post–9/11 crisis.* But each proved immensely costly to the reputation of the United States, as well as to President Bush. More recently, President Obama's inability to close Guantanamo and his increasing reliance on killing by drones was likely to further alienate opinion in many parts of the world.

President Bush and President Obama were both honorable leaders; they had different perceptions of the world but, confronted with the nihilism of Al Qaeda, each faced similar, painful, and overwhelmingly sad choices between lesser evils. Sympathy for both presidents is more appropriate than condemnation.

This continuing crisis is not of America's making. It stems, to a substantial extent, from the struggle within the Muslim world for the soul of Islam. As this book went to press, the liberalizing potential of the "Arab Spring" was far from realized—indeed the region was racked with instability and violence. At the same time, Al Qaeda and its Salafist Jihadist associates continued their pitiless campaign of mass murder across the world.

Whatever America's mistakes since 9/11, its strength is that it is a nation of laws founded on individual liberty. It is the world's strongest and most vital democracy and its errors are being constantly corrected. In the question of justice for the enemy, the subject of this book, there is every reason to believe that the nation and its courts—military and civilian—will continue to interpret the law in an exemplary fashion, and with the defendants enjoying far more rights than their predecessors did at Nuremberg.

---

* In September 2011, Eliza Manningham-Buller, the former director general of MI5, Britain's internal security service, strongly criticized the waterboarding of Al Qaeda detainees. She went on to say, "The argument that lifesaving intelligence was thereby obtained, and I accept it was, still does not justify it." [Reith Lectures, 2011, www.bbc.co.uk.]

I have written this before, but in an age where anti-Americanism is so easy, so fashionable, and so widespread, it needs repeating: America's commitment and sacrifices have, since the beginning of the twentieth century, been essential to the world's ability to resist nihilism. That is still true today. America needs the consistent support of its allies. Only America has the power and the optimism to defend the world against what really are the forces of darkness.

# ACKNOWLEDGMENTS

Many people have helped me on this book, in many different ways. They include:

Marc Abramowitz, Mort Abramowitz, Kenneth Anderson, Anne Applebaum, Gerard Baker, John Barrett, John Bellinger, Peter Berkowitz, Paul Berman, Nigel Biggar, Michael Burleigh, Christopher Caldwell, Carole Corcoran, Devon Cross, Michael Doran, Charles Duelfer, Eric Edelman, Charles Elliot, Jordana Friedman, Victor David Hanson, Roger Hertog, Christopher Hitchens, Thomas Joscelyn, John Lloyd, Andrew McCarthy, Alexander Meleagrou-Hitchens, Alan Mendoza, Larry Morris, Philip Mudd, Michael Mukasey, Douglas Murray, Melanie Phillips, Seamus M. Quinn, Carlos Rivera, Robin Simcox, Tim Spicer, Anthony Smith, Bret Stephens, Amir Taheri, Strobe Talbott, George Weidenfeld, Benjamin Wittes, Juan Zarate. I thank them all very much indeed. And I commend www.lawfareblog.com, created by Benjamin Wittes, as an invaluable resource for any study of law and war today.

I have relied heavily, at times, upon the works of several prominent scholars whose expertise far outweighs my own. Notable among those are Gary Bass, author of *Stay the Hand of Vengeance*; Michael Burleigh, author of *Blood and Rage*; and Terry McDermott, author of *Perfect Soldiers*. I can only hope I have faithfully represented their views and have given proper credit where due.

I was greatly helped in London by the excellent research work of Julia Pettengill, and towards the end, Stephanie Leutert did invaluable research under great pressure in the United States. Lynn Nesbit was, as always, my kind agent. At PublicAffairs, it has been a pleasure to work again with Peter Osnos, old friend and quondam colleague from Saigon; Clive Priddle was once again a gifted and supportive editor; Melissa Raymond and Susan Weinberg were much more tolerant of my delays than I deserved and Marco Pavia was a skilled and adaptive copy editor.

My family, and in particular my wife Olga, had a lot to tolerate in the course of my writing this book.

My grateful thanks to everyone. Any mistakes are of course my own.

WILLIAM SHAWCROSS
*London, July 2011*

# NOTES

## INTRODUCTION

1. *Der Spiegel* online, "The Long Road to Eichmann's Arrest: A Nazi War Criminal's Life in Argentina, April 1, 2011," quoted by Norman Geras, April 3, 2011, normblog.com.

2. D. J. R. Bruckner, "Talk with George Steiner," *New York Times*, May 2, 1982, www.nytimes.com/1982/05/02/books/talk-with-george-steiner.html.

3. Ibid.

## CHAPTER 1–PRECEDENTS

1. The official transcript of the daily proceedings in court. *Trial of the Major War Criminals before the International Military Tribunal: November 14, 1945–October 1, 1946*, 22 Volumes (Nuremberg: International Military Tribunal, 1947).

2. White House News Release, "Roosevelt's Statement on Punishment of War Crimes," August 21, 1942.

3. Cordell Hull, *The Memoirs of Cordell Hull*, Vol. II (Whitefish, Montana: Kessinger Publishing, 2010), 1289–1290.

4. Winston Churchill, *Closing the Ring* (New York: Houghton Mifflin Company, 1951), 330.

5. *Morgenthau Diary*, Vol. I (September 4, 1944), 448; quoted in Gary Bass, *Stay the Hand of Vengeance* (Princeton: Princeton University Press, 2000), 152.

6. Ibid., 490; ibid., 153.

7. Ibid.

8. Bass, *Stay the Hand*, 154.

9. Ibid., 170–172.

10. Anne Tusa and John Tusa, *The Nuremberg Trial* (London: BBC Books, 1995), 63.

11. Hartley Shawcross, *Life Sentence* (London: Constable, 1995), 90–92.

12. Ibid.

13. "Aid Memoir from the International Conference on Military Trials," Yale Law School: Lillian Goldman Law Library, April 23, 1945, http:avalon.law.yale.edu/imt/jack02.asp.

14. Alpheus Thomas Mason, *Harlan Fiske Stone: Pillar of the Law* (New York: Viking, 1956), 716; quoted in Bass, *Stay the Hand*, 25.

15. Tusa and Tusa, *Nuremberg Trial*, 69.

16. Justice Robert Jackson (speech to the American Society of International Law, Washington, D.C., April 13, 1945); quoted by Andrew C. McCarthy, *National Review* online, February 4, 2010.

17. Shawcross, *Life Sentence*, 94.

18. Ibid., 93.

19. Ibid., 94–95.

20. "Minutes from the International Conference on Military Trials," Yale Law School: Lillian Goldman Law Library, June 29, 1945, http: avalon.law.yale.edu/imt/jack17.asp.

21. Tusa and Tusa, *Nuremberg Trial*, 72.

22. Ibid., 77–78.

23. Francis Biddle, *In Brief Authority* (Garden City, NY: Greenwood Press, 1976), 385.

24. Tusa and Tusa, *Nuremberg Trial*, 89.

25. *Trial of the Major War Criminals before the International Military Tribunal: November 14, 1945–October 1, 1946*, Vol. 2, 100.

26. Ibid.

27. Ibid.

28. Ibid.

29. Robert E. Conot, *Justice at Nuremberg* (New York: Harper and Row Publishers, 1984), 337.

30. The Rt. Hon. Lord Shawcross, "Robert A. Jackson's Contributions During The Nuremberg Trial" (lecture to the American Bar Association), (New York: Columbia University Press, 1969).

31. Shawcross, *Life Sentence*.

32. See http:www.crimesofwar.org/a-z-guide/persecutions-on-political-racial-or-religious-grounds.

33. Hannah Arendt, *Eichmann in Jerusalem* (New York: Penguin Books, 1994), 221.

34. Bass, *Stay the Hand*, 205.

## CHAPTER 2–CRIMES

1. Justice Jackson's closing address, *Trial of the Major War Criminals before the International Military Tribunal: November 14, 1945–October 1, 1946*, Vol. 19 (Nuremberg, 1947), 400, www.loc.gov/rr/frd/Military_Law/NT_major-war-criminals.html.

2. Reuel Marc Gerecht, "Democracy in Egypt: Why the West Should Welcome a Political Upheaval in the Middle East," *The Weekly Standard*, February 14, 2011, Vol. 16, No. 21, www.weeklystandard.com/articles/democracy-egypt_541410.html.

3. Ibid.

4. John Calvert, *Sayyid Qutb and the Origins of Radical Islamism* (New York: Columbia University Press, 2010), 89.

5. Amin al-Husseini, Radio Berlin, March 1944.

6. Sayyid Qutb, "The America I Have Seen" (1951), 16, www.tawhed.net/dl.php?i=070410Iv.

7. Sayyid Qutb, "Aduna al Awal: al Rijal al Abid," al Risala, November 3, 1952; quoted in John Calvert, *Sayyid Qutb and the Origins of Radical Islamism* (New York: Columbia University Press, 2010), 149.

8. National Commission on Terrorist Attacks, *The 9/11 Commission Report* (New York: Norton, 2004), 51.

9. Sayyid Qutb, "Our Struggles with the Jews," 1951, quoted in John Calvert, *Sayyid Qutb*, 169.

10. Thomas R. Mockaitis, *Osama bin Laden: A Biography* (Santa Barbara, CA: ABC-CLIO, LLC, 2010), 9.

11. Michael Burleigh, *Blood and Rage: A Cultural History of Terrorism* (New York: Harper Collins, 2009), 374.

12. Osama bin Laden, "Jihad against Jews and Crusaders," World Islamic Front statement, February 23, 1998, www.fas.org/irp/world/para/docs/980223-fatwa.htm.

13. *The 9/11 Commission Report*, 47, www.911commission.gov/report/911Report.pdf.

14. Roger Scruton, *The West and The Rest* (Wilmington, DE: ISI Books, 2002), 118.

15. Ibid., 132–133.

16. Ibid., 125–134.

17. Terry McDermott, *Perfect Soldiers* (New York: HarperCollins, 2005), 111.

18. Rolf Mowatt-Larsen, "Al Qaeda's Pursuit of Weapons of Mass Destruction," *Foreign Policy*, January 25, 2010.

19. Michael B. Mukasey, *How Obama Has Mishandled the War on Terror* (New York: Encounter Broadsides, 2010), 1–6.

20. McDermott, *Perfect Soldiers*, 149.

21. "Proud Terrorist Gets Life for Trade Center Bombing," CNN News, January 8, 1998, http:articles.cnn.com/1998–01–08/us/9801_08_yousef.update_1_yousef-trade-center-bombing-airliner-bombing?_s=PM:US.

22. *The 9/11 Commission Report*, 148–149.

23. *The 9/11 Commission Report*, 189.

24. Osama bin Laden, "Jihad."

25. Ibid.

26. Mowatt-Larssen, "Weapons of Mass Destruction."

27. *The 9/11 Commission Report*, 70.

28. Paul Harris and Burhan Wazir, "Al-Qaeda's Bombers Used Britain to Plot Slaughter," *The Guardian*, April 21, 2002, www.guardian.co.uk/world/2002/apr/21/terrorism.religion.

29. Ibid.

30. Marc A. Thiessen, *Courting Disaster: How the CIA Kept America Safe and How Barack Obama Is Inviting the Next Attack* (Washington, D.C.: Regnery, 2010), 81.

31. The United States District Court, "Indictment of Khalid Sheikh Mohammed," *Wall Street Journal*, 2009, http:issuu.com/wsj.com/docs/ksm2009indictment04042011.pdf.

32. Tony Blair, *A Journey: My Political Life* (London: Hutchinson, 2010), 342.

## CHAPTER 3–CONVENTIONS

1. Justice Robert H. Jackson, "Nuremberg in Retrospect: Legal Answer to International Lawlessness," address before the Canadian Bar Association, September 1, 1949, *American Bar Association Journal* (1949), 813, http: www.roberthjackson.org/the-man/speeches-articles/speeches/speeches-by-robert-h-jackson/nuremberg-in-retrospect-legal-answer-to-international-lawlessness.

2. Ibid.

3. Victoria Toensing, "KSM Deserves Military Justice," *Wall Street Journal*, March 2, 2010.

4. Ibid.

5. John C. Yoo and James C. Ho, "The Status of Terrorists," New York University–University of Virginia Conference on Exploring the Limits of International Law, *Virginia Journal of International Law* 44 (2003), 207.

6. Jack Goldsmith, *The Terror Presidency: Law and Judgment Inside the Bush Administration* (New York: W.W. Norton, 2007), 109–113.

7. President Bush, transcript of speech on terrorism, *New York Times*, September 6, 2006.

8. Marc A. Thiessen, *Courting Disaster: How the CIA Kept America Safe and How Barack Obama Is Inviting the Next Attack* (Washington, D.C.: Regnery, 2010), 31.

9. Goldsmith, *Terror Presidency*, 111.

10. Ibid., 111–113.

11. Thiessen, *Courting Disaster*, 208.

12. Ibid., 31–33.

13. Noah Feldman, *Scorpions* (New York: Twelve Publishing, 2010), 215–225.

14. Ibid., 215–225.

15. Francis Biddle, "Cases Adjudged in the Supreme Court of the United States at July Special Term," *Ex Parte Quirin Et Ali* (1942), 12.

16. Jack Goldsmith, "Justice Jackson's Unpublished Opinion in *Ex Parte Quirin*," *The Green Bag: An Entertaining Journal of Law*, Spring 2006.

## CHAPTER 4–RESPONSES

1. Jack Goldsmith, *The Terror Presidency: Law and Judgment Inside the Bush Administration* (New York: W.W. Norton, 2007), 107–108.

2. Ibid., 118.

3. Ibid., 119–120.

4. Tom Bingham, *The Rule of Law* (London: Allen Lane, 2010), 146.

5. Donald Rumsfeld, *Known and Unknown*, (New York: Penguin Group, 2011), 570–571.

6. Alain Grignard, "Guantanamo Better than Belgian Prisons: OSCE expert," *Reuters*, Brussels, March 6, 2006.

7. Michael B. Mukasey, *How Obama Has Mishandled the War on Terror* (New York: Encounter Broadsides, 2010), 29–32.

8. Goldsmith, *Terror Presidency*, 120.

9. Quoted by John Lloyd, "Does Torture Work?," *Financial Times*, November 5, 2010.

10. Ibid.

11. Ibid.

12. Christopher Hitchens, "Believe Me, It's Torture," *Vanity Fair*, August 2008.

13. George W. Bush, *Decision Points* (New York: Crown Publishers, 2010), 171.

14. Ibid.,169.

15. Donald Rumsfeld, "How WikiLeaks Vindicated Bush's Anti-Terrorism Strategy," *Washington Post*, May 12, 2001.

16. "Pelosi News Conference on Waterboarding Disclosure," *Washington Post: CQ Transcriptwire*, May 14, 2009.

17. Benjamin Wittes, *Law and the Long War* (New York: Penguin Group, 2008), 29–30.

18. Alan Dershowitz, interview with Wolf Blitzer, CNN, March 4, 2003.

19. Elihu Lauterpacht and C. J. Greenwood, *International Law Reports* (Cambridge: Cambridge University Press, 1980), 198.

20. Nigel Biggar, letter to *Financial Times*, November 20-21, 2010.

21. Anne Applebaum, "The Torture Myth," *Washington Post*, January 12, 2005; and "Torture Is Counterproductive," *Slate*, March 20, 2007.

22. Michael Walzer, "Political Action: The Problem of Dirty Hands," *Philosophy and Public Affairs* 2 (1973), 160–180.

23. Marc Thiessen, *Courting Disaster: How the CIA Kept America Safe and How Barack Obama Is Inviting the Next Attack*, (Washington, D.C.: Regnery, 2010), 410–411.

24. Ibid., 23.

25. Ibid., 89; and John Kiriakou, quoted in Joby Warrick and Dan Eggen, "Waterboarding Recounted," *Washington Post*, December 11, 2007.

26. Bush, *Decision Points*, 169.

27. Thiessen, *Courting Disaster*, 5.

28. Bush, *Decision Points*, 170.

29. Scott Shane, "Inside a 9/11 Mastermind's Interrogation," *New York Times*, June 22, 2008; Peter Finn, "Retired Officers Meet with Obama Aides on Interrogation Policy," *Washington Post*, December 4, 2008; and Steven Swann, "What Happened in Europe's Secret CIA Prisons?" BBC News, October 8, 2010.

30. Bill Hutchinson, "WikiLeaks Reveals Al Qaeda Thug Khalid Sheikh Mohammed Vowed 'Nuclear Hellstorm' Tied to Bin Laden," *New York Daily News*, April 25, 2011.

31. Bush, *Decision Points*, 170.

32. Paul Owen, "George Bush Admits U.S. Waterboarded 9/11 Mastermind," *The Guardian*, June 3, 2010.

33. C.I.A. Inspector General Report (PDF), "Khalid Shaykh Muhammad: Preeminent Source on Al-Qaeda (PDF)," *Washington Post*, August 24, 2009, ccrjustice.org/files/CIA%20KSM%20Preeminent%20Source.pdf.

34. George W. Bush, "President Bush's Speech on Terrorism," *New York Times*, September 6, 2006.

35. Donald Rumsfeld, *Known and Unknown*, (New York: Penguin Group, 2011), 593.

36. Bush, "President Bush's Speech."

37. John Reid, "Twenty-First Century Warfare–Twentieth Century Rules," *RUSI Journal*, June 2006, 151, 3; ProQuest Research Library, 14.

38. Ibid.

39. Bush, *Decision Points*, 279.

40. "Military Commission, 9/11 Murder and Conspiracy Charges to Be Re-sworn Against KSM," Liberty Rocks, www.libertyrocks.us, May 30, 2011.

41. "9/11 Military Commission Charge Sheet," National Institute of Military Justice, June 2, 2011.

42. Associated Press, "Accused September 11th Mastermind 'I Wish to Be a Martyr,'" quoted on Fox News, June 5, 2008.

43. Robert Spencer, "9/11 Defendants Claim Divine Praise Even While They Plead Guilty," *Washington Post*, December 9, 2008; and Human Events, December 10, 2008.

44. Peter Berkowitz, "The Insanity of Bush Hatred," *Wall Street Journal*, November 14, 2007.

45. Tony Blair, *A Journey: My Political Life* (London: Hutchinson, 2010), 348–349.

## CHAPTER 5–COURTS

1. Campaign speech by Senator Obama in Pennsylvania, June 16, 2008, www.stjohns.edu/media/3/b001e52d8635402c933a628ab179faab.pdf?d=20080.

2. Ed Whelan, "*Boumediene*—Justice Scalia's Dissent," *National Review* online, June 12, 2008, www.nationalreviewonline.com/bench-memos/50907/boumediene—justice-scalias-dissent/ed-whelan.

3. *Johnson v. Eisentrager*, 339 U.S. 763 (1950), caselaw.lp.findlaw.com/cgi-bin/getcase.pl?friend=%3C%20riend%3E.

4. Telford Taylor, *The Anatomy of the Nuremberg Trials* (New York: Knopf, 1992), 56–77.

5. Donald Rumsfeld, *Known and Unknown*, (New York: Penguin Group, 2011), 596–598.

6. Ibid.

7. Marc A. Thiessen, "The Dean of the Gitmo Bar," *Weekly Standard*, Vol. 15, No 27, March 29, 2010, http://www.weeklystandard.com/articles/dean-gitmo-bar.

8. Michael Ratner, "Gonzales Has His Hand Deep in the Blood of the Conspiracy of Torture," *Democracy Now*, January 28, 2005, http://www.democracynow.org/2005/1/28/michael_ratner_gonzales_has_his_hand.

9. Carol Rosenberg, "Critics Assail Pentagon Plan for Terror Trials," *Miami Herald*, November 18, 2006, http://www.miamiherald.com/2006/11/18/320155/critics-assail-pentagon-plan-for.html.

10. Andrew C. McCarthy, "The Corner," *National Review* online, March 14, 2010, and "Here's to al-Qaeda," *National Review* online, April 30, 2011.

11. Ibid.

12. Benjamin Wittes, *Detention and Denial* (Washington D.C: Brookings Institution Press, 2010), 17.

13. Richard Cohen, "What if Cheney's Right?," *Washington Post*, May 12, 2009.

14. Charles Bolden, "The NASA Administrator and Astronaut in Conversation with Al Jazeera's Imran Garda," Al Jazeera English, July 1, 2010, http://english.aljazeera.net/programmes/talktojazeera/2010/07/201071122234471970.html.

15. Jane Mayer, "The Trial," *New Yorker*, February 15, 2010.

16. Ibid.

17. Scott W. Johnson, PowerLine blog, November 18, 2009.

18. Terry Frieden and Chris Kokenes, "Accused 9/11 Plotter Khalid Sheikh Mohammed Faces New York Trial," CNN, http://edition.cnn.com/2009/CRIME/11/13/khalid.sheikh.mohammed/index.html.

19. Alan Dershowitz, "America Is on Trial as Much as Khalid Sheikh Mohammed Is," *Globe and Mail*, November 13, 2009, http://www.theglobeandmail.com/news/opinions/america-is-on-trial-as-much-as-khalid-sheikh-mohammed/article1363102/.

20. Thomas Sowell, "Bowing to World Opinion," *Jewish World Review*, November 17, 2009.

21. Michael Makasey, *How Obama Has Mishandled the War on Terror* (New York: Encounter Books, 2010), 43.

22. Letter from Carolyn B. Lamm, president of the American Bar Association, to Attorney General Eric Holder, November 25, 2009.

23. Michael Elliott, "The Shoe Bomber's World," *Time*, February 12, 2002.

24. Richard Reid, "I am at war with your country," partial transcript of court hearing (CNN), January 31, 2002, http://www.cnn.com/2003/LAW/01/31/reid.transcript.

25. Pam Belluck, "Threats and Responses: The Bomb Plot: Unrepentant Shoe Bomber Is Given a Life Sentence," *New York Times*, January 31, 2003.

26. John B. Bellinger, III, "Prisoners in War: Contemporary Challenges to the Geneva Conventions," lecture at the University of Oxford, December 10, 2007.

27. "Obama Expresses Confidence KSM Will Be Convicted; Says He Isn't 'Prejudging' Verdict" (video), Realclearpolitics.com, November 18, 2009.

28. Robert Hochman, "*Brady v. Maryland* and the Search for Truth in Criminal Trials," *The University of Chicago Law Review* 63 (1996).

29. Victoria Toensing, "The Case for Military Trials," *Weekly Standard*, February 1, 2010, http://www.weeklystandard.com/blogs/where-try-ksm.

30. Ibid.

31. Eric Holder on Osama bin Laden, Associated Press, March 16, 2002.

## CHAPTER 6—REALITIES

1. Clifford Krauss, "Witnesses Recount the Mass Murder at Fort Hood," *New York Times*, October 13, 2010.

2. "A Hero's Recovery," PowerLine blog, January 23, 2011.

3. Thomas Joscelyn, "See No Evil: The Pentagon's Fort Hood Investigation Is a Pathetic Whitewash," *Weekly Standard*, February 1, 2010.

4. Daniel Pipes, "Major Hasan's Islamist Life," Frontpagemagazine.com, November 20, 2009.

5. Christopher Hitchens, "Multicultural Masochism: The War on Terror Didn't Cause the Fort Hood Shootings," *Slate*, November 23, 2009.

6. Senator Joe Lieberman and Senator Susan Collins, "Ticking Time Bomb: Counterterrorism Lessons from the U.S. Government's Failure to Prevent the Fort Hood Attack," Senate Homeland Security and Governmental Affairs Committee Report, February 1, 2011.

7. Spencer Hsu and Carrie Johnson, "Fort Hood Suspect's Links to Imam Under Scrutiny," *Washington Post*, November 9, 2009, http://www.washingtonpost.com/wp-dyn/content/article/2009/11/08/AR2009110818405.html.

8. Dorothy Rabinowitz, "Major Hasan, 'Star Officer,'" *Wall Street Journal*, February 16, 2011.

9. Lieberman and Collins, "Ticking Time Bomb."

10. Joscelyn, "See No Evil."

11. Heather Somerville, "Fort Hood Attack: Did Army Ignore Red Flags Out of Political Correctness?," *Christian Science Monitor*, February 3, 2011, http://www.csmonitor.com/USA/Military/2011/0203/Fort-Hood-attack-Did-Army-ignore-red-flags-out-of-political-correctness.

12. Rabinowitz, "'Star Officer.'"

13. John Hinderaker, "A Hero's Recovery," PowerLine blog, January 23, 2011, http://www.powerlineblog.com/archives/2011/01/028195.php.

14. Jane Mayer, "The Trial," *New Yorker*, February 15, 2010.

15. Ibid.

16. Ibid.

17. Alexander Meleagrou-Hitchens and Michael Weiss, "Terrorism and the British Academy," *Weekly Standard*, October 22, 2010.

18. Thomas Joscelyn, "Al Qaeda's Trojan Horse," *Weekly Standard*, December 31, 2009.

19. Victor Morton, "Awlaki Personally Blessed Detroit Attack," *Washington Times*, December 29, 2009.

20. Eric Lipton and Scott Shane, "Questions on Why Suspect Wasn't Stopped," *New York Times*, December 28, 2009.

21. Stephen Hayes, "What We Lost While Abdulmutallab Clammed Up," *Weekly Standard*, February 3, 2010, http://www.weeklystandard.com/blogs/what-we-lost-while-abdulmutallab-clammed.

22. Ibid.

23. Kathryn Jean Lopez, "Move Abdulmuttalab, Senators Insist," *National Review* online, January 25, 2010.

24. Editorial, *Washington Post*, January 23, 2010.

25. Michael Mukasey, "Where the U.S. Went Wrong on the Christmas Day Bomber," *The Washington Post*, February 12, 2010, http://www.washingtonpost.com/wp-dyn/content/article/2010/02/11/AR2010021103331.html.

26. Eric Holder, letter to Senator Mitch McConnell, February 3, 2010.

27. Mayer, "The Trial."

28. Ibid.

29. John McCormack, "KSM Trial Decision Put Off Until After Midterms," *Weekly Standard*, June 21, 2010, http://www.weeklystandard.com/blogs/ksm-trial-decision-put-until-after-midterms.

30. Joshua Durkin and Ray Storez, "Military Commissions: 'An Enormous Practical Failure,'" *The Public Record*, March 20, 2010.

31. Ibid., March 21, 2010.

32. Mayer, "The Trial."

33. Zahid Hussain, "From Suburban Father to a Terrorism Suspect," *New York Times*, May 4, 2010.

34. "Faisal Shahzad Made Suicide Video: Al Arabiya Airs Failed Times Square Bomber's Tape," Al Arabiya, July 14, 2010.

35. Daniel Pipes, "Faisal Shahzad, Jihadi, Explains Terrorism," *National Review* online, June

25, 2010, http://www.nationalreview.com/articles/243333/faisal-shahzad-jihadi-explains-terrorism-daniel-pipes.

36. Ibid.

37. Ibid.

38. Document, "Government's Memorandum in Connection with the Sentencing of Faisal Shahzad," September 29, 2009, www.nypost.com/r/nypost/2010/09/29/news/media/usavshahzad13.pdf.

39. Barry Rubin, Rubin Reports blog, www.rubinreports.blogspot.com, October 23, 2009.

40. Sunlen Miller, "Obama Honors Daniel Pearl with Freedom of the Press Act," ABC News, May 17, 2010.

41. "Verbatim Transcript of Combatant Status Review Tribunal Hearing for ISN 10024," March 10, 2007, www.aclu.org/pdfs/safefree/csrt_ksm.pdf.

42. Benjamin Wittes, "So KSM Really Did Kill Daniel Pearl?," January 20, 2011, Lawfareblog.com.

43. "Eric Holder Refuses to Say Radical Islam," Keep America Safe, May 13, 2010, http://www.youtube.com/watch?v=HOQt_mP6Pgg&feature=player_embedded.

44. Mark Steyn, "Nicking Our Public Discourse," *National Review* online, May 15, 2010.

45. "Lieberman and MPAC Face Off Over Terror Terminology," The Investigative Project on Terrorism, June 18, 2010, http://www.investigativeproject.org/2016/lieberman-and-mpac-face-off-over-terror.

46. Joseph Lieberman, "Democrats and Our Enemies," taken from a speech given at a dinner hosted by *Commentary* magazine, May 18, 2008, http://patriotpost.us/reference/democrats-and-our-enemies/.

47. Peter Finn, "Guantanamo Bay Detainee Brought to U.S. for Trial," *Washington Post*, June 10, 2009.

48. Thomas Joscelyn, "Smearing America in Defense of a Terrorist: On the Anti-Americanism of Ghailani's Pro Bono Counsel," *Weekly Standard*, November 18, 2010, http://www.weeklystandard.com/blogs/smearing-america-defense-terrorist_518167.html?page=1.

49. Benjamin Weiser, "Judge Bars Major Witness from Terrorism Trial," *New York Times*, October 6, 2010.

50. Ibid.

51. Benjamin Weiser, "Report Shows Detainee's Insight into Legal Process," *New York Times*, September 26, 2010.

52. Benjamin Weiser, "Ghailani's Lawyers Detail Terror Defense Strategy," *New York Times*, January 17 2011.

53. Benjamin Weiser, "Trial Omitted Statements by Ghailani," *New York Times*, November 17, 2010.

54. Joscelyn, "Smearing America."

55. Ibid.

56. Weiser, "Ghailani's Lawyers."

57. Chad Bray, "Tanzanian Man Was Active Member of Bomb Plot, Prosecutor Says," *New York Times*, November 8, 2010.

58. Chad Bray and Evan Perez, "Man Convicted in '98 Attacks," *New York Times*, November 18, 2010.

59. Thomas Joscelyn, "Holder's Sham Trial," *Weekly Standard*, November 29, 2010.

60. Jocelyn, "Smearing America."

61. John Podhoretz, "Center for Constitutional Rights," *Commentary*, November 18, 2010.

62. Diane Marie Amann, "A Proper Conviction," *New York Times*, November 18, 2010.

63. Elise Cooper, "How the Feds Bungled the Ghailani Trial," FrumForum, November 26, 2010, www.frumforum.com.

64. "Bush AG Attorney General: Eric Holder Made 'Wrong' Decision," Real Clear Politics, November 19, 2010.

65. Benjamin Wittes, "Lawfare: Hard National Security Choices," December 2, 2010, Lawfareblog.com.

66. Personal conversation.

67. Michael Walzer, "Symposium: The Killing of Bin Laden," *Dissent*, May 10, 2011.

## Chapter 7—Verdicts

1. Scott Shane, "U.S. Approves Targeted Killing of American Cleric," *New York Times*, April 6, 2010.

2. "Terrorists Believed to be Planning Attack in Berlin," *Der Spiegel*, November 20, 2010, http://www.spiegel.de/international/germany/0,1518,730236,00.html.

3. Andrew Lebovich, "The LWOT: AQAP Releases New 'Inspire' Magazine; Germany Attack Fears Intensify," *Foreign Policy*, November 23, 2010.

4. "Gordon Brown: 75% of UK Terror Plots Originate in Pakistan, Gaby Hinsliff in Islamabad," *The Guardian*, December 14, 2008, guardian.co.uk.

5. P. W. Singer, "We, Robot," *Slate*, May 19, 2010.

6. Ibid.

7. Ibid.

8. Laurie Goodstein, "A Nation Challenged: The American Muslims; Influential American Muslims Temper Their Tone," *New York Times*, October 19, 2001, http://www.nytimes.com/2001/10/19/us/nation-challenged-american-muslims-influential-american-muslims-temper-their.html?pagewanted=2&src=pm.

9. "New Evidence suggests Radical Cleric Anwar al Awlaki Was an Overlooked Key Player in 9/11 Plot," Fox News, May 20, 2011, http://www.foxnews.com/politics/2011/05/20/new-evidence-suggests-radical-cleric-anwar-al-awlaki-overlooked-key-player-11/.

10. Anwar al-Awlaki, *Inspire* magazine, January 2011.

11. Alexander Meleagrou-Hitchens, "The Voice of Terror," *Foreign Policy*, January 18, 2011, http://www.foreignpolicy.com/articles/2011/01/18/voice_of_terror.

12. "Keynote Address at GEOINT Conference by Charles E. Allen, Under Secretary for Intelligence and Analysis/Chief Intelligence Officer," Department of Homeland Security, October 28, 2008.

13. Anwar Awlaki, interview on Al Jazeera, December 24, 2009.

14. Thomas Joscelyn, CBS News, May 24, 2010.

15. Lebovich, "The LWOT."

16. "44 Ways to Support Jihad," February 5, 2009, www.nefafoundation.org.

17. Meleagrou-Hitchens, "The Voice of Terror."

18. *Inspire* magazine, January 2011.

19. Marc Thiessen, "Al Qaeda's American Bred Leadership," *Washington Post*, March 10, 2011, http://voices.washingtonpost.com/postpartisan/2011/03/al-qaedas_american-bred_leader.html.

20. CSIS Report, "A Threat Transformed: Al Qaeda and Associated Movements in 2011," 22–23.

21. Editorial, "U.S. Approves Targeted Killing of American Cleric," *New York Times*, April 6, 2010.

22. David Sanderson, "BA Worker Jailed for 30 Years for Plotting to Blow Up Plane," *The Times* (London), March 19, 2011.

23. Ibid.

24. Margaret Coker, "Al Qaeda in Yemen Publishes Attack Details," *Wall Street Journal*, November 21, 2010.

25. Lebovich, "The LWOT."

26. David J. Rusin, "Everybody Remember Molly Norris Day," May 20, 2011, www.is-lamist-watch.org.

27. Ibid.; and David J. Rusin, "On the Advice of the FBI, Cartoonist Molly Norris Disappears from View," *Seattle Weekly*, September 15, 2010.

28. Chris McGreal, "Prime Suspect in Cargo Plane Bomb Plot: Anwar al-Awlaki," *The Guardian*, October 31, 2010, http://www.guardian.co.uk/world/2010/oct/31/cargo-plane-bomb-suspect-anwar-al-awlaki.

29. "Al-Awlaki urges American killings," Al Jazeera, November 9, 2010. U.S.-born Islamic cleric Anwar al-Awlaki calls in a video message upon Muslims around the world to kill U.S. citizens.

30. Lebovich, "The LWOT."

31. Benjamin Wittes, "Initial Thoughts on the ACLU-CCR Al-Aulaqi Brief," October 9, 2010, Lawfareblog.com.

32. Thomas Joscelyn, "Anwar al Awlaki's License to Kill," *Weekly Standard*, November 11, 2010.

33. Ibid.

34. Kenneth Anderson, "Judge Bates Dismisses Al-Aulaqi Case," Opinio Juris, December 2010, opiniojuris.org.

35. Barack Obama, "Speech on National Security and American Values," May 21, 2009, http://www.dailykos.com/tv/w/001364/.

36. "Obama Ratifies Bush—The Administration embraces military tribunals at Gitmo," *Wall Street Journal*, March 8, 2011.

37. Benjamin Wittes, "Time for Obama to Embrace Guantanamo," January 21, 2011, Lawfareblog.com.

38. Thomas Joscelyn, "Gitmo Recidivism Rate Soars," *Weekly Standard*, December 7, 2010.

39. Thomas Joscelyn, "State Department Designates Former Gitmo Detainee Turned AQAP Commander," *Long War Journal*, June 16, 2011.

40. Thomas Joscelyn, "John Brennan is Still Wrong on Gitmo Detainees," *Weekly Standard*, May 13, 2011, http://www.weeklystandard.com/blogs/john-brennan-still-wrong-gitmo-detainee_560982.html?page=2.

41. Joscelyn, "Gitmo Recidivism."

42. Thomas Joscelyn, "Ex Gitmo Detainee Training Libyan Rebels in Derna," *Long War Journal*, April 2, 2011.

43. Thomas Joscelyn, "Supreme Court Shuts Door on Gitmo Detainees' Appeal," *Weekly Standard*, April 19, 2011.

44. Editorial, "A Right without a Remedy," *New York Times*, February 28, 2011.

45. Richard A. Serrano, "Obama to Resume Military Trials for Guantanamo Bay, Cuba Detainees," *Los Angeles Times*, March 8, 2011.

46. Clive Stafford-Smith, "This Plan Just Perpetuates the Prisoners' Legal Limbo," *Independent* (London), March 9, 2010.

47. Peter Finn and Anne E. Kornblut, "Obama Creates Indefinite Detention System for Prisoners at Guantanamo Bay," *Washington Post*, March 8, 2011.

48. "Guantanamo: The Prison That Won't Go Away," *New York Times*, March 8, 2011, http://www.nytimes.com/2011/03/09/opinion/09wed2.html.

49. Dahlia Lithwick, "Cowardly, Stupid, and Tragically Wrong," *Slate*, April 4, 2011.

50. Editorial, "Is Obama a War Criminal Yet?," *Washington Times*, March 8, 2011, http://www.washingtontimes.com/news/2011/mar/8/is-obama-a-war-criminal-yet/.

51. Benjamin Wittes, "Is Guantanamo Just a Legacy Problem?," December 27, 2010, Lawfareblog.com.

52. Daniel Halper, "While Announcing KSM Decision, Holder Attacks Congress," *Weekly Standard*, April 4, 2011.

53. Peter Fedynsky, VOA News, April 15, 2011.

# CHAPTER 8–JUSTICE

1. Bob Fertik, "Dick Cheney Had a Death Squad," Democrats.com, March 9, 2011, www.democrats.com/dick-cheney-had-a-death-squad.

2. Luiza Ch. Savage, "Did Torture Help the U.S. Find bin Laden?," Macleans.ca, May 25, 2011.

3. Ken Dilanian, "From Attorney General: McCain 'Simply Incorrect' on Interrogations That Led to Key Bin Laden Intelligence," *Los Angeles Times*, May 12, 2011.

4. John Yoo, "From Guantanamo to Abbottabad," *Wall Street Journal*, May 4, 2011.

5. Michael Hayden, "Birthers, Truthers, and Interrogation Deniers," *Wall Street Journal*, June 2, 2011.

6. Ibid.

7. Ilya Somin, "Admiral Yamamoto and the Justification of Targeted Killing," May 13, 2011, lawkipedia.com.

8. Harold Koh, Opinio Juris, May 19, 2011, opiniojuris.org.

9. Joe Coscarelli, "Noam Chomsky on Osama Bin Laden: George W. Bush's Crimes 'Vastly Exceed' Bin Laden's," *Village Voice* blog, May 9, 2011.

10. Judith Miller, Fox News, May 9, 2011.

11. Gerald Steinberg, "Human Rights Watch Challenges bin Laden Killing: Odious Immoral Equivalence," NGO Monitor, May 4, 2011.

12. "Germany's Moral Warriors," *Wall Street Journal* online, May 6, 2011.

13. Steven Erlanger, "In Europe, Disquiet over Bin Laden and U.S." *New York Times*, May 5, 2011, www.nytimes.com/2011/05/06/world/europe/06europe.html?pagewanted=all.

14. Robin Simcox, "Amnesty International is Keeping Dubious Company," Radio Free Europe, Radio Liberty, May 16, 2011.

15. Ibid.

16. Christopher Hitchens, "Death of a Madman," *Slate*, May 2, 2011, http://www.slate.com/id/2292687/.

17. Michael Walzer, "Symposium: The Killing of bin Laden," *Dissent*, May 10, 2011.

18. Quoted by John Q. Barrett, Jackson List, May 3, 2011. Justice Jackson, speech to the American Society of International Law, April 13, 1945, www.roberthjackson.org/the-man/speeches-articles/speeches/speeches-by-robert-h-jackson/the-rule-of-law-among-nations/.

# EPILOGUE

1. George Orwell, "Who Are the War Criminals," *Tribune*, October 22, 1943, http://orwell.ru/library/articles/criminals/english/e_crime.

2. Ibid.

3. Lord Shawcross, GBE, QC, letter to Arthur Suzman, QC, Johannesburg, South Africa, May 3, 1977, 229.

4. Ibid.

5. John Yoo, *War by Other Means* (New York: Atlantic Monthly Press, 2006), 20.

6. Gabriel Schoenfeld, "Legalism in Wartime," *National Affairs*, No. 7, Spring 2011, www.nationalaffairs.com/authors/detail/gabriel-schoenfeld.

7. Robert Chesney, "Consensus at the HASC Hearing on the Need for Flexibility?," July 30, 2011, Lawfareblog.com.

8. Jack Goldsmith, "Mark Martins to be Chief Prosecutor, Military Commissions," June 23, 2011, Lawfareblog.com.

9. Willy Stern, "Rebrander in Chief," *Weekly Standard*, October 3, 2011.

10. Benjamin Wittes, "The Next Step in Establishing the Legitimacy of Military Commissions," July 1, 2011, Lawfareblog.com.

11. Ibid.

12. Michael Mukasey, "Testimony of Michael B. Mukasey in Front of the Senate Armed Services Committee," July 26, 2011.

13. Chesney, "Consensus at the HASC Hearing."

14. Ibid.

15. Bill Roggio, "Pakistani Taliban Kidnap Young Girl to Turn Her Into a Suicide Bomber," *Long War Journal*, June 20, 2011.

16. Reinhold Niebuhr, *The Irony of American History*, (New York: Charles Scribner's Sons, 1952); cited in Abe Greenwald, "What We Got Right in the War on Terror," *Commentary*, September 2011.

17. "Killing Awlaki," *Wall Street Journal*, October 1, 2011.

18. John Bellinger III, "Will Drone Strikes Become Obama's Guantanamo?," *Washington Post*, October 2, 2011.

19. Keith Johnson, "Al Qaeda Remains Top Threat to U.S.," *New York Times*, June 30, 2011.

20. "U.S. Favorable Ratings Plummet Across the Arab World, a Zogby Poll," Al Jazeerah, July 19, 2011, www.aljazeerah.info/Opinion%20Editorials/2011/July/18%20o/US%20Favorable%20Ratings%20Plummet%20Across%20the%20Arab%20World,%20a%20Zogby%20Poll.htm.

21. Pascal Bruckner, *The Tyranny of Guilt: An Essay on Western Masochism* (Princeton: Princeton University Press, 2010), op. cit., 218, 202.

# INDEX

# ABOUT THE AUTHOR

CONRAD SHAWCROSS

WILLIAM SHAWCROSS is an author and journalist who has covered international conflicts and conflict resolution for many years. He has written several books including *Sideshow: Kissinger, Nixon and the Destruction of Cambodia; The Quality of Mercy: Cambodia, Holocaust, and Modern Conscience; Deliver Us from Evil: Warlords, Peacekeepers, and a World of Endless Conflict; Allies;* and the bestselling *The Queen Mother: The Official Biography.* He was a founding member of the International Crisis Group and served on the board and executive committee from 1995-2006. His father, Hartley Shawcross, was Britain's lead prosecutor at the Nuremberg Trials. He appears regularly on television and radio, and his articles have appeared in leading newspapers and journals throughout the world. He lives in London.